MW01633166

IF ONLY THEY COULD SPEAK

ALSO BY THE AUTHOR

Dogs Behaving Badly

The Cat Who Cried for Help

The Dog Who Loved Too Much

IF ONLY THEY COULD SPEAK

STORIES ABOUT PETS AND THEIR PEOPLE

DR. NICHOLAS H. DODMAN

W. W. NORTON & COMPANY
NEW YORK LONDON

The stories in this book are true, but in most instances the names have been changed in order to provide anonymity to the pet owners. The photographs used at the beginnings of chapters are not necessarily the animal/s depicted in that chapter. Although various medical treatments are referred to throughout the work, it is vital to note that no drugs or medications should ever be administered to pets by their owners except under the direct supervision of a veterinarian.

Printed in the United States of America
First Edition

Frontispiece: © Eunice Pearcy/Animals Animals. Chapter openers: 1: Courtesy of Rose Beneski. 2: Courtesy of Linda Eber. 3: Courtesy of Britain Hill. 4: Courtesy of Janice-Porter Naber. 5: Courtesy of Ingsu Liu. 6: Courtesy of Daniel Baxter. 7: Courtesy of Nicholas Dodman. 8: Courtesy of Beth Hyder. 9: Courtesy of Britain Hill. 10: Courtesy of Joanne O'Connor. 11: Courtesy of Nicholas Dodman. 12: Courtesy of Lisa Boyle. 13: Courtesy of Jodie Krumpfer. 14: Courtesy of Timothy Murray. Epilogue: Courtesy of the Lazovitz-Blaskslee Family.

The text of this book is composed in Minion
with the display set in Charlemagne
Composition by Molly Heron
Manufacturing by The Haddon Craftsmen, Inc.
Book design by Chris Welch
Production manager: Andrew Marasia

Library of Congress Cataloging-in-Publication Data
Dodman, Nicholas H.
If only they could speak : stories about pets and their people /
Nicholas H. Dodman
p. cm.
ISBN 0-393-05100-5 (hardcover)
1. Dogs—Massachusetts—Anecdotes. 2.Dogs—Behavior—Massachusetts—Anecdotes. 3. Dog owners—Massachusetts—Anecdotes. 4. Dodman, Nicholas H. 5. Veterinarians—Massachusetts—Anecdotes. I. Title.
SF426.2 .D59 2002
636.7—dc21
2002000523

W. W. Norton & Company, Inc., 500 Fifth Avenue, New York, N.Y. 10110
www.wwnorton.com

W. W. Norton & Company Ltd., Castle House, 75/76 Wells Street, London WIT 3QT

1 2 3 4 5 6 7 8 9 0

To my sister,
Angela Shaw

CONTENTS

ACKNOWLEDGMENTS

I would like to acknowledge the support I have had from my immediate family as I have worked to complete this book. I would also like to thank my agents, Glen Hartley and Lynn Chu of Writers' Representatives Inc. in New York, for their patience and wisdom. Finally, I would like to thank my editor, Bob Weil, for his hard work and dedication during the preparation of this manuscript and for having faith in me.

IF ONLY THEY COULD SPEAK

INTRODUCTION

Until he extends his circle of compassion to include all
living things, man will not himself find peace.
—*Albert Schweitzer*

Did you hear about the dog who always arranged exactly six pieces of kibble in buttonhole depressions in the couch and one piece by the leg of the couch before it would lie down? Or the dog who would always take one piece of kibble out of his dish and place it on the carpet in the den before going back into the kitchen to eat? Both these true stories remind me of a Christmas card I once sent to a friend and obsessive-compulsive disorder (OCD) researcher at the National Institute of Mental Health. The card showed Santa making his gift list. On the front it said, "He's checking it once, he's checking it twice. . . ." And then inside the card it read, "It sounds as if Santa's a little obsessive-compulsive to me." Constant checking, a preoccupation with symmetry, excessive concerns over personal safety, and hoarding are all typical variations of obsessive-compulsive disorder in human beings. It is surprising to some people that these are also signs of OCD in nonhuman animals.

Animal intelligence, emotions, and self-awareness have always been highly controversial subjects that have led to centuries of, to this point, somewhat fruitless debate. The last fifteen years have continued to produce evidence to support the contention that animals are thinking, sentient beings who appreciate their own and others' circumstances and emotional state. Naysayers, however, simply elevate the bar each time field scientists find evidence to refute the objections du jour. At one time, animals' lack of an opposing thumb and their supposed inability to fashion and use tools was considered to be a principal differentiating factor. Such dexterity and the physical and mental opportunities it afforded were uniquely human endowments, the anthropocentrists said. But Jane Goodall demonstrated that chimps fashion tools out of twigs and use them in their efforts to extract juicy termites from their mounds. Many other examples of tool use in animals have been documented since that time. Next, objectors tried to distinguish humans from animals on the basis of language. But now this supposed distinction has been blurred. From parrots to primates, elementary language and cross-species communication between humans and animals has been shown to occur. Irene Pepperberg's work with her famous parrot, Alex, and the signing abilities of orangutans at the National Zoo in Washington, D.C., provide elegant testimony to this. One dog I know, Hogan, understands forty-four words of American Sign Language. Add to this his ability to communicate by means of body language and he is probably due a Pulitzer Prize sometime soon. Of course, employing language as sophisticated as our own necessitates a more advanced brain, but nonhuman animals can and do understand rudimentary language, so the language/no language distinction is no longer valid.

The wonderful thing about being an animal behaviorist is being able to observe animals in their modern-day ethological niche. While laboratory scientists struggle in sterile environments to prove that domestic animals are sentient creatures, behaviorists get to observe the daily goings-on in the lives of a variety of animal species under much more normal circumstances. When I started out in behavioral medicine nearly two decades ago, little was known about many of the behavioral conditions and treatments that are now well documented. In those days, if a veterinarian had diagnosed obsessive-compulsive disorder in a person's pet, people would have looked at him as if he had three heads. But what other reasonable explanation is there for a dog who compulsively grooms (washes) his paws until the skin is raw or a cat who compulsively hoards shiny objects? And why, if not because of an inner compulsion, does a captive bear pace mindlessly or constantly drink by cupping water in its paws? Of course, not all repetitive behaviors are compulsive disorders or even resemble them, but some are dead ringers for the human condition and respond to antiobsessional medicine almost precisely the same way as people with OCD. Recently, Prozac and the like have found considerable application in veterinary medicine, especially for the treatment of hitherto virtually untreatable conditions like excessive feather picking in birds, cribbing in horses, tail chasing in dogs, and wool sucking in cats.

Fifteen years ago, Prozac was unknown as a treatment for aggression in man and animals. In fact, many of the behavioral medicines in use today, including Prozac, were not even available at that time. It had only just been discovered that urine marking, the foremost behavior problem in cats and a leading cause of their surrender, was amenable to treatment with Valium. The implications of this breakthrough—that urine marking in neutered cats was an anxiety-based problem—had yet to be fully appreciated. At the time, we were still struggling with definitions of behavior problems and treatments, and the full impact of these problems on pet longevity was only just surfacing. Then as now, "real scientists" were trying hard to think of ways to prove that humans are unlike nonhuman animals in anything other than the most basic ways.

Emotions have been another stumbling block, as we have not been allowed to give domestic animals credit for what they feel. Even as recently as last year I was told by a reviewer for the *Journal of the American Veterinary Medical Association* that I couldn't use the word "fear" in the context of "fear aggression." Fear, the reviewer said, is a subjective feeling that is impossible to prove in nonverbal species. Instead he suggested that I say the animal (a dog in this case) was showing certain physical signs in the presence of an aversive stimulus (a person) and that a human exhibiting equivalent signs in a similar situation would be experiencing fear (i.e., no direct reference to fear could be made). I published the article elsewhere. This obtuseness in failing to recognize that animals may share human emotions stems from a blinkered, anthropocentric view marked by extreme conservatism. "Show me data and I will believe," say the doubting Thomases. But when the tools of the cognitive behaviorist include oranges, bananas, rope, and cardboard cylinders (with and without holes), and the object of the research is to verify love or jealousy, the experiment is already destined for failure. Like all the other good things in life, like beauty and the universe, the correct interpretation of abstract notions is in the eye and imagination of the beholder. Unfortunately, as in the case of the half-full glass, there is always room for more than one interpretation, and the bias is to stick with the existing mantra. Those who step outside the boundaries of what can be "scientifically proven" have been disparagingly labeled "anthropomorphic" as if it were some sort of disease or weakness.

But animals do feel emotions, just like us. Take Mona, for example, the cat I describe in the chapter entitled "A Second Chance." Mona became so anxious when her owner went away to England that she began to pull her fur out in clumps. Or how about another cat who became clinically depressed and started hair pulling after her cat buddy died? That cat did eventually recover, but only to start pulling out her fur again the following year on the anniversary of her buddy's demise. Of course, some would argue that animals can't tell time or date, but they obviously can—not from clocks or calendars but from other more fundamental inputs, like daylight and temperature. Another cat refused to enter a room in which its lady owner died—for one year to the day. When it finally did return to the room it curled up on the woman's pillow and died. Separation anxiety, described in "The

Willing Prisoner," is a common disorder of hyperattachment that affects dogs and cats (and some people). There is no doubt from recent observations that higher animals experience basic emotions, like fear and anger, but extrapolating from their complicated interactions and behaviors within the home, it is quite plausible that they are also capable of more complex secondary emotions. For example, they seem to be able to empathize with other creatures, ostensibly able to pick up on another animal's emotional state, and may well be capable of feelings such as jealousy and guilt.

That dogs are aware of the emotional and physical status of people is a fact well known to many intelligent dog owners. One of the chapters in this book, "The Dog Who Hated Men," is about a dog who saved his owner from a diabetic coma on more than one occasion. Some therapy dogs warn their owners of seizures and are able to detect impending seizures long before the owner is aware of what is going on. One canine patient of mine saved its male owner from falling as a result of a heart attack when it saw him swaying in front of his shaving mirror. The dog ran and got the man's wife to the scene in seconds, dragging her Rin Tin Tin style to the bathroom so that she caught her husband before he hit the deck. Also, many dogs seem to know when their owner is feeling down or is ill and will completely change their behavior toward them. My wife's dog, Pascra, lay next to her for two days when she, a vet student at the time, was ill and confined to bed. The corollary to this observation is that chronic human ailments can sometimes sap a pet's energy and lead to neurotic behaviors in the pet. This may have been part of the problem with Lenny in the chapter "Life with Lenny," as his owner carried and radiated a good deal of anxiety concerning his own ill health and misfortune.

In the chapters "Biting the Hand That Feeds" and "The Pit Bull from Hell," we see dogs who have sudden mood swings and violent, uninhibited responses to unwelcome advances. Call it rage, call it anger, it seems to involve a considerable emotional response on the part of the dog. Cats display similar extreme mood swings, too. In

Seths's case, in the chapter "For the Love of Seth," his mood swings had biological underpinnings, but some apparently normal cats show signs of high arousal, virtually at the drop of a hat. Fortunately for Seth, his owners remained devoted to his cause. Sam, in "Sam's Story," started out rebellious, but his mood swings and behavior modified over time when he received proper attention. He was clearly a lost soul looking for direction. Osaka, the Akita in "Somerset Farm," could also react with an emotional outburst when pressed by other dogs, much to the dismay of his caring, emotionally invested owner. Good control was the key to his containment.

That people love and need their pets there is no doubt. But do the pets love their people? I believe some do, to the point of exhibiting jealousy, rebellion, and extreme attention-seeking behavior. "Ménage à Trois" describes an awkward three-sided relationship between a formerly single, highly successful businesswoman, her constant companion cat, and her new husband. Jealousy was likely at work here. Romeo, in the chapter "Romeo and Julie," was so attached to his owner that he constantly acted out in unmentionable ways in order to gain her attention. With Ginger, in "Midlife Crisis," it was a case of immediate bonding for his doting owners, who later learned the price of their devotion. And Merlin in "Poltergeist in a Fog" couldn't have survived long in this bustling world without his adoring owner, the only one he trusted and on whom he depended. Then there was poor Bonnie, in "The Two Dogs of Mrs. Spinelli," a dog who relied on her controlling owner's support—but that reliance went a shade too far.

In my work, I see a complicated series of actions and interactions between people and their pets and between pets and their people. No one will convince me that pets do not have feelings or that they don't appreciate their own (or others') existence. In my practice, I work on the basic principle that pets are as emotionally invested as we are, experiencing anger, fear, boredom, loneliness, jealousy, and other sophisticated emotions. Acting on this firm belief, I am able to diagnose and explain behaviors to myself and to owners, and furthermore, this approach lends itself to the development and application of successful treatment strategies.

The very success of pharmacologic treatments, which feature prominently throughout this book, is testimony to the basic similarity between the mental processes of humans and nonhuman animals. While some readers may consider the use of psychotropic drugs in pet behavioral medicine to be unnecessary, trendy, or just plain misguided, I hasten to point out that without these new and developing treatments there would be even greater unnecessary loss of animal life than already occurs. We are not merely listening to Prozac in terms of what the success of such treatment implies; we are also saving lives that would otherwise be lost.

1

THE TWO DOGS OF MRS. SPINELLI

A dog never lies, but when was a wolf known to speak the truth?—*James Fenimore Cooper*

As a veterinarian who specializes in treatment of behavior problems in animals, I routinely meet stimulating people, and Caroline Spinelli definitely fell into that category. A confident but kindly-looking fifty-year-old woman with a heart-shaped face, expensively coiffed blond hair and oversized blue-tinted spectacles, Mrs. Spinelli cut an imposing figure that practically demanded undivided attention. She clutched a small, rather straggly-coated, nervous-looking black poodle to her chest with one arm while her pocketbook swung lazily from the other. As we made our way to the consulting room, her considerably younger consort, Teddy, who was tenuously holding the lead of a shifty-looking, midsized German shepherd, walked a couple of paces behind us. The poodle's rhinestone collar and the shepherd's shifty eyes glinted under the glare of the fluorescent lights in my office.

It was a freezing cold January day when Mrs. Spinelli, Teddy, the two dogs, and I got together to discuss what for her was a pressing problem, a feud that had broken out between her two dogs. Outside the ground was frozen hard like iron, the Massachusetts landscape was dusted white with frost, and tree branches glistened with frozen rain, giving them an appearance of glass. We were glad to be inside. Mrs. Spinelli took center stage as she made introductions all around, still clutching the timorous poodle, whose name, I was informed, was Bonnie. Teddy sat in the wings keeping a close hold on Tina, the German shepherd. Both dogs were neutered females. Bonnie was seven years old, and Tina just over two. Bonnie was Mrs. Spinelli's original dog and was clearly her favorite. I saw a kind of nervousness in the shepherd that comes from a lack of proper schooling and direction, and in the poodle I saw uncertainty and dependency.

As Mrs. Spinelli spoke about the dogs' problems, pausing occasionally to sigh and gaze heavenward, I puzzled over her thick South American accent and wondered how she had come to be living in the Boston area. My curiosity didn't prevent me from hearing every word she was saying.

"Dr. Dodman," she proclaimed, "I don't know what's got into Tina. She's suddenly become extremely jealous of Bonnie and I think she's going to kill her. I'm a busy woman and worrying about these two dogs is wasting a lot of my precious time. I'm not sure I can continue on like this. Is there any way you can help or do I have to find a home for Tina?"

My mind raced through the myriad cases of infighting between family dogs that I had seen over the years, searching for a parallel situation. As common a problem as such infighting is, each case has its own unique dynamic involving not only the dogs themselves but also the owner. Often the problem stems in part from a power struggle between the dogs involved, in part from subtle alliances between one or the other dog and the owner. Sometimes the problem is more symbolic than serious, and at other times it is downright deadly.

"I should be able to help you," I said cautiously. "This problem is normally referred to as sibling rivalry, whether the dogs are actually siblings or not. I will need some more information from you first before I can tell you how to proceed and give you some idea of the likelihood that you will be able to turn things around."

"Very well," Mrs. Spinelli sighed. "Let me start the ball rolling by telling you that the problem has been going on for the last two months. . . . That's about right, isn't it, Teddy?"

"Yes, it was November, I think, when the first incident occurred," Teddy replied quietly.

This was the first time I had paused to survey Teddy carefully. A slim ascetic type, he had aquiline features framed by a full head of curly black hair. His expression was drawn and I could tell from his countenance that he shared Mrs. Spinelli's grave concern.

"It is terrible, Dr. Dodman, just terrible," Mrs. Spinelli said, shaking her head and removing her glasses to clean them. "With all the love I give these dogs, I can't imagine why there would be any reason for them to fight."

"Tell me about the November incident," I prompted.

She drew a deep sigh and led off with what was for her an extremely painful account.

"Well, I had just come back from food shopping and I opened the door and put the bags down on the floor, turning to Bonnie to greet her first. I always greet Bonnie first, and then I go over to Tina and make a fuss of her, too. This time they both approached me excitedly, and suddenly, with no provocation at all, Tina lunged and attacked Bonnie, seizing her by the head and thrashing her from side to side. I screamed out something like, "My God, Tina, stop it," and grabbed Tina by the collar in an attempt to pull her off Bonnie. Bonnie did get free, yes, for a short time, but Tina then ran after her, pulling me down on the floor and dragging me across the living room floor before grabbing Bonnie again. I knew I had been injured but somehow I managed to summon the strength to pin Tina against a desk and then I jammed my hand into her mouth to stop her from biting Bonnie. Bonnie scampered off into another room, leaving a trail of blood behind her. I threw Tina out into the backyard while I caught my breath and took stock of the situation.

"I was trembling all over like jelly and was breathless with the exertion and pain," she continued. "Tina had punctured my hand with her sharp teeth, and my right rib cage, in fact, the whole right-hand side of my body, was throbbing as I limped over to find out what had happened to Bonnie. I found Bonnie sitting in a corner shivering and picked her up to find large gaping wounds all over her head. One of her ears had been almost ripped off," she said, dabbing her eyes with a handkerchief. "I called for Teddy and we jumped into the car and headed for the vet's right away. My poor Bonnie, she had more than twenty stitches. Look at these photographs. These were taken right after the surgery." She pushed an envelope containing photographs toward me and the room fell silent as I surveyed the damage.

Tina certainly had done a butchering job on Bonnie. Red incision lines and rows of stitches ran across the top of her small head and down the side of her cheek, behind her ear, and across her neck. If you didn't know you were looking at the picture of a dog, you would have thought it was an aerial shot of a railroad junction. This was real reconstructive surgery.

"Goodness!" I exclaimed, whistling through my teeth. "She really did a number on Bonnie, didn't she."

"Oh, it was vicious, Dr. Dodman, just vicious."

"Tell me about the other incidents. Were they just as bad?"

"Oh yes, they were terrible, too. We were trying to keep the dogs separate. We spent the whole time carrying Bonnie around whenever Tina was around, but Teddy made one mistake in December and that was all it took. He was standing guard at the French doors, waiting for Bonnie to come back from her nighttime walk, and was ready to pick her up. But as Bonnie crossed the threshold, Tina left her bed under the stairs, flew at her, and grabbed her by her little body. Teddy had to nearly choke her to death to get her to release Bonnie. The commotion woke me from a deep sleep, and as I attempted to come down the stairs, I stood on the edge of my silk kimono-style nightdress that was billowing out behind me, slipped, and fell, crashing into a gate that I had installed to keep the dogs apart at night.

"The third attack was similar, but this time I had taken some liberties, allowing the dogs to interact together outside because Tina, Dr. Dodman, seemed to be in such a good mood. I had her on lead and she seemed quite happy until we decided to go back into the house. But as that dreaded threshold appeared, she once again lunged at Bonnie, and this time, I swear, she would have killed her if Teddy and I hadn't separated them by hauling Tina off her by the tail."

"I gather you don't have them together at all now, is that correct?"

"That's correct, Dr. Dodman. You know, we just can't risk it. Since that last attack, Tina is restricted to the living room, kitchen, and an area downstairs near the garage. She is no longer allowed upstairs, even though she used to sleep on our bed at night. Whenever we want to bring Bonnie downstairs we lock Tina in the garage area before we even think about bringing Bonnie down. She can then go out into the yard to do her business and is confined in her area again before Tina is allowed back into the house."

"What a way to go on," I exclaimed.

"Yes, it's almost intolerable. If this continues I may even have to get rid of Tina."

Before giving Mrs. Spinelli the fundamentals of treatment, I asked a few more questions about both dogs' backgrounds and found out that both had what I call dysfunctional histories. Bonnie had been a pound dog and Mrs. Spinelli had acquired Tina at a pet store when she was three or four months of age. To me, both these backgrounds were relevant to the dogs' underlying fears, though Tina's aggression toward Bonnie was certainly also a feature of her struggle for dominance. She was vying with Bonnie for the alpha position in the home, and with her young-adult confidence and larger physical size was bullying Bonnie over valued resources (such as Mrs. Spinelli's attention) and privileges (the right to cross the threshold first). I suspected that the situation had been some time in the making and that Mrs. Spinelli's constant support for Bonnie, and the fact that Bonnie was allowed to sleep in her bed—her nest, in essence—had finally roused what could reasonably be construed as jealousy on the part of Tina.

At that time in the Tufts Behavior Clinic, we were advising clients to support the dog who normally was the aggressor and the one who, through size and confidence, would probably be the natural leader. Nowadays we factor in age and incumbency as important considerations (not that it would have changed the advice that I supplied in this particular case). I determined that Tina was unlikely to accept any rank other than top dog, so I knew I had to advise Mrs. Spinelli to change her tack completely. I could tell that Mrs. Spinelli was not going to like the treatment I was about to suggest.

First I explained to her that it was only prudent to keep both dogs separated for the time being, until she could establish better control over them, Tina in particular. I also instructed her on our leadership program and fitted Tina with a head halter so that Mrs. Spinelli would have better physical control over her when a reintroduction was eventually attempted. In addition, I advised Mrs. Spinelli to support Tina over Bonnie in all matters, greeting her first, feeding her first, and allowing her to come through doorways first. Strict physical control of both dogs would be essential at all such times. Bonnie, who loves her crate, was to be crated while the Spinellis were away, and Mrs. Spinelli was to make a tremendous fuss over Tina on her return. The same would apply to mealtime, with Bonnie being fed second, and inside her crate. Lastly, Tina would be ceremoniously walked through the door, using her head halter to guide her, and the carefully chaperoned Bonnie would bring up the rear. Finally, since the behavior Tina had shown was so severe, I suggested that we should treat her with Prozac to reduce the likelihood of serious aggression should the two dogs inadvertently come into direct contact. I warned Mrs. Spinelli of the exorbitant price of Prozac for a dog of Tina's size, but she dismissed this concern with a wave of her hand and gave Teddy a knowing sideways glance. It was at about this time that I noticed the fine clothes Mrs. Spinelli was wearing and the huge, stunning ruby that she sported on her wedding finger.

"I will do whatever you suggest, Dr. Dodman. If the word is Prozac, so be it. These dogs are my family and I will spare no expense to resolve this problem."

As we prepared to leave, I asked Mrs. Spinelli whether she would be able to go through with the treatment program, and with a broad smile she informed me that there was basically nothing that she couldn't do if she put her mind to it. This was a refreshing prospect for me, to find a client who understood everything I had said, and was determined to see it through. Also, it was good that she could afford top-of-the-line treatment, since many of my clients cannot afford expensive medication and their pets do not qualify for drug insurance. I must admit I felt reasonably optimistic at that time that she would succeed in her quest.

As the three of us sauntered out to the front desk to settle the bill, we started chatting about things that were going on in our lives. It is often the case that after an hour and a half cooped up in the consulting room, focusing intently on the problem in hand, people seem to want to unwind by discussing more general matters as they exit. Mrs. Spinelli was no exception, and a social exchange began and continued at a much more open level than I normally expect from a client. Perhaps the frankness of the discussion reflected the genuine affection and appreciation we seemed to have developed for each other during the consultation. After Mrs. Spinelli commented that I looked slightly off-color, I mentioned to her that I had not been well and had been in the hospital the month before for an operation. She was genuinely concerned and said that she had some excellent medical connections if I needed other opinions. Whatever was wrong with me, she said, I deserved only the very best doctors in town, and there were plenty of them close by. Then she started to drop the names of some of the most famous doctors in Boston and said that she would call them for me to make sure that no worthwhile treatment was spared. I thanked her very much for her concern and asked how she came to have such strong ties to the medical community.

"That's easy," she replied. "My first husband was a urologist—head of a clinic at one of the major teaching hospitals in Boston. He and I got to know practically all of the medical community, anyone with any serious credentials or influence anyway, and we are on first-name terms with most of them, too."

Mrs. Spinelli kindly wrote down two or three doctors' names on a piece of paper and said she would call them and get back in touch with me. I thanked her very much for the kind gesture, not sure whether this might be locking the stable door after the horse had bolted (I had already been operated upon).

As Mrs. Spinelli left the hospital, I walked with her to her car—an old Cadillac that she kept for transporting the dogs. She told me she had another new Cadillac but was having some teething problems with it so she had ordered another. Though her first husband was extremely well placed financially, she volunteered that she had not taken a penny from him following their divorce, only one of the two Cadillac sedans. In fact, she had bought their three-level, red sandstone Charles River apartment from him and released him from all obligations. The two of them, she announced, had remained good friends, and though she could afford as many new cars as she wanted, her "ex" had purchased the new Cadillac recently as a gift. I was out of my depth in this conversation and merely smiled feebly and remarked, "How nice."

As Mrs. Spinelli and Teddy drove off, I realized that I had enjoyed talking to them. They both seemed very honest and, believe it or not, unpretentious. I assumed Teddy was around because Mrs. Spinelli found him attractive and perhaps interesting to talk to, though clearly he was not the decision maker. Mrs. Spinelli was a character of the first order, and her self-assuredness, obvious intelligence, and kindness had made an impression on me. I hoped profoundly for the best for her with her two dogs.

Mrs. Spinelli, good as her word, called me up within days of her visit with more detailed contact information for the physicians that she had mentioned to me. Unfortunately, though I tried several times, I kept missing the clinician I decided to contact, and when I learned that he had left the country for a couple of weeks to attend a conference, I finally gave up my pursuit. Mrs. Spinelli's kindness in even trying to put us in contact was still much appreciated, but I decided to go it alone and take my chances.

A few days later I found a message from Teddy on my clipboard saying that things were going much better with the two dogs. I was extremely pleased to receive this information. I relayed a message back to Teddy and Mrs. Spinelli that I would like them to come for a follow-up appointment so that we could take detailed stock of recent events. This was agreed.

When Mrs. Spinelli returned, she was without Teddy and strode into the consulting room with Bonnie in her arms and Tina trailing far behind on a long lead. She smiled engagingly at me across the consulting room table and began, "Well, Dr. Dodman, I think my problem is solved. There is no longer any aggression between these two dogs. In fact, they're both as good as gold, but I want to share something with you. I didn't do at all what you said. I did exactly the opposite." I knew, as I sat there, that I was going to hear exactly how and braced myself for the education. The tables were completely turned. Instead of me, the behaviorist, informing her, the client, how to proceed, I had Mrs. Spinelli lecturing to me on the way she had solved her problem despite my advice. Beaming as she began her monologue, she reminded me of the sentiment in Frank Sinatra's song: *I did it my way.* I sat wide-eyed, almost disbelieving, as I took in what she had to say.

"Dr. Dodman, I did understand what you were telling me to do, but I just couldn't bring myself to do it. Bonnie's my best friend. She was here first, she's a wonderful pet, and she needs me. Don't get me wrong, I like Tina, too, but Tina came into my house as a young puppy, how do you put it, a "dysfunctional" young puppy, and I gave her a home. Now that she's gotten all grown up and surly, I'm *not* going to have her picking on my Bonnie. I decided after we spoke the last time that enough is enough. She just isn't going to get away with it anymore."

"So what did you do?" I asked.

"I put her on that thing, that head halter, or whatever you call it, and every day I would take them both out to the yard and make them walk through the door at the same time. The head halter gave me control, and if there was even so much as a growl from Tina, I would immediately pull the lead straight up in the air so that Tina's nose was pointing at the sky. Then I would scold her, and I would take her out into the garage where she would stay for the rest of the day. If she was lucky, she'd get fed that night. Then I'd bring Bonnie inside and pet her and praise her and give her a nice meal, supporting her as the number one dog, which, Dr. Dodman, she is to me."

"That *is* different from what I suggested," I responded. "Diametrically opposite, in fact. That's what I thought caused the problem in the first place, going against the flow of nature."

"I'm telling you, Dr. Dodman, I wasn't taking it anymore from Tina, and she knew it. I came down on her like a ton of bricks. The minute there was the slightest hostile expression toward Bonnie, the minute there was a growl or forward movement, I was able to apprehend her mid-flight, thanks to the new control that I had. Eventually, as you see, she got the message." I glanced across at Tina, who, I must admit, looked very sorry for herself, sitting silently on the other side of the room as her absolute leader told the tale.

There was no hostility or animosity between Mrs. Spinelli and me. I was pleased that she had achieved what she set out to achieve, peace between her feuding dogs, though possibly a brittle one. What Mrs. Spinelli had done was to establish her own control over both dogs so that, almost literally, when she opened her mouth, no dog (in the entire neighborhood) dared bark. Then she indulged whichever dog she chose, whenever she wanted to and on her own terms. That sounded like the Caroline Spinelli that I was beginning to know. Trust her to stand the world on its head to suit herself and not to take no for an answer. It was tough love at its most extreme. Mrs. Spinelli, as nice as she was and as kind as she was (at least outwardly), was strong, forceful, and determined. I don't know how she came to be so confident and self-assured or to have such tremendous control. Perhaps success in the world of business or personal triumphs had contributed. More recently, perhaps success with her dogs factored in. For whatever reason, she was a leader among men and a leader among dogs. A commendable state of affairs, in a way, but not one many people can achieve. What I found so surprising was that with all of this control, determination, and willpower, she indeed was still one of the nicest and most compassionate people you could hope to meet. Though Mrs. Spinelli was firm, her strictness was tempered with a deep affection, not only for her two dogs but also for animals in general. I learned that she also shared her home with several exotic parrots and made philanthropic donations to a number of animal charities. Her love of animals practically consumed her. They were her friends, her passion, her raison d'être. Any animal that crossed her path would find itself in luck—as long as it toed the line. But if the pet started to misbehave, strict mother that she was, she would not stand for it and would make her will known. Tina found this out the hard way with a lesson in tough love from "the one who must be obeyed."

There was a sad epilogue to this tale of ferocious leadership. One day some months later, I received a message saying that I had to call Mrs. Spinelli right away. It was an emergency. I called her at home, and as I began to speak I heard her sobbing uncontrollably on the other end of the phone. I paused, and then, when the sobbing diminished somewhat, I said, "Whatever is the matter, Mrs. Spinelli? Please tell me."

"Dr. Dodman," she started, "Bonnie's dead. Tina killed her. It was as if Tina had held it all inside for so long that she just exploded. I normally do not allow them to be together unattended, but this time I left a door unsecured and Tina pushed through it. It was horrible and I saw it all happen. Tina just picked Bonnie up and shook her like a rag doll until she stopped breathing. I tried screaming at Tina but she wouldn't listen, and I—I'm only a small woman, Dr. Dodman—could not pull her off. When I finally did get her attention, it was too late. Poor, poor Bonnie. What have I done?"

"I'm so sorry," I said. I was stunned by this bad news. As I caught my breath, Mrs. Spinelli continued between sobs.

"But that isn't all. I didn't know what to do with Tina afterwards. I wanted to get rid of her but then couldn't bring myself to do it, so I let her stay, even though I could barely bring myself to look at her. And then, guess what? Didn't she go after my beloved parrot, Joey. Oh my god, Dr. Dodman, she did. She grabbed her one day while I was hand-feeding her and she killed her, too. One moment that beautiful green and blue bird was sitting on my hand and the next I saw feathers flying. Tina just crushed her between her jaws, and within two seconds there were her tail feathers protruding from Tina's mouth. Of course, I pried what was left of Joey out of Tina's jaws, but it was too late. She was already gone. That was the final straw. I marched Tina down to the vet's office and, I'm sorry to have to tell you this, I had her put to sleep. I couldn't stand to keep her, and with her aggression problem, I could never have found a home for her without worrying constantly. I'm so, so sorry. I should have listened to you in the first place."

Although the motivation for Tina's parrot-killing spree may in part have been predatory, and thus slightly different from that of the attacks on Bonnie, this was no time to start a discussion of biological motives. Sure, jealousy could have played a role, too.

Since this incident, I have insisted with a lot more conviction that clients support the alpha dog of the pair, often the older one and the incumbent, but not always, as in this case. The penalty for supporting the wrong dog can be very steep, as Mrs. Spinelli painfully learned. Perhaps I should also have insisted that Mrs. Spinelli not interact with her parrot, Joey, in front of top dog Tina—but I didn't know of Joey's existence at the time, and then again, Mrs. Spinelli might not have listened anyway.

Is there a conclusion we can draw from this disaster? I think so. It is that although people may love their dogs dearly, dogs will always be dogs and not human facsimiles. As near human as dogs sometimes seem, they will always have a canine agenda, a canine "take" on things, if you will. It is imperative to appreciate and accept this fact. Therefore, I believe it is every pet owner's responsibility to learn more about the natural behaviors of their pet and to try to cast their animal's existence and their interactions with and between their pets with this truism in mind. If unadulterated love and unmitigated human agendas are substituted for a more biologically appropriate approach, problems can and often do arise. We just can't make up our own rules and fly in the face of thousands of years of evolution. Mrs. Spinelli's insistence on going against the flow brought to mind the legend of King Canute of England, who, around 1000 A.D., sat on a throne by a tidal shore and commanded the waves to retreat. Like Canute, Mrs. Spinelli was unsuccessful and got her feet more than a bit wet, paying an excruciating price for her hubris.

2

BITING THE HAND THAT FEEDS

Every dog is a lion at home.—*Italian saying*

The receptionist handed me the record for the next case as an extremely busy day drew to a close. I looked at the top left-hand side of the case record to find the client's name and saw the single word "Pethuggers." Pethuggers, I thought. What on earth is that? I surveyed the crowded waiting room for a few seconds as I pondered the rather unusual name. A large woman cradling a somewhat distraught cat glanced at me hopefully from the feline enclave. A short balding man with a huge Great Dane in tow looked toward me with eyebrows raised. People coughed, feet shuffled, and pets whimpered or moaned as they awaited their fate. I looked down at the chart again.

"Pet huggers, is pet huggers here?" I asked gingerly. Everybody looked up at once, perhaps thinking I was going to say something really profound. One of the assembled, a tallish, slimmish, bearded man, rose slowly to his feet, turning his head sideways toward a woman who was accompanying him. This must be them, I thought. As the two of them approached me, I noticed the dog behind them.

He was a well-behaved, calm-looking beagle who gave no clues as to the problem at issue.

After some perfunctory handshakes, the three of us headed into the rather stark, windowless consulting room where, in the customary fashion, we situated ourselves around my partners-style steel-trimmed desk. A dim table lamp was positioned to counter the somewhat intimidating effect of overhead striplighting, and a synthetic washable rug, in lieu of a carpet, was strategically positioned to create a homey effect. I glanced at the owners' written description of the problem before surveying them more carefully. "Unpredictable aggression," it seemed, was the problem to be addressed. I cast another glance at the dog, and once again he gave no clues as to the mercurial side of his personality, appearing nonchalant, if not a little curious, about his new surroundings. I looked up and smiled hello at his guardians.

"Allow me to introduce myself," said the confident-looking, forty-ish man, inching forward on his seat and leaning in toward me. "My name is Andy Smith. I'm an attorney and founder of Pethuggers, a nonprofit animal rescue organization. Mikey," he said, gesturing toward the indifferent animal, "was rescued by us some time ago and is presently in a foster care situation with Beth."

I cast my eyes to the woman next to him, who acknowledged that she was indeed Beth.

"Beth Gardner," she said with a faint smile. "I would really like to be able to keep Mikey, if at all possible. I haven't had him long but he is a dear and I've grown quite fond of him. I really don't think he can help himself when he gets into one of those moods."

She might have been right. Beth was around forty, had strawberry blond hair, a pale complexion, flatish features, and wore a gentle expression. I immediately picked up that she was a sensitive and caring person. She seemed smart, too, and was clearly looking for serious help with Mikey. Though all three of us were united in our desire to help this dog, conversations such as the one that lay ahead are never easy for owners, or even their agents. Most people feel a little uneasy about discussing their pet's problems in front of a "pet psychologist," even worse, a "pet psychiatrist," perhaps because the aberrant behavior may somehow be a reflection of their own mismanagement or ignorance, or perhaps because of the supposedly "fringish" nature of behavioral medicine. Beth and Andy were no exception to this general rule, so before the proceedings proper, we had a small side conversation to break the ice. During this conversation we introduced ourselves and settled in for what turned out to be a lengthy and intriguing session.

Andy was not simply along for the ride but had a vested interest. He was a dyed-in-the-wool animal activitist who really put himself out on behalf of dogs and cats to spare them unnecessary suffering, and Mikey was one of his protégés. Apparently Mikey had been abused by his first owners prior to being abandoned at one year of age. After some weeks of wandering, an emaciated, matted Mikey was apprehended by a dog officer and brought to the local shelter, where he was put up for adoption. A month or so passed, but nobody seemed to want Mikey because he was not house-trained. Prospective adopters always hesitated at that incriminating line in his transcript and then moved on. Eventually Mikey's card was flipped over—an indication that he was slated for "humane destruction" (talk about an oxymoron). This is when Andy and his organization came to the rescue of Mikey, who graduated to the risk-free luxury of Andy's no-kill shelter. During his stay, he was housed in an indoor/outdoor commercial kennel, all bills paid, while Pethuggers searched for a foster home for him. He was there for a year before they located an owner willing to tolerate and work to correct his defect. Beth was that person. Mikey was just over two years old at the time of his trial adoption by Beth.

Beth, a professor of anthropology at a local university, was obviously completely smitten with Mikey, and her attachment was immediate. Both Beth and her husband, Fred, also a successful academic, were career people. They had made a conscious decision not to have children. Instead, when they first married, some twenty years earlier, they had acquired a dog, one of those once-in-a-lifetime dogs, who lived to be fifteen years old. When this dog, Rusty, eventually died, they couldn't bear to have him buried in the backyard because they knew they would move sooner or later. So they had him cremated and his ashes put in an urn that would travel with them everywhere. Those ashes were still on Beth's mantelpiece and she talked to her deceased friend daily. When Rusty died, for reasons that only serious dog owners can fully understand, she could not bear to replace him with another dog. There was, and never would be, any substitute for Rusty's unique personality. But time, as usual, tempers all, and it was well into this healing phase that the long-bereaved Beth encountered Andy from Pethuggers. Mikey was about to get a new life.

At the time of the consultation, Beth had owned Mikey for about two and a half months. During that time, despite his introverted, dour attitude, he would occasionally erupt into apparently unpredictable fits of aggression. The aggressive bouts lasted mere seconds, but there was no doubt that whatever message he was trying to transmit, he was really serious about it. These incidents only occurred three to five times a week, but, understandably, that was three to five times a week too often for Andy and Beth. Both were extremely concerned about the way things were going.

I asked Beth to describe in detail some of the situations that brought on Fred's aggression, and she told me that there were four categories of circumstance in which he might show aggression. The first was when she tried to remove some object from him that he had "stolen." The second was when she pulled on his collar or otherwise told him to do something he didn't want to do. The third was when she or Fred lifted him up, and the fourth was when he was cornered and, as she said, "felt closed in." She added that yelling at him seemed to make things worse, though she could sometimes distract him with a penny can or food treat. Having itemized the problems, she then proceeded to relate details of Mikey's most recent incident of aggression. This happened while she was sitting on the couch and Mikey slithered up next to her. She started to pet him, which initially he seemed to enjoy, but then, as she leaned over him and put her arm around him, he snapped at her and then bit her arm. I saw Andy, the lawyer, squirm mentally.

Beth, apparently oblivious to Andy's discomfort, proceeded to describe Mikey's lifestyle. Mikey, I learned, spent most of his time in the house with Beth and Fred. The couple, however, also had a kennel on their property (a ten-by-ten-foot room with wall-to-wall carpeting, large windows, well insulated and heated) with a dog door leading to a fenced run of approximately twenty-five by fifteen feet. They put Mikey in the kennel when they both had to be absent for more than a couple of hours, which occurred approximately four times a week, but he spent the rest of the time in the house. The primary reason for his sequestration at certain times was Mikey's ongoing housebreaking problem. Confined in this way, he would bark his head off, causing the neighbors to complain, so Beth had fitted him with an antibark collar. I presumed that this was a "shock collar," but chose not to delve too far into the matter for fear of diverting her from the theme of her story. As she continued, I learned that she had a calico cat called Rainbow, whom Mikey seemed to enjoy and tried his hardest to interact with. Despite his best efforts, however, Rainbow simply ignored his attempts at friendship and would generally saunter off in search of seclusion.

I asked Beth for, and received, a full report on a day in Mikey's life. On a typical day he would wake up in his dog bed in Beth and Fred's bedroom, have his breakfast in the kitchen, and then spend a couple of hours hanging around the house or resting in a sunny spot before being put in the indoor kennel. He was confined to the kennel, with its outdoor run, for about five hours when Beth and Fred were away. In the kennel, Mikey would mostly sleep, seldom playing and usually refusing to eat. When Beth and Fred returned home, Mikey was allowed back in the house and was fed dinner between 5 and 7 P.M.

Following this, Beth indulged him for a while before the nighttime getting-ready-for-bed routine started. Mikey's life was a simple one. He liked playing in the yard, chasing sticks, and going for the newspaper, but was never allowed off leash except when in the fenced-in kennel area during the day. Around the house he enjoyed playing with toys, running around, and, according to Beth, being cuddled. No wonder Mikey wanted Rainbow to play. He must have been truly bored. Too many dog owners, Beth included, think that if they provide their dog with two square meals per day, a roof over his head, and their warmth and affection, their pet will be fully satisfied and eternally grateful. This is not the case. Dogs, like people, have more diverse biological imperatives than survival. They need social structure, direction, and outlets for various natural behaviors. Mikey was not leading a real dog's life.

Obedience-wise, Mikey was somewhat lax. Beth hedged on my questions regarding his responsiveness to commands.

Does he reliably respond to a stay command?
"Sometimes," Beth replied.
Does he perform a "down" when instructed?
"When he wants to."
Does he come when called?
"He knows the word."

And so on.

When asked about situations in which Mikey was less likely to obey her, Beth said, "When he's got something that he's decided should be his or when he's otherwise intent on some pursuit." In other words, whenever she *really* needed him to respond. She added, "He's got a beagle mentality."

I was beginning to learn of another side of Mikey that wasn't apparent from his amiable in-office disposition. I turned the page of the questionnaire to the dominance profile that Beth had been kind enough to fill out for me and noticed that Mikey's aggression, though confined to certain circumstances, was severe and fully committed. Specifically, rather than growling, lifting a lip, or otherwise threatening when ticked off, he would escalate immediately to a bite. Beth had checked off that he would be likely to bite if a real bone or rawhide chew was taken away from him, and that he would bite if a "stolen" object was taken away against his will, if his collar was grabbed or he was pulled back by the scruff, and, finally, if anyone tried to *make* him respond to a command. The intensity of his response gave Mikey a dominance score (80 out of a possible 240 points) considerably higher than that of the average dominant aggressive dog we see at Tufts (34).

Most worrisome was not the score per se but the way he attained it—by biting. Some dogs bite halfheartedly, leaving delicate imprints and barely puncturing the skin. In Mikey's case, the bites were forceful and liable to cause serious damage. He displayed no bite inhibition—a bad omen for the future if ever there was one. At least one thing was clear: the diagnosis of dominance-related aggression. Mikey was a typically dominant dog and his aggression was selfishly motivated to preserving his own best interests. Typically, dominance aggression displays itself as overzealous protectiveness of objects or food, in response to perceived invasions of personal space, or when a dog is forced to do something against its will or is chastised. Mikey's aggression manifested itself in all three of these classical situations. Also typical of dominance aggression was the fact that his acts of aggression were sudden, seemingly without warning or threat, and immediately afterward, he seemed contrite or remorseful, or was seemingly unaware of what had gone before.

But it wasn't only Mikey's commitment to a full crushing bite that worried me. Beth's warm and forgiving disposition also posed a problem, I thought, for Mikey's rehabilitation. When I asked her why she took Mikey on, she said, "To love and be loved." As good a reason as that was, it wasn't what I wanted to hear, bearing in mind the problem I was about to address. The kind of loving relationship she was looking for is possible with many dogs but wasn't possible with Mikey. He was a tough and willful dog who was relatively independent and self-sufficient. Beth's attempts to curry his favor and draw him into her "circle of love" would be construed by Mikey as a sign of weakness and would allow him to perceive himself as ranking higher in the family pack. Her practice of giving food treats to him unconditionally, lavishing him with sycophantic affection, and responding to his demands for attention with alacrity would all foster his perception of her as a low ranker—because this is how low rankers behave in the pack. Catering to a dominant dog's every need leads to the initiation and sustenance of owner-directed dominance aggression. Whether I would be able to persuade Beth to change and act in ways counter to her instincts was by no means certain.

"So what do you think, Doc?" Beth said cheerfully. "I am determined to do whatever I have to do to turn this around because I love this little sucker despite himself."

I mused for a second. At least the commitment was there. I would give it a try, assuming she was that willing to work with the program. There weren't too many other options for poor Mikey. It seemed unlikely that he would find any better opportunity than to be in a home with a loving and intelligent owner who was determined to stay the course with him. I outlined for Beth the so-called Nothing in Life is Free dominance modification program. As both Beth and Andy sat there scribbling notes, I explained the "how to" essence of what I refer to as the Ten Commandments.

Ten Commandments for Dominance Control

1. Engage in consistent (daily) nonconfrontational obedience training with an appropriate reward for a job well done.
2. Require all food and treats to be *earned* by having the dog sit or lie down on command before these assets are made available.
3. Have the dog work (obey a command) to receive petting.

4. Initiate and terminate all games, using one-word commands.
5. Cache toys and other objects the dog is likely to steal and only provide them under certain terms and conditions.
6. Do not supply real bones, rawhide chews, or delicious food that the dog might want to protect.
7. Do not force a dominant dog to do anything.
8. Never reprimand the dog but rather ignore it, turning a cold shoulder when it behaves badly.
9. Prevent the dog from getting onto furniture or beds.
10. Provide adequate exercise and a low-protein, artificial-preservative-free diet.

I thought some of the directives were going to be easy for Beth to follow, but I could see Beth swallowing hard at the idea of curbing her interactions with Mikey and making her love conditional. As I saw her struggling to come to grips with this new concept, I decided that it would be opportune to describe the type of success we have had with this program and the likely time frame for Mikey's improvement.

"Nine out of ten people who engage in this dominance control program see improvement in their dogs within a period of two months," I told her, "and seven out of ten believe their dog's behavior is so much improved that they would consider their problem with the dog cured."

I saw a flicker of a smile cross her lips as she held my gaze. Andy was slowly nodding as he imbibed these impressive figures. I assured Beth that not all aspects of this austere "tough love" program would need to be continued indefinitely and that she might be able to cut Mikey some slack sometime in the future, once he was toeing the line.

"So the improvement is maintained?" Andy asked.

"It is," I was able to reply with confidence, as we had just completed a long-term study of dogs treated by means of this "dominance control" program. "We have studied dogs six to eighteen months out from this program and found that their dominance scores have remained consistently low once people have learned how to master their interaction with their dog."

"And what about medication?" Andy asked. "Is there ever any cause to use drugs in a case like this?"

"Yes," I replied. "We often prescribe medicines to curb pets' aggression while owners come to grips with the behavior modification program. But I always suggest that they try the behavior modification alone first, because it's often effective on its own. I would suggest that Beth try behavior modification alone for about two months, and then, at that time, we can talk about whether medication would be necessary. The medicine we usually prescribe is Prozac, one of the selective serotonin-enhancing drugs. This drug has the effect of curbing any residual aggression and facilitating the dog's eventual rehabilitation."

Beth looked a little disappointed that I was not going to prescribe Prozac right away. Her look prompted me to make another suggestion.

"There is a sort of halfway house treatment that sometimes helps to reduce aggression," I ventured.

"Oh," said Beth, her face brightening a little.

"It's 5HTP—a dietary supplement, an amino acid, actually, that you can buy in health food stores or pharmacies as a mood stabilizer. 5HTP is a precursor of serotonin, the neurotransmitter that all our behavior modification strategies are designed to augment. When dogs are fed 5HTP, it enters the bloodstream and is converted into serotonin. A high concentration of serotonin will reduce Mikey's impulsivity and increase his threshold for aggressive behavior. It might be worth a try."

"It certainly would," Andy said, glancing at Beth. "I think that's a very fair compromise, and personally, I prefer the idea of a dietary supplement."

"Me, too," said Beth. "Whatever we need to do, I'm prepared to do for this dog. Fred and I are fully committed to do what we need to do to help him."

On this note, the consultation terminated and we departed for the reception area. I bid them farewell at the front door of the hospital, watched them climb into a car after they put Mikey into the rear seat, and then they left the campus. Back in the sanctuary of my office, I sat staring out of my window as I pondered Mikey's case. It's always so tragic when a dog's and an owner's personalities are so ill matched, as they appeared to be in this case. To Beth, a kindly, intelligent, childless woman, Mikey was to be enjoyed and indulged as the waif that he was. If Mikey had known which side of his bread was buttered, he would have gone along with Beth's indulgences. He had it "made in the shade" with both Beth and Fred. Love and affection, a beautiful home, and a veritable cornucopia of food and other goodies. What else did he want? What a pity he didn't understand the way things really were. What a pity we couldn't explain it to him. Because of his behavioral myopia, he just didn't see the big picture. He was preoccupied with the moment, overly protective of what he jealously regarded as his own, and was both intolerant and irascible. This mind-set was virtually the opposite of Beth's. Beth wanted to share everything with Mikey and, in return, sought only his love.

A couple of days after Andy and Beth came to see me, I was approached by NBC to help them put together a program about behavior problems in pets. One of the subjects they were interested in illustrating was canine aggression. Naturally, Mikey's case sprang to mind. Somewhat tentatively, I called Beth at home and asked her if she would be willing to cooperate by allowing Mikey to be filmed. She was extremely enthusiastic about the project, feeling that by sharing her story she could somehow help dog owners everywhere. This was the motivation from my perspective, too, and between us we began to figure out how best to depict Mikey's behavior and her present plight. Though in the early stages of treatment, Mikey was still likely to show some aggression, but the problem was how to demonstrate his worst side without Beth getting hurt.

Beth bravely and generously agreed to give this matter some thought before the camera crew's visit. Unbeknownst to me, the scheme she came up with was to have husband Fred film her with their camcorder while she provoked Mikey. When she called me a few days after our conversation, I thought she wanted to discuss how to proceed, but I was in for a dreadful surprise.

"Dr. Dodman, I got the tape that you wanted," she said jubilantly, "but unfortunately Mikey bit me and it was quite a serious bite this time."

"Oh no," I said, groaning at the thought of what might have occurred. "Tell me what happened."

"Well, I took the commission a little too seriously, I suppose," she said. "I had Fred film me as I laid next to Mikey petting him. Then I tried picking him up, and so on. Everything was going well for a while, he did growl a couple of times, but then I put him on the couch next to me and went to hug him. That's when he bit me . . . in the hand."

"Did he actually puncture the skin?" I asked, horrified.

"Oh yes, he did a real number on me. His tooth went clean into my palm, there was blood everywhere. It's okay now, though. I washed it well and had it bandaged. It's throbbing a bit at the moment but I'll be okay."

"Good heavens," I said. "I wish you hadn't pushed him that far."

"Well, I must admit, I didn't quite realize that he would respond so violently, but at least we've got the incident on film so the producer will be happy."

Sure enough, when I told the producer she was ecstatic. High drama of this magnitude makes good television, so I could understand her reaction.

"Excellent," she replied. "That really illustrates the point well. I am sorry for the woman, though. Please give her my condolences. We'll go to the house next week and film an interview with her to complete the segment. It's great to have the aggression already on tape. At least we won't have that problem to deal with."

I didn't feel as enthusiastic about the aggressive incident as the producer, but what was done was done. The film was in the can. When the camera crew arrived for the interview, Beth was able to demonstrate the techniques she had been practicing with Mikey. She was able to show him sit on command in order to gain access to the yard and lie down before receiving his food. These measures, involving having him work for privileges and resources, were components of the leadership program I had recommended to Beth and Fred.

The weeks ticked by and the program aired showing Beth being bitten and trailing off to the bathroom, blood dripping from her hand. We all lived the nightmare a second time. Beth was very disappointed that many of the comments she had made during the television interview were not aired, particularly those relating to her reason for wanting to work with Mikey to resolve his problem. She said she'd encountered so many people who just said, "Why don't you just put that dog down?" or "For goodness' sake, Beth, it's just a dog. Why don't you get a different one?" Apparently Beth had mentioned this attitude in the interview and wanted her response to be documented. Reasonable person that she was, she acknowledged these other people's points of view, agreed to disagree, and then stated her case. Basically, she felt, as I do, that a commitment is a commitment and if problems arise they should be corrected rather than avoided or passed on to someone else by placing the pet in a new home. Getting rid of Mikey was not an option, she told the interviewer. She would do what she could until either a satisfactory result was achieved or until there was no further hope of improvement for Mikey.

I appreciated Beth's sentiments and philosophy, but I was definitely concerned about her personal safety and her own apparent disregard for it. Andy, I knew, felt the same way as I did. The three of us stayed in contact by e-mail, monitoring events as they unfolded, with Andy and me full of trepidation. The following excerpts from our e-mail correspondence, in chronological order, illustrate the difficulties we encountered.

In an effort to prevent him from urinating on her deck, Beth said she gently took hold of his purple collar and spoke softly to him, trying to direct him toward the steps.

> Then, all of a sudden, I mean, with absolutely no warning at all, he got this look in his eyes like something out of a Stephen King movie (wide eyed and sort of glazed), snarled, and while baring his teeth, went for the hand that I had on his collar. I was able to pull my wrist away before he inflicted more than just tooth marks but if I hadn't been able to disengage myself I don't know what would have happened. I had to leave for an appointment and was shaking all over as I went. Believe me, I did not yell or even pull. I was gentle. He had been in a good or neutral mood until the second he went for me.

On another occasion, noticing some matter around his eyes, Beth reported:

> I got a tissue and gently began to wipe around his eyes. He snarled at me and snapped but I was out of there before he made any contact. This happened at least once before when I've tried to wipe stuff away from his eyes but that was a long while ago. It was probably my fault.

And then, a week later,

> Mikey just bit down hard on both my forearms. . . . I was taking a break from grading papers and decided to brush his coat. He went from one arm to the other. I was wearing long sleeves but still have raised welts on both arms.

Then there were encouraging messages.

> Mikey was a sweet little dog this weekend. What a strange contrast. The nice weather makes it easier to get him the exercise he needs. Fred is willing to let me take the lead on this. I want to give Mikey every chance. As long as my patience and my fingers are still there, I'd like to keep trying.

But things never stayed good for long, and the nice/nasty pattern reminded me of what abused women often go through with abusive men.

> Mikey just tried to attack both of us, rather viciously. I was trying to coax him to go outside before bedtime so that he wouldn't wake up Fred in the middle of the night, as he has for the last two nights. I used a soft, gentle voice to coax him. When he looked uninterested, I tried to attach his leash and walk him. Then he went for me and wouldn't quit. Luckily, I got away before he did much damage. A few minutes later, Fred tried the same thing with the same result, except that he got Fred in the stomach as well as the hand (no skin broken though, Fred got away, too). Twice, earlier that evening, he appeared to want to be petted, nuzzling, pawing and wagging his tale, and then, when I went to oblige, he growled at me menacingly. Just when you think there's a little progress . . .

Things deteriorated further.

> Mikey has been on a tear this morning. Tried to bite me when I attempted to brush his coat. Tried to bite Fred when he went to put the leash on him. Ate a disgusting litter-encrusted turd out of the cat's litterbox. Absolutely ignored all commands. Life's just a bowl of cherries with this Mikey man. What did I do to deserve such happiness?

As I expected and feared, Beth was not able to follow through with all aspects of the program. For example, she somehow couldn't help trying to make him do things by speaking to him softly and guiding him by his collar. I had advised her against this and other coercive measures. Along similar lines, she couldn't resist the temptation to tug at his lead to make him go somewhere. Also, she consistently invaded his personal space, seemingly acting on the hypothesis that her kindness and patience would eventually be repaid. I don't believe she meant to disregard what I was saying; she couldn't help herself. She had worked on some mild-mannered obedience training at Mikey's mealtimes and tried to make him sit before he went out the French doors to the deck, but it was impossible for her to implement a full-fledged, boot-camp-style retraining program. She just wasn't up to it. She was too kind.

Quite apart from that issue, another unexpected factor crept in. One evening Beth and Fred woke up to hear Mikey's tags jingling. They wondered what had happened and got a flashlight so that Mikey could go outside. He was out of his dog bed, shaking all over, drooling heavily, and unable to stand. He kept trying to stand up, but each time collapsed and exhausted himself in the effort. He seemed unable to attend to what they were saying or to move in a deliberate way. The tremors and other signs lasted about three minutes, after which he slowly regained the ability to stand and then staggered to the door, falling several times in the process. Eventually he managed to get outside and took care of business on the deck before stumbling back in and trying to bite Beth when she attempted to towel the wet snow off him, a routine he usually enjoyed. The situation was tense. Mikey had two or three other attacks like this one, and had another bizarre spell where he began licking the carpet and wood trim in the gazebo non-stop before vomiting half a dozen times. Beth took him outside after this attack and he began to eat a great deal of grass, then vomited two large amounts of grass before appearing a little easier. Beth then gave Mikey his evening meal, most of which he ate, but when he came back into the house, he began licking the carpet and acting nervous again, following which he vomited four more times. All of the above signs, including the shaking and inability to stand, the carpet licking, and vomiting are attributable to seizures. This was an unexpected turn of events, although in retrospect, Beth and Fred remembered detecting drool on the carpet at other times, which could indicate that he had previous attacks when they were not around.

As I was in the process of trying to decide which medication to use to control his seizures, Mikey attacked Beth one more time and this turned out to be the final straw for Andy, who insisted on bringing Mikey back to the kennels. Once again, Beth had contravened the rules, petting Mikey while he was on the living room couch. All of a sudden, he burst into the most explosive aggression she had ever seen, worse by a factor of ten, according to her account. During the attack he bit her in the chest and did not let go. Fred had to step up to the plate and pry Mikey away from Beth, but not before the damage was done. I heard about this horrific event the next day when Beth, in her usual lighthearted way, took the blame for what had happened and tried to play down the incident. "Before this," she quipped, "I had a perfect pair of breasts." I had no reason to doubt this.

This last aggressive incident was a turning point for Mikey because Andy as Mikey's trustee and legal owner, felt that he could no longer justify leaving Mikey in Beth's care. He explained to her that it would be better to have Mikey's problems treated in the safety of a kennel environment under my direction than to risk any further attacks directed toward her. Husband Fred supported this view and Mikey was duly transported back to the Pethuggers kennels. The first thing I asked Andy to do was to have Mikey checked by the local veterinarian. The vet reported no physical problems and ran blood work, the results of which were unremarkable. Then, from a distance, I instituted treatment with Prozac and phenobarbital—the former to control Mikey's aggression and the latter to suppress his seizures. This combination of medications had proven effective in similar cases, so I thought that it would be worth trying again.

I didn't hear from Pethuggers or Beth again for a couple of months because I was on the road and no doubt they were busy, too. However, news did eventually come. When it came, it was good. Andy reported that since Mikey had been at the kennel he had not had any seizures and there had been no side effects from the medications, which he appeared to be tolerating well. He added that Mikey's behavior was also very good, but noted that he was in a totally controlled environment and that a full assessment was not really possible under these circumstances. Nonetheless, Mikey had enjoyed interactions with the staff and had played with a few of the other dogs without incident. This was indeed good news.

Eight months elapsed before I next heard about Mikey. I called Beth because I knew that she would be intimately involved in his fate. As it turned out, although she had not been able to readopt him on the advice of Andy and Fred, Mikey had found placement on a large farm owned by a dog lover who had advanced multiple sclerosis. The man really needed a friend, and so did Mikey. The two of them hit it off perfectly, and though it may sound a little maudlin, the fact is that Mikey now enjoys life on the farm with his new owner, a life free from aggression and seizures. Reading between the lines, Mikey's new owner must have been a no-nonsense individual and a strong leader to whom Mikey could look for direction. It is often the case with dominant dogs that when their owner takes proper control of them, they appear relieved and are visibly less stressed. It is almost as if they are saying, "Thank goodness. For a horrible moment I thought I was going to have to be in charge here."

Knowing how Beth felt about Mikey, I asked her how she felt about the situation. As you may have guessed, she was just happy for him that he had found his niche. She didn't say that she was sad that she wasn't the one to love and be loved by Mikey. She was just thankful for the things she had. A good home, a good job, and a loving husband. Secretly, I hoped that one day she would find another dog to replace the two that she had lost and to complete her family circle. Until then she had husband Fred and Rusty's ashes to keep her company.

3

POLTERGEIST IN A FOG

We are shaped and fashioned by what we love.—*Goethe*

Sometimes, perhaps once in a lifetime, dog owners find that they have a truly remarkable dog, a dog who understands them as perfectly as they understand him. Dogs like this seem almost human in their ability to recognize their owners' moods, needs, and wishes, and freely give their undivided loyalty and trust to all family members. They seem both wise and loving and would have a caring home forever were it not for the curse of the canine species: that their lives are unfortunately all too short. When such dogs die, they leave a huge gap in the family ranks which is impossible to fill.

Rufus was such a dog to the Collins family. When he died one miserable muddy March day in Massachusetts, his family grieved. In Rufus's case, it was not just his human family that missed him but also his lifelong canine companion, Sammy, an eleven-year-old Akita–Bernese mountain dog crossbreed, who had a profoundly hard time coming to grips with his old friend's sudden demise. His owners, John and Martha Collins, were not the type of people to just fold. They would not collapse under the weight of their grief; they would find a solution to their mutual suffering, a remedy for themselves and for Sammy. The only solution they could come up with was to get another dog to make their family whole again and to provide a diversion from their anguish. They knew the new dog could not replace the irreplaceable Rufus, but they also knew they had scant choice in the matter. They intended to wait a respectable period of time before acting on their pained impulse, out of respect for Rufus, but vowed that when the time seemed right, they would cut their losses and start looking for his replacement.

A month later, the Collinses went to the New Hampshire SPCA in Stratham, New Hampshire, looking to adopt a husky, malamute, or some other northern breed of dog in an attempt to replace the dog they had lost. Merlin wasn't at all what they were looking for, but his exotic blue merle coloring caught their eye and they asked if they could take him out of the pen to check him out. The people at the shelter were delighted to find someone interested in him and told them that he was extremely timid, a "rescued" animal, as they say. They believed that he was approximately six months old, no one knew for sure. They weren't able to share many details of his early life but indicated he had been neglected and possibly abused. He didn't have a name at the time and the SPCA workers had dubbed him "Stanley."

When the SPCA volunteer went into the pen to leash Stanley and bring him out, he was, true to his young nature, terrified. He had to be dragged out, and cowered with his belly just a few inches off the floor and his tail so tight between his legs that the Collinses weren't even sure he had one. He wouldn't make eye contact with anyone, just kept his head down low, trembled, and kept trying to turn back into the pen. With patience, the Collinses managed to coax him outside the immediate kennel area, and he walked along on the leash submissively, trembling slightly, never raising his head or his tail. The Collinses tried to be as unintimidating as they could be, but nothing they could do would allay Stanley's all-consuming fear.

The Collinses had owned a lot of dogs between them and considered themselves to be proficient "dog people." In addition, they had a great doggy environment—a large fenced-in yard with a dog door into the house, another friendly and outgoing companion dog, and no kids, so that their dogs were the most important members of their family and received a lot of attention. Neighbors said the Collinses treated their dogs better than most people treat their children, which was undoubtedly true. Confidently, though somewhat naively, the Collinses assumed that they'd be able to take this timorous mutt home, win his confidence, and show him that life was wonderful. They thought that, with their help, he'd get over his fears and become a happy and confident dog. Also, in the back of their minds, the Collinses knew that most folk would probably not consider adopting a dog as fearful as Stanley and that the SPCA wouldn't, couldn't, hold on to unadoptable animals forever. A combination of these factors—overconfidence and compassion bordering on pity—led the Collinses to take Stanley home and give him a chance.

If potential adopters already own a dog, the SPCA will not let them take a dog home unless they bring their other dog to the shelter and introduce the dogs to each other. The Collinses' first visit to the shelter was on a Saturday, so the next day, Sunday, they returned with Sammy in tow. Stanley, more tremulous than before, again had to be coaxed from his pen, and the two dogs were subsequently introduced. Sammy was one of those happy-go-lucky dog-loving dogs. He loved people too. Naturally he thought Stanley was great, and that came as no surprise to the Collinses. Stanley was scared of all people, but not of Sammy, and actually sniffed him a little, showing his first signs of interest in anything or anyone. The SPCA workers were impressed by how mellow Sammy was and thought he might be instrumental in bringing Stanley out of his shell. So, even though Stanley wasn't a malamute, the Collinses filled out the adoption forms and took him home. Right away they knew "Stanley" wasn't going to work for a name, so they came up with "Merlin" because of his merle coat, and because they'd just watched a movie about Merlin and King Arthur, and Martha was a big fan of *The Once and Future King* legend. They always had nicknames for their dogs, so they thought he'd be "Merlin the Magical Dog."

After adopting Merlin, the Collinses learned more about Merlin's history from a friend who volunteered for the New Hampshire SPCA. Merlin was a seized dog from an animal-hoarding case, a tragic situation that I've encountered before. This case involved a woman who collected cats, dogs, and various farm animals—goats and sheep mostly. In all, there were over one hundred animals. The woman provided minimal care for her animals, and it's believed there was some abuse, probably by her boyfriend and directed mostly at the dogs. Apparently all of the dogs, fifteen or twenty of them, were penned together in a large dog run. Merlin was one of the youngest dogs, so he was at the bottom of the pack order. Eventually the woman and her boyfriend moved away, and the animals were left in the charge of the woman's elderly mother, who was incapable of properly caring for herself, let alone the animals. Concerned neighbors contacted the SPCA, which investigated the situation and ended up confiscating all the animals. The animals were divvied up among several shelters. Merlin ended up in Stratham. Apparently he had a sister who looked just like him but was not quite as timid. She was adopted a few weeks before the Collinses went to the shelter, and Merlin, responding to this abandonment, became even more terrified and withdrawn once she had gone. It often happens that fearful or timid dogs become extremely attached to another dog or person and sometimes suffer intense anxiety if they become separated from their attachment figure. The very fact that Merlin displayed this attachment and suffered so terribly following his sibling's departure was yet more evidence of his fearful disposition and shed some light on his likely future behavior.

At the Collinses' home, Merlin rapidly bonded with Sammy and within a week the two of them were playing and tearing around the yard together. It was heartwarming to see Merlin so happy, bobbing and weaving as Sammy came thundering toward him in mock battle, sometimes knocking him over. But all the activity was in the spirit of fun, and the two dogs would later rest together, Sammy with his head or one paw draped across Merlin's back. They made a happy pair. That part of Merlin's rehabilitation went well, and since the primary objective of his adoption was to get a companion for Sammy, in this respect the exercise was an unqualified success.

Merlin displayed no fear at all while playing with Sammy, although Sammy was definitely the dominant one. The problem the Collinses had was that Merlin wasn't getting over his fear of people as they had hoped. He slowly became attached to Martha, but in a subordinate way, and remained absolutely terrified of her husband, John. Strangers visiting the house caused him to panic.

After a couple of months, it seemed that Merlin's fearful behavior was getting worse instead of better. He was friendlier and less shy of Martha, but would still panic if she picked up anything that could conceivably be used to strike him—a flyswatter, stick, rake, or even a piece of rope. Clearly he had received many a good beating from his former owners; beatings that would remain indelibly imprinted on his mind. Early events always have a profound and lasting effect on dogs' personalities, particularly in the first three months of life, with the eighth to the tenth week particularly critical with respect to the development of fears. That's exactly when things were worst for Merlin. Bad experiences at this time in particular should be avoided, as they will likely never be forgotten. Merlin obviously did not manage to dodge this bullet, or rod in his case, and his beatings as a youngster were probably largely responsible for his fearful demeanor. When he was around anyone other than Martha, Merlin would cower, shake, and urinate submissively, or attempt to run away and hide. Not helping the situation, Merlin suffered from panosteitis—a painful condition affecting his bones—and suffered several distressful episodes during his first few months in the Collinses' home. During one occurrence, he appeared even more timid and fearful than usual and cowered and shrank away if approached by anyone, even Martha. It was as if he thought that people were somehow causing him the pain. Luckily he outgrew this condition, so that by the time I saw him he had been free of such painful attacks for months.

On very rare occasions Merlin displayed aggressive behaviors. He once bit a veterinary technician who was giving him an intramuscular injection. He also barked ferociously and snapped at a six-year-old girl, the daughter of friends of the Collinses. He didn't actually bite her but clacked his teeth together very close to her face the minute she strayed from her parents' side. The girl was terrified of Merlin, who, like so many other fearful dogs, capitalized on the situation and went on the offensive. It was as if she was the only person in the world he could dominate and he was making the most of it. Needless to say, his behavior toward her made her even more frightened, and a vicious cycle involving her fear and his aggression was activated. The girl's family had two other children who pretty much ignored Merlin, and he wasn't at all aggressive toward them. Such experiences go to show how sensitive dogs are to our feelings toward them.

Desperate to relieve Merlin's fearfulness, the Collinses talked with their local veterinarian, Dr. Leger of New Haven, Connecticut, who suggested dog-training classes as a first step toward putting Merlin on the road to recovery. The Collinses duly enrolled Merlin in a series of classes early in the summer of 1999, but, despite the "tuition," there was no improvement in his behavior. Actually, the Collinses came to the conclusion that Merlin was too scared to learn anything in the class. Again, other dogs were not a problem for him, only people.

The dog days of summer passed slowly as the Collinses sweated their way through scores of training sessions. Despite all their efforts, they didn't feel they were making much headway. Then they began grasping at straws, following various suggestions from almost anyone who had advice to offer. Martha summarized for me the measures she had taken at this stage and the consequences of her actions:

John and she shared responsibility for feeding the dogs to help endear John to Merlin. However, when John did the feeding, Merlin would approach his dish only after John had put it down and walked away. This situation never improved. John tried randomly offering Merlin special tasty treats and even carried a plastic bag of meat scraps around with him for a while. Merlin would approach John gingerly to receive the treat, but would snatch it from him and take it to the other side of the room to eat it. Not much trust there.

The Collinses had gone out of their way to keep visitors from frightening Merlin. They told strangers to ignore him, to get seated as quickly as possible, and not to make any sudden movements. Socialization was never forced on him. The whole time strangers were there, they had the dog door to the outside open as well as the bedroom door ajar so that Merlin could retreat to a "safe place" if he felt at all threatened. Sometimes he would hang around and watch Sammy being petted and talked to by the visitors, and if the visitors managed to ignore him totally, he might sneak up behind them and sniff their hands or legs. But the minute someone spoke to him or reached out a hand to him, he would retreat to the bedroom or outdoors. This never changed.

Neither John nor Martha ever scolded or punished Merlin, even when he chewed furniture, shoes, or anything else he could get his teeth into, or when he stole food off the counter. Instead they tried to avoid setting him up by not having stuff around that he could chew or steal. Whenever he had done something wrong, the Collinses could tell because he would roll onto his back and pull back his lips, exposing his teeth in a grin—even before they discovered the damage. The Collinses appreciated that this toothy display was a submissive gesture and not an aggressive one. Following this, Merlin would wag his tail as fast as he could and then slink along the ground, not letting Martha get anywhere near him. It was as if he knew he'd done something wrong and was sorry, but at the same time was afraid that she might punish him (even though she never had). What's odd is that when he was doing this slinking, he would turn to John and hide behind him or sometimes lean up against him as if he wanted protection from Martha's potential wrath.

By the end of the summer the Collinses felt that Merlin's improvement had stalled. He was in a veritable behavioral doldrums and the Collinses were beginning to lose hope that he would make any more gains. But then a close friend of theirs who happened to be a veterinarian asked if they'd considered some type of antianxiety medication. This was a new avenue to pursue. They spoke with Dr. Leger about this prospect and he agreed that medication was probably needed, but instead of simply prescribing something on a trial basis, he suggested that they visit me at Tufts. The leaves had just started to turn color in Massachusetts when the Collinses came for their initial consultation but their thoughts were far from the scene of orange, red, and gold beauty that surrounded them on the trip.

My first impression of Merlin was that he had been abused. As attractive as he was to look at, his shyness of people radiated like a somber beacon and it was clear to me that he was dysfunctional. I had only seen a couple of dogs as severely affected as Merlin over the previous ten years—he really stood out in the crowd. The Collinses, two of the most well-balanced people you could hope to meet, narrated Merlin's tragic tale and I sat and listened intently. At the conclusion of their story, I deliberated on the best way to help Merlin. I ran through the usual potpourri of background measures, ranging from appropriate exercise, a healthy diet, and improved communication through training, and dwelled for some time on a specific behavioral modification practice known as desensitization and counterconditioning. I realized, however, that the Collinses had already tried some of what I was suggesting and agreed with the referring vet that it was probably time for some antianxiety medication to grease the wheels of success. Casting my mind back to a similarly dysfunctional pit bull I had once treated highly successfully with the antidepressant amitriptyline, I decided to try this medication first. I prescribed a fairly robust dose with all due advice and caveats. Amitriptyline, I thought, should lift Merlin's spirits, stabilize his mood, and reduce his fearfulness. It was, potentially, a "threefer" deal.

The Collinses took my training and behavioral modification suggestions, and simultaneously started Merlin on amitriptyline. After about three weeks, they reported back to me that Merlin was noticeably less frightened than he had been previously, but had started displaying aggressive behavior to other dogs as a side effect. Unfortunately such overconfidence does sometimes occur when amitriptyline is prescribed, and I had warned the Collinses about this possible paradoxical effect. The most alarming aggressive incident took place one evening when the Collinses took both dogs for a walk at a nearby park. For the first time since they had owned him, Merlin became ferocious with other dogs, barking, growling, jumping, and acting as if he wanted to kill them. We stopped the amitriptyline immediately and switched him to Prozac.

About two weeks after beginning the Prozac, and before it had time to produce any meaningful effect, the Collinses' house caught fire while the dogs were penned outside. Apparently, spontaneous combustion of oily rags was responsible for the conflagration. Whatever the cause of the fire, John came home from work one day to find the fire department in his driveway and one end of their house in flames. One section of the dog fence had burned down and Sammy (whom they referred to as "the intelligent dog") had run out of the yard away from the house and was mingling affectionately with the firefighters. Neighbors finally nabbed him and put him in their yard, but they couldn't find Merlin anywhere and believed he had gone into the burning, smoke-filled house to hide. Merlin's favorite safe place, reserved for hiding from the most frightening experiences, was in the Collinses' spare bedroom, under a computer table. John told the firefighters that that's where they'd find him. Thankfully the fire department had some dog-loving firefighters, and three of them went into the house to get Merlin out. He was precisely where John told them he would be, hunkered down and shaking violently, drooling from the corners of his mouth. The Collinses were having some carpeting laid on the day of the fire, so they'd filled their spare room with small pieces of furniture from the other end of the house—end tables, chairs, chests, stereo speakers, etc. The room was absolutely crammed. Merlin was in the far corner, under the computer table. The house was completely filled with smoke at this point—an atmosphere the firefighters described as "oatmeal." Three of them went into the crammed, smoke-filled room in their full fire-fighting regalia, including breathing apparatus, and tried to coax Merlin out. Surprisingly, he didn't want to come! He put up a fight, not biting, just refusing to come out, twisting every which way every time they got hold of him and acting like he had twelve legs to hold on with instead of four. In fact, Merlin did everything in his power to stay under the computer table, where he thought it was safe. Later Martha spoke with the firefighter leading the rescue mission and he said, "It was like fighting a poltergeist in a fog." When they were finally able to go into the house, they saw what he meant. It looked like there had been an earthquake in that room. Pictures were knocked off the wall, furniture was overturned, and stereo speakers were on top of the counter. Merlin had indeed put up an impressive fight.

It took the firefighters about fifteen minutes to wrestle Merlin out, and they only succeeded because by that time he was overcome by smoke. The lead firefighter carried him out, laid him down on the lawn, and then flopped down beside him, totally exhausted from the battle he'd just been through. Eight people ran over and crowded around Merlin, who was semiconscious, making sure he was breathing while trying to revive him. Nearby, an incapacitated firefighter who lay sprawled out on the grass, coughing and wheezing noisily, was totally ignored.

John knew that Merlin probably needed some sort of medical attention, so he put him in his pickup truck and drove off to the vet's office. The Collinses heard several comments later about how much they must love their dogs because John drove off with Merlin while flames were still coming out of one end of their house and the fire department was actively battling the fire. John's response was that he couldn't do anything to help the fire department—they'd either get it out or not. Merlin needed some attention right away and that was something he could do something about. Fortunately Merlin's smoke inhalation wasn't too bad. He was given an injection of corticosteroid and sent home on a short course of antibiotics as a precautionary measure. While John was at the vet's office, the staff was asking him how bad the fire was. To their surprise, John said he just didn't know—the firemen were still putting it out when he left. When Martha got home, the fire was almost out and the neighbors rushed up to her to tell her where John and Merlin were and that Sammy was safe and at their house.

Fortunately the fire didn't completely devastate the Collinses' home. Damage was confined to the cellar and one end of the house. However, because of the smoke and water damage, John and Martha were unable to return to the house for a week, so they went to stay with some friends nearby. Unfortunately these friends had cats and neither of the Collinses' dogs did well with cats, so the dogs could not come with them. Instead their neighbors, the ones who'd taken Sammy to their house during the fire, volunteered to keep both dogs with them until the Collinses could get the fence fixed and the house boarded up enough to let the dogs back in. Martha was concerned about Merlin's response to being in a strange house without her, but the neighbors said he did fine. Sammy was there with him, and the neighbors had a mild-mannered husky-type dog of their own. Merlin did not seem stressed at all and was content to follow both dogs around all day. The neighbors were dog-savvy people and didn't try to force Merlin to interact with them; they just let him be and things worked out well. However, at the end of his stay, a week later, he was definitely glad to see Martha when she showed up to bring them home.

After the fire, the Collinses' life was anything but routine. There was a continuous flow of contractors, carpenters, plumbers, and electricians through their house. They were living in one end of the dwelling, in only two bedrooms and the kitchen, and a plastic wall separated them from the part of the house where the reconstruction was taking place. Because of the presence of the workers, the Collinses had been putting the dogs out in their fenced-in yard during the day and blocking off the dog door to prevent them from entering the house. Merlin did better than they expected with all this commotion going on. The workers told Martha that he sometimes barked at them through the windows, but by all accounts he did not freak out. He loved running around in the yard with Sammy. When the Collinses came home after work and opened up the dog door, the two dogs would often stay outdoors playing.

Several months after the appointment at Tufts, and several months after Merlin began taking Prozac, Martha came back in for a "recheck" appointment to let me know how he was doing. He was apparently showing no ill effects from the house fire episode and Martha was able to relay some positive changes in Merlin's behavior, though she had expected Merlin to be much better at this stage. Merlin remained quite frightened of John, slinking away if John tried to touch him or talk to him. He would accept treats from John sometimes but would grab the treat and run off as before. Merlin would also leap up and run away if John walked past him while he was resting. He definitely loved Martha more than anyone else in the world, except for maybe Sammy, whom he adored. Sometimes Merlin was even scared of Martha, especially if she was carrying anything he thought she might use to strike him. He would also become frightened and would slink away and hide if Martha played with Sammy, perhaps because Sammy would often play ferociously and did a lot of growling when tugging on a rope. Merlin also became frightened if John and Martha were talking and raised their voices. Martha kept thinking that Merlin's natural curiosity would help him overcome his fears, but it never did. He often hovered around John when John was interacting with Sammy, or when visitors were at the house, and the Collinses could tell he wanted to be part of things but just lacked the courage to join in. This was a new experience for the Collinses who were used to dogs who wanted to be part of everything and to be with them all the time. In contrast, Merlin seemed to prefer being by himself. If Martha and John rented a movie and sat down to watch it, Sammy would come and join them (and often demand his fair share of the couch), but Merlin would always stay in the other room, curled up on the bed by himself. The Collinses felt sad because he seemed so lonely.

During the course of the follow-up appointment, Martha gave me some examples of the unpredictable nature of Merlin's fear. She said that Merlin loved to ride in the car and usually jumped right in when she opened the back door. One day she parked the car in a different location—on a slope. She took Merlin, on leash, around to the passenger side of the car and opened the door. Because of the slope, the door swung open faster than it would normally. This terrified him and she could not coax him in through that door no matter what she did. She ended up walking him around to the other side of the car and when she opened the door, he jumped right in. Another curious thing was that Merlin could be lying on the floor and Martha could step over him ten times in a row and he wouldn't flinch. Then, the next time she went to step over him, he would get scared, jump up, and run off. Had she stepped faster or slower that time than the other ten times? Was she two inches closer to his head? She just couldn't figure it out.

Martha never knew what was going to scare Merlin. As part of the reconstruction of their house, the Collinses had to pick paint colors. For some reason Merlin was terrified of the Sherwin Williams paint-color wheel. This unpredictability made it impossible to shield him from things that scared him, and since they didn't know what object would frighten him next, training by desensitization was not feasible. The Collinses had no margin for honest mistakes either. If they tripped over him by accident, he would interpret the event as a kick and react as if it were deliberate. It seemed that as much as he loved Martha, he just couldn't bring himself to trust her.

In an attempt to win Merlin's confidence, Martha had started encouraging Merlin to sleep in bed with John and her at night. This strategy actually had been partly successful, she acknowledged. Sammy slept on their bed too, and Martha joked that the four of them must have looked pretty ridiculous all curled up together. Merlin seemed to enjoy this new privilege and would relax, stretch out against both John and Martha, and wasn't frightened of John as long as John was in bed first. Merlin would even allow John to pet and stroke him while they were both on the bed. However, if Merlin was on the bed when John tried to get in, Merlin would leave.

"Merlin's not a bad dog," Martha said at one point. "He does some hysterical things and makes us laugh a lot, like stealing big chunks off the gingerbread house that we foolishly left sitting on the counter, bounding around the yard like a gazelle, or being totally amazed at the snow and digging in it and biting it."

Apparently he was also the first dog they'd owned who even faintly resembled a watchdog. He would howl and bark at things in the driveway almost incessantly. The only problem was that the things he howled at were usually rustling leaves, squirrels, or the wind. Sammy was always running over to see what Merlin was barking at and seemed confused when, like his owners, he couldn't figure it out. With people, Merlin reacted somewhat differently. As they came up the drive he would bark for a few seconds and then run and hide. As Martha clarified, "I said he *resembles* a watchdog, not that he *is* a watchdog."

In an attempt to make Merlin a tad less fearful, I tried him on a different anxiety-reducing medication, buspirone, for a while following the appointment. The new treatment led to some further improvement in his condition, but still things were far from ideal. One problem Merlin and I had to contend with was that the Collinses had an open home, with friends coming and going with great frequency. All the dogs they'd owned previously had been friendly and outgoing ("ferociously friendly" is how one friend described them). With Merlin, it was difficult for their friends, especially children, to grasp that he was so different and didn't want to play or take part in whatever was going on. Everyone was used to the Collinses' dogs being big friendly mutts.

John and Martha were both very active in their local town government. John was a selectman and Martha was chair of the conservation commission and a member of the planning board. So, in addition to their friends, there was usually a steady stream of townsfolk tramping through their home. All this visiting had slowed down for a while during reconstruction of the Collinses' home, but Martha told me that she expected it to resume in full force before too long. She didn't want to overexpose Merlin to things that were going to scare him, but she wasn't prepared to live a monklike existence to cater to his misanthropy, either. Merlin was going to have to get used to visitors one way or another. Martha hoped that Merlin's current method of coping, by hiding under the computer table, wouldn't last forever because she wanted him to be happy and have fun.

Just when we had all resigned ourselves to Merlin's skittish nature, an unexpected change in family dynamics occurred in the Collins household. Martha got a new pup, Uther (named for the father of King Arthur), a small, blue-eyed, white-coated snowball of a pup that she just couldn't resist. The new acquisition was a source of much play and fun for Merlin, and as a result, he eventually gained in stature. Uther, a husky-type pup, would mouth Merlin's head and Merlin would run around with his head "all crispy" with Uther's saliva. Slowly but surely, Merlin started to display more confidence and to stand up for himself. One day Merlin was lying down resting and when Uther approached Merlin growled. Uther's expression said it all—"Yeah right." But then Merlin snapped and actually made contact with Uther's nose. Uther yelped, scared by this surprise turn of events. Merlin was so proud. Following the encounter, he strutted around the yard, his tail held high, almost saying, "Look at me. I am no longer at the bottom of the totem pole. I am a force to be reckoned with."

Merlin's recovery started at this precise point in time and went forward from there immeasurably.

In my last conversation with Martha, she acknowledged that Merlin was a new dog. He had learned to hold his ground with strangers and even allowed himself to be petted on occasion. John also seemed to have benefited by gaining a measure of Merlin's trust. Merlin no longer balked when John approached and no longer hopped off the bed at night when John got in. This was a remarkable turnaround. Merlin felt better, it seemed, when he was not the pariah of the pack.

If I had known that getting Merlin his own puppy would do so much for his ego, I would have told the Collinses to adopt one much sooner. The acquisition of Uther was undoubtedly the most significant single factor in Merlin's astonishing recovery. However, the Collinses' dedication and good, caring leadership, and the dog-friendly environment, also must have played a significant role in Merlin's recuperation. Perhaps some of the measures I suggested contributed as well. I like to think so. The medication may have played a role in Merlin's recovery by giving him enough confidence to make the necessary adjustments when Uther invaded his territory. When I withdrew the medication, the improvements in Merlin's frame of mind were sustained and the Collinses were delighted. This almost storybook ending was most likely attributable to a combination of factors, but the Collinses' dedication was essential in allowing them all to come together. It was indeed lucky for Merlin that they found him and lucky for them that they managed to rehabilitate such a very special dog.

4

A SECOND CHANCE

There are two means of refuge from the miseries of life: music and cats.—*Albert Schweitzer*

Debbie Simmons, M.D., was engrossed in thought about her troubled friend Mona as she made her way to the lumberyard early one Saturday morning in the spring of 1993. On Debbie's advice, Mona had finally left her husband and was desperately trying to organize a new life. The previous few years had been disastrous for Mona, and Debbie was relieved that her friend had finally gathered up enough courage to make the right decision.

Debbie's red Toyota pickup crackled up the graveled drive of the lumberyard, coming to rest by a large stack of two-by-six-foot planks. She turned off the engine, wound down the window, and took a deep breath before focusing on the task at hand. She needed deck wood but required a little assistance in selecting just the right type. Two brown-coated lumberyard employees were standing several feet away peering at a clipboard when one of them, Fred, noticed Debbie staring blankly out of the truck window.

"Hi, Dr. Simmons, how're you hitting 'em?" said Fred, a tall gangling man sporting a goatee, as he strolled toward the truck.

"How are you cutting 'em, more like," his colleague chortled, referring to Debbie's occupation as a general surgeon.

"Oh, I'm doing just fine, thank you. I was spacing out—forgot what I came for for a second—but I would like your help if you can spare a few minutes."

"Sure, Doc, anything for you. Is it more deck wood?"

"Yes. I need a few more planks, but I was thinking of picking up cedar this time, for the steps."

Debbie eased herself out of the vehicle and stood beside Fred, trying to follow his line of vision.

"Well, let's see what we've got," Fred said thoughtfully, surveying a distant stack of wood.

As Debbie and Fred meandered toward the stack, Debbie suddenly became aware of a plaintive meowing sound coming from a nearby shed.

"Have you got a kitten in there, Fred?"

"Ah, that I do, Doc," Fred replied. "There were a couple of them but there's only one left now. The mom deserted them when we started shifting things around with the forklift. We found 'em right here," he said, pointing toward the ground beneath the stack of planks. "Watched them for a while but the mother never came back, so we thought we'd better help them out."

"That was kind, Fred," Debbie said. "Can I take a look at the one you have left?"

"Sure can," Fred said, and escorted her to the shed.

Inside, in the arms of a seven-year-old girl, was a tiny gray and white kitten. Debbie surveyed the scene for several long seconds without saying a word. The girl, her long dark locks falling forward over her face, was sitting on an upturned orange box silently stroking the wee one.

"I've been trying to take care of her," said the girl without looking up, "but she doesn't seem to want to eat."

Debbie glanced at an untouched bowl of moist, fishy-smelling cat food lying on the floor.

"Maybe she needs to be fed," Debbie said. "She is rather young, you know."

The girl looked puzzled for a second but then shrugged her shoulders and resumed petting the kitten.

"Do you mind if I hold her?" said Debbie. "I'd love to say hi."

"Okay," said the girl, sweeping the hair back from her brown eyes and offering Debbie the kitten with her outstretched arm.

Debbie gently took the kitten from the girl and cradled it in her arms. There was no doubt that this was a very young kitten, probably no more than three weeks of age, and also that it was in need of more help than this young girl could provide. As the kitten gazed up at Debbie with its unfocused blue eyes, she made an instantaneous decision to take it home and help it. Debbie had always had a deep affection for animals and had even considered becoming a vet before she went into human medicine. A caring cat owner already, Debbie felt she had to step into the breach.

"Would you mind if I looked after her for a while?" Debbie said to Fred, closely watching the girl's reaction. She wanted to help the kitten but didn't want to disappoint the girl, who had obviously given her all to help the little one.

"She's yours if you want her," Fred said. "We were just wondering what we were going to do with her."

The girl looked almost relieved and looked directly at Debbie for the first time.

"I think it would be best if you took her," the little girl chipped in, "because my mom won't let me take her home and she really shouldn't be staying here in a lumberyard."

"That's very kind and very thoughtful," said Debbie. "You're a good girl and I want you to know that you can come and visit her anytime. Fred has my address. Just give me a call and swing by whenever you want to see her."

The girl nodded in approval and petted the kitten one last time.

Debbie cradled the little kitten all the way back to the truck, where she placed it on the passenger seat beside her. The wood was of secondary importance now, so she told Fred she'd be back later and headed off to set things up for the little kitten. On the way home she began to wonder what her husband would think when he discovered that she had gone out for wood and come back with a kitten, especially since they already had two cats. She also wondered what her other two cats, Samantha and Alex, would think about the new addition. Debbie arrived home about thirty minutes later after swinging by the pet store to pick up a cat bed, a litter box, and some KLM kitten food. Her husband, Jim, a slim, fifty-year-old, Mr. Rogers look-alike, met her at the door and helped her in with the stuff.

"What's this I see?" he remarked. "A visitor or a new family member?"

"A new family member," Debbie admitted. "She was abandoned by her mother down at the lumberyard and I just couldn't leave her there. A little girl was trying to feed her solid food, but really she didn't have a clue. I thought the best thing to do was step in."

"Sounds like you did the right thing," her husband said. "You and that soft spot for cats. I just hope Samantha and Alex don't mind."

"I'm not going to take the chance that they do. Not to start with anyway. I'm going to keep her separate and take care of her myself."

So saying, Debbie walked into the small family room off the kitchen, where she deposited the kitten in the center of the floor and surrounded her with all kinds of cat paraphernalia. There were Koosh toys, whiffle balls, cotton-stuffed mice, bunches of feathers, and some crinkly paper bags. Debbie called her husband into the room and the two of them sat there and watched the kitten explore. After a brief spell inside one of the bags, the kitten investigated the feathers and then started batting at the whiffle ball, which rolled away tantalizingly. The Simmonses were delighted to see that the youngster was both active and curious and appeared relatively independent, even at this tender age. Debbie sat on the floor and encouraged some interaction from the kitten. To her great surprise the kitten became animated at this point, rolling on its back, ears flat to its head, and with a wild look in its eyes as it mouthed her finger and scratched at the palm of her hand with its back feet.

"Ow!" Debbie exclaimed, withdrawing her hand rapidly. But the kitten sprang forward and attacked her hand again. It had found a new plaything. In the course of a few minutes, the youngster had demonstrated its skill at crouching, stalking, and various diving maneuvers, occasionally retreating a short distance and flattening its body against the floor before springing back into action.

"Boy, she's a hot ticket, Debbie!" her husband exclaimed. "You're going to have fun with her."

"I guess I will," Debbie replied thoughtfully, "but I have a good feeling about her. I think she'll work out just fine."

"What are you going to call her?" Debbie's husband asked.

Debbie mused for a second, her mind darting back to her good friend Mona's plight. "I think I'll call her Mona because, like my friend Mona, she has got a second chance . . . a new beginning. This little baby complains a lot when she gets wound up, so the name is doubly applicable."

The pair left the room, leaving Mona to sleep off her excitement, but not long afterward Debbie returned for the first of what would be many feedings. For the first couple of days Debbie had to bottle-feed Mona every two to three hours, day and night.

On Monday morning, when it came time for work, Debbie had to bring Mona and all her accoutrements to work with her. A few eyebrows were raised as Debbie, the head of her department and chief of surgery, had to take time out between consultations and surgeries to bottle-feed young Mona. But despite the raised eyebrows, Mona's presence at the office was, in general, a positive experience for all concerned, including the occasional patient who caught a glimpse of her.

A couple of weeks later, when Mona was reckoned to be about four to five weeks of age, Debbie started to introduce her to solid food. Initially Mona wasn't quite sure what to do with it, and would sit on top of the food, occasionally lowering her head to suck on it. Although a somewhat unconventional method of ingestion, this sucking method had the desired effect, and Mona began to make the transition to solid food. Three weeks later her weaning was complete and she had learned to gulp her food as well as the next cat. It was now time for Debbie to introduce Mona to Samantha and Alex face-to-face. Until this time, Mona had been sequestered in the family room off the kitchen. Although the other cats undoubtedly knew of her presence, they had yet to actually set eyes on her, and since vision is such an important sense in cats, this was obviously a big step.

The first stage of the introduction was to bring Mona into a bathroom in the main part of the house and to gate it off so that the cats could all see each other but could not physically interact. Mona seemed quite happy with this new arrangement and was kept occupied with frequent visits from Debbie and her husband and with an assortment of cat toys, including her favorite, a "Cat Dancer" attached to the back of the bathroom door. Samantha and Alex were suspicious at first, but then curiosity overcame fear and they approached to get a closer look at their new housemate. All in all, the introduction went well, and within a week or two, Debbie took the gate down and allowed the cats to interact freely. Samantha, who was a little skittish, was no problem at all and basically kept her distance, though she always appeared interested in what Mona was doing. Alex also adapted quite well but insisted on asserting his dominant alpha status. He would occasionally swat at Mona to keep her in line if she took any liberties, but these minor skirmishes never developed into full-scale war and Mona remained duly deferential.

During Mona's juvenile period, the bond that formed between her and Debbie strengthened to the point where the two of them became almost as one, fully in tune to each other's needs. Debbie seemed to know, telepathically, just when Mona wanted her attention or needed access to some place. Mona sought out Debbie and paid extra attention to her when she was feeling "blue." The two of them had probably developed a silent form of two-way communication through the subtle medium of body language. True, Mona did display a dislike for being restrained in any way, but apart from that, she turned into what Debbie regarded as the perfect cat. During the bonding process she developed such endearing habits as giving Debbie an exuberant greeting when she came home, rolling on her back and enjoying "belly kisses," and sleeping on Debbie's bed tightly curled up close to her face. Nobody could deny that Mona was Debbie's cat, which is hardly surprising considering the maternal role Debbie played in the first few weeks of Mona's life. The critical period of development in cats is between two and seven weeks of age, during which time they learn much about their environment that will stay with them forever. I suspect that Mona's dislike of physical encroachment stemmed from her feral roots, but that her deep affection for Debbie resulted from the close and rewarding experiences she had with her in the early days.

Several months passed by uneventfully and Mona reached ten months of age. Then Debbie was summoned to an international meeting in England and, deciding to combine business with pleasure, had her husband join her on the trip. In their absence, the cats were to be well looked after by a cat-sitter, who fed them, cleaned their litter boxes, and attended to their every need. A satisfactory situation, it would seem. However, when Debbie and Jim returned ten days later, they opened the door to the house to find white fluff scattered everywhere, all over their navy blue rugs and furniture. It looked as if it had been snowing.

"What the—!" Jim exclaimed, and they both got down on bended knee to inspect the foreign material.

"It's hair," said Debbie.

"Cat hair?" asked Jim, incredulous.

"I think so. And who's the only cat with white hair?" Debbie said, narrowing her eyes.

They looked at each other and simultaneously exclaimed, "Mona!"

Mona was most definitely a little depressed when they found her. Instead of greeting Debbie exuberantly as she normally would, she had sequestered herself underneath a couch in the room off the kitchen where she had been bottle-fed as a youngster, and just sulked.

"My poor girl. What's happened to you?"

Coaxing her out from under the couch, Debbie picked Mona up, lifting her under her front legs, and raised her high in the air, inspecting every inch of her limp body. Her first and only observation was that huge chunks of hair were missing from her white bib and along her underbelly.

"What have you been doing, my angel?" Debbie said soothingly. "Have you been fighting with the other cats?"

It was a reasonable thought that the cats might have been fighting, but that wasn't the cause of the hair loss. It took the Simmonses a couple of days to figure out what was going on. As they relaxed after their trip, they noticed that Mona was now spending an inordinate period of time grooming herself and was physically removing tufts of her own hair by pulling it out with her teeth. After each bout of intense grooming, Mona would emerge with a bunch of hairs protruding from her mouth. She would then shake her head from side to side to free the prehended hair, which would then float down to the rug like duck's down. It was time for a visit to the vet to find out what was causing this aberrant behavior.

On the way to the vet's office, Mona was anxious, moaning and salivating before throwing up several times, and depositing a fresh stool sample on the backseat just before they reached their destination. The vet, an enthusiastic fresh-faced recent graduate, examined the distraught specimen before him as he listened to Debbie's tale of woe. In the process of conducting his examination, the young vet plucked a hair sample from Mona's skin and examined it under the microscope behind him as Debbie finished her tale. A minute or two of silence passed and Debbie, who was not used to being kept waiting, began to fidget. Eventually she felt compelled to speak up in the hope of expediting what seemed like an overlong inspection.

"Did you find anything yet?" she said, trying to sound calm.

"A lot of these hair shafts are broken and look as if they've been chewed," he replied, cleaning his glasses on his tie and peering down the scope for a second look. "This appearance, plus the absence of any obvious skin problem, makes me think that Mona's condition is psychological rather than medical. The history you gave, of her starting to pull her hair out when you left for vacation, is also suggestive of a neurotic disorder, perhaps related to separation anxiety."

Debbie stared in astonishment. "So what can we do, Dr. Smith?" she practically stammered.

"Well, to rule out the possibility of skin disease I would like you to see a veterinary dermatologist first, but if the dermatologist doesn't find anything, I suggest that you make an appointment to see someone in the behavior service at Tufts Veterinary School."

Debbie agreed, happy to grasp at these straws of help. "That's a plan."

She asked for an appointment with the dermatologist immediately and was lucky enough to be scheduled for the following week. When the duly appointed time arrived, she brought Mona to the specialist. The specialist agreed that the problem was likely psychological in origin, but also wondered whether there might be an allergic component. He suggested an allergy test, but Debbie declined the option, preferring instead to have Mona treated with a short course of steroids. The results were underwhelming, with Mona showing only the briefest abatement of her hair pulling before continuing with renewed vigor. Debbie now proceeded to the next stage of the plan, and made an appointment to see a behaviorist at the veterinary school.

The first person she saw was my German resident, Dr. Petra Mertens, imposing figure, almost six feet tall, pale skin, ice blue eyes, and outrageous copper-colored hair that fitted her head like a Harley rider's motorcycle helmet. Despite her forebidding appearance, Mertens, who spoke perfect English, was a superb doctor who never missed a diagnosis. Mertens smiled confidently as she greeted Debbie and welcomed her to the clinic. Debbie immediately knew that she had come to the right place and that her precious Mona would be well cared for. Mona, as usual, was none too happy after the car ride and was still acting quite stressed. She had moaned the whole way to Tufts, finally throwing up her breakfast as Debbie pulled into the parking lot. Mertens took a thorough clinical history, gathering some important ancillary information, such as the continuing bouts of aggressive behavior between Alex and Mona and the more recent development of aggression by Mona toward the skittish Samantha. By this time, Samantha had become something of a pariah. Debbie also noted that Mona would occasionally attack her hand or arm quite viciously if she persisted in petting her for too long. She then quite correctly summed up the whole situation by saying that she believed Mona was a dominant "wannabe" who was ruled by Alex and took out her frustration on Samantha. Mertens noted this with a nod, recording that the "interfeline" problems, as well as Mona's apparent devotion to Debbie, might be responsible for the anxiety underlying Mona's compulsive self-grooming. She then relayed this interpretation to Debbie, indicating a possible psychosomatic origin of the behavior, and recommended by way of therapy that Debbie attempt to insulate Mona from her stressors, enrich Mona's environment by providing additional distractions, and in addition treat Mona with some antiobsessional medication. Mertens explained that to isolate Mona from her stressors might require separating her from the other cats for a while to give all parties a rest from the constant feuding. She also suggested that Mona sometimes accompany Debbie to the office and advised Debbie to keep Mona separate from the other cats during future absences from the home.

Debbie agreed with most of the above strategies and came up with a few ideas of her own, but she resisted the idea of putting Mona on antiobsessional medication. That was fine with Mertens, who wanted to see how Mona would fare in the aftermath of these modifications to her environment.

Early follow-up by Mertens indicated that Mona's condition failed to improve following the behavioral appointment, and after two or three months she lost contact with Debbie. From what I learned later, Debbie just decided to let Mona live with her problem. Seasons came and seasons went, and so did personnel. Mertens heard that a job had opened up at her alma mater in Munich and felt compelled to take the position. She therefore departed her residency program prematurely, before it came to its formal conclusion. With her gone, I now assumed responsibility for Mona's case management.

Almost a year to the day after Debbie's initial appointment, and not long after Dr. Mertens's departure, I called her up to check on Mona's progress, or lack thereof. As I suspected, Mona was still pulling away, and I suggested that Debbie might want to come back in so that I could take a look at Mona. She agreed to do this, and not long after that we met face-to-face. I had a camera crew visiting during Debbie's follow-up appointment, so the whole interview was conducted under bright arc lights with various cameras peering into our faces, but it was business as usual for Debbie and me.

I ran through Dr. Mertens's notes and agreed with her findings and then examined Mona from nose to tail. She certainly had the classical distribution of baldness associated with psychogenic alopecia, and I generally concurred with the final diagnosis. But I wanted to establish that no allergy was involved. Knowing that Debbie was averse to intradermal allergy testing, I suggested a RAST intravenous allergy test instead. When she realized that this entailed no more than taking a blood sample, she acquiesced and one of our technicians skillfully siphoned a few milliliters from Mona's jugular vein.

"If the results of this test are negative," I informed Debbie, "I would like to have you try Mona on a low dose of the antiobsessional, antidepressant drug Prozac—at least for a while. The medication will help control her anxiety and thus the hair pulling."

Though Debbie had previously resisted the suggestion of using drugs to help treat Mona's condition, when I emphasized the antianxiety component of Prozac's action, she agreed to give it a try. We awaited the results of the blood test before instituting this therapy. Several days later the results of the RAST test came in and there were no positive results for any of the common allergens. With allergies ruled out, I called in a prescription of Prozac for Mona, and Debbie started treating Mona immediately.

The first report came back three weeks later, when Debbie called to say that Mona was doing extremely well and that her licking and hair pulling had decreased substantially since the institution of the Prozac therapy. There were, however, some unfortunate side effects. Mona had become slightly more withdrawn and somewhat lethargic as a result of the medication. In this new state, she disliked petting and simply refused to be held. Knowing that the side effects of Prozac are usually temporary, we decided to tough it out for a while in hopes that they would dissipate. As predicted, Mona did rally after a week or two, but, in Debbie's words, still did not appear to be as "vibrant" as she normally was ("vibrancy" was a quality Debbie enjoyed in all of her cats). Though Debbie appreciated the positive effects of Prozac in curtailing Mona's hair pulling, she eventually decided that Mona's loss of joie de vivre was too great a price to pay for the improvement, so she tapered off the medication and Mona's hair pulling resumed at its previous level of intensity.

Another year slipped away. Mona had now became more hostile toward Alex, so Debbie began taking her into work every day as she had done initially. Mona was quite comfortable with this new arrangement and had little reason to hair-pull and no opportunity to be aggressive toward the other cats. It must have been quite a sight for the patients entering Dr. Simmons's consulting room to find a rather forward, if slightly anxious, alopecic cat wandering around the room during the consultation and occasionally hopping up onto the good doctor's desk. When Debbie told me about this state of affairs, I asked her how the patients reacted to sharing the consultation room with an animal. She replied that most people were delighted to have the pet around as it made the whole environment seem warmer and friendlier. There was one exception, however, when a kind, elderly woman patient went to pet Mona and was savagely swatted. The woman screamed and clutched her bleeding hand as nurses poured into the room to see what was causing the commotion. Luckily Debbie was right there to stanch the bleeding and repair the damage. Perhaps even more fortunately, the lady's finger healed without medical complications or a lawsuit.

Debbie had another session with a veterinary dermatologist who prescribed a course of desensitizing injections for Mona against an allergen that had come up positive on a second RAST test. I told her that when the course of injections was complete, if there was no improvement in Mona's condition (which I anticipated), she should come and see me again to discuss trying a different antiobsessional medication, such as Paxil. It was a deal and we agreed to stand by for the results of the desensitization injections.

"I will come back for a recheck in March," she promised.

I had spent many hours on the phone with Debbie and always marveled at her profound dedication to her cats. Before we signed off from this most recent conversation, I felt compelled to ask her why she had such a devotion to cats in general and Mona in particular. After all, she had spent thousands of dollars on veterinarians, behaviorists, dermatologists, and now an allergist, not to mention pet-sitters and car upholstery cleaners. Debbie thought for a while before answering.

"I like cats because they're independent yet they all have distinct personalities. All the cats I select are vibrant personalities and have a sort of unique individuality. They are my very good friends and companions, and I find them intriguing and full of mystique. Alex says 'hi' in his own macho way and I know he adores me. Samantha is the only one who licks my nose, as a bonding gesture, I think. As skittish as she is, she's easily lovable. And then there's Mona. Yes, Mona is my favorite. I just love the way that when I come in after a long day's work, I can always look forward to having Mona to greet me. She runs right up to the door, rolls on her back, and wants to be kissed. Of course, I get down on my hands and knees and kiss her all over her tummy. It's really wonderful, the interaction that we have."

"And she still sleeps on your bed at night?"

"She does," said Debbie. "Curled up like a spring right next to my head, same as she always did."

"You must dote on her very much."

"I certainly do, Dr. Dodman, and that's why I want to continue to work with you and try to come up with new ideas that will make her feel better—be less anxious."

"By the way," I said, "how's your friend Mona, the woman Mona was named after?"

"Oh, she's doing fine. She got remarried and now she also has three cats, a super husband, and she's as happy as can be."

"I'm so glad," I said. "I'm glad there was a happy ending to that story. I just wish we could get this Mona's problem under control, too."

"We will, Dr. Dodman," Debbie replied. "I feel sure we will. If there's no improvement in the next three months I'll bring her back to see you, as promised."

During the follow-up visit that March, Debbie admitted that the course of desensitizing injections had done nothing to resolve Mona's condition and that she had been considering taking me up on the Paxil treatment offer. But something had occurred in the meantime to change her mind. Cat person that she was, Debbie had befriended a feral kitten at a nearby shelter and had decided to take it home with her. Of course, the mom cat would have to come along, too. Debbie was happy with her decision but worried about how Mona would take to the new arrival. The answer was well, as it turned out. Although the mom cat initially spent her time under a couch, her kitten soon came out of its shell and started trying to play with Mona. Mona wasn't thrilled at first, hissing and swatting when approached, but the kitten wouldn't leave her alone. Gradually Mona developed a curiosity about where the kitten was and what it was doing. Some jealousy seemed to emerge, too, in that any toy the kitten started to play with suddenly became the one Mona wanted. Amid all this social activity, some good, some not so good, Mona's hair pulling stopped completely. Debbie was delighted but wanted to know why there had been such a turnaround.

"Because compulsive hair pulling is a condition fueled by stress and boredom," I replied. "It is genuinely psychogenic. Whatever interaction these two cats have going on, it's enough to take Mona's mind off her preoccupation with hair pulling."

"Really," said Debbie. "Is that the case with people who pull their hair out, too?"

"It is," I was able to say with confidence, having recently been down to the OCD clinic at Massachusetts General Hospital to observe some patients with trichotillomania, the equivalent human condition.

I told her the story of a beard-pulling Harvard undergraduate whose compulsion abated when he went backpacking across the United States. During the trip, because of genuine concerns about his own welfare, he left his beard alone for the entire two-week period, but he started pulling his beard out again when he got back to Cambridge and resumed life in front of a flickering screen. I also told Debbie about an anxious woman who plucked her eyebrows every day to the point of baldness but who ceased when she went on a cruise, only to resume as the cruise ship reentered Boston Harbor.

Upon hearing these tales, Debbie realized that while Mona was not pulling her hair out now, the danger of her starting again was real because Mona had an anxious, nervous temperament. The doctor and the vet sat there across the table at the end of the appointment, both marveling at the similarities between their two fields. Perhaps Mona's and Debbie's maternal feelings toward their respective infant surrogates somehow fulfilled and enriched their lives in a similar way. For Debbie, owning cats may have been a positively therapeutic exercise that she stumbled on almost by accident. For Mona, her interest in the kitten apparently enriched her life to such an extent that she stopped the hair pulling entirely, and in so doing narrowly avoided being medicated. Debbie and Mona, were, in a way, kindred spirits.

5

THE DOG WHO HATED MEN

He who takes a strange dog by the ears is likely to be bitten.—*Chaucer*

Sandra Belle Miller, a German shepherd owner, came to see me one hot July day in the summer of 1999. In her late twenties, with a pasty complexion and noticeably overweight, Sandra struck me as having some problems of her own. Her sad expression and the absence of a sparkle in her eye or a spring in her stride told me that she might be somewhat depressed. She struggled to make her way into the consulting room, dragging her unwilling female shepherd behind her, and wedged herself into one of the narrow seats across from me. I flipped the switch of a small brass table lamp on my desk to soften the fluorescent lighting in the otherwise clinical consulting room. As I shuffled through the paperwork and started to settle in for what would be an hour-and-a-half-long consultation, I glanced casually and nonthreateningly at her dog, Belle (perhaps significantly, Sandra's maiden name), who was pacing anxiously along the edge of the room furthest from me. The problem probably had something to do with nervousness or fear, partly because of Belle's demeanor but also, playing the odds, because conditions involving fear are common in German shepherds: conditions such as fear of people or other dogs, thunderstorm phobia, or anxiety-driven compulsive behaviors, like compulsive self-licking and tail chasing. Belle would be no exception.

During the preconsultation pleasantries I learned a lot about Sandra's personal predicament as well as her problems with Belle because the two were intertwined. Sandra lived with her husband, Frank, in a remote corner of northwestern Massachusetts and was leading a relatively eventless life. She had always been a German shepherd person. Her family had owned several shepherds while she was growing up, but when she moved into the Massachusetts "boondocks" with Frank, she found herself dogless for a few years. Two things happened that helped propel her back into the ranks of the dog-owning public. The first was a rash of break-ins in their area, with their own dwelling being broken into on more than a dozen occasions. The second was the birth of an extremely attractive litter of German shepherd puppies at Sandra's nearest neighbor's home, right behind her own dwelling. Knowing shepherds as she did, and fearing another robbery, Sandra decided that a guard dog would be in order and duly arranged to adopt one of the females, later named Belle, as soon as the pup had reached an appropriate age. That was the explanation she gave her husband for the acquisition of her new charge, but in retrospect, there was another more personal reason. There seemed to be something of a hole in Sandra's life at the time, and Belle filled an important social and nurtural void.

By the time Belle was physically transported to Sandra and Frank's home, Sandra and Belle were already the best of friends and virtually inseparable. At this time Sandra's mother was living in an apartment in the house and the two women took great pleasure in the entertainment Belle provided throughout the day. They took turns with housebreaking runs, correctly taking Belle to a particular location in the garden and confining her to a restricted area if she didn't make an attempt to eliminate outside. They also started to teach Belle a few necessary words and saw the pup's ability to understand begin to blossom. About two weeks after Belle moved into the house, both Sandra and her mother began to notice something very strange about husband Frank's behavior. Every time Belle approached him in a playful way with her head cocked and tail wagging, Frank would stand up and move to some other part of the house, or even go outside and sit on the steps. He appeared to have no time for the youngster, and try as Belle might, she could not get Frank to play with her, pet her, or even speak to her. Sandra was unhappy about the situation and wondered why Frank was so cold toward Belle. Frank, a man of few words, did not communicate his reason for dismissing Belle, but he wore his dislike of her like a badge.

When Belle was four months old, Sandra took her to a training class for a couple of weeks in the nearest town. The training was going reasonably well, though Sandra felt the training style was "rough." From her description, I pictured lessons that were heavy on discipline, with much jerking of a "choke" collar. For a sensitive dog like Belle, this was exactly what she did not need. After about three weeks of this punitive approach, during a socialization or free-play period in which the pups were allowed to run around and interact with each other, the trainer called Belle to her but Belle didn't come.

"This dog's just not listening," the woman trainer huffed in a loud voice, and strode across the room toward Belle. She then seized Belle by the collar with both hands and lifted her clear off the ground. Belle howled in terror, urinated, and discharged her anal glands.

"What do you think you're doing?" Sandra exclaimed in horror.

The trainer was mortified by this rude intervention and Sandra wondered if she was next in line for discipline.

"I'm teaching her who's the leader," the woman replied with venom in her voice. She then let go of Belle's collar, causing the pup to plummet to the ground. "If you don't show them who's boss, they'll walk all over you," she said, leaving Sandra speechless and shaking with emotion.

Belle ran under a chair and hid for what remained of the so-called socialization period, and from that moment on seemed to regard strangers with considerable trepidation. These events heralded the end of the training classes for Belle. Sandra took her home that day, never to return—but the damage had been done.

Unfortunately for Belle, the rough treatment she got at the obedience trainer's was not the only harmful experience she suffered at an early, impressionable age. Shortly after that incident, Frank, a very large, bearded man standing six feet three in his stocking feet and weighing 260 pounds, suddenly began to pay Belle some unwelcome attention in the name of play. He started to chase Belle around the house, stomping his feet and hollering. Whether this was a form of play or teasing, Sandra wasn't sure, but she begged Frank to stop these antics. During this entire period and beyond, Belle had no contact with men other than the negative experience of being approached by this lumbering giant whom Sandra herself described as looking like Paul Bunyan. Frank eventually got tired of the chase-and-holler game, but not before Belle had developed a complete mistrust of him, and eventually, as a natural progression, fear of all men. Sandra tried to encourage Frank to speak kindly to Belle to repair the fractured bond, but he refused and never made any attempt to reconcile with her. It was at this time that he informed Sandra that he had always been terrified of German shepherds and wanted nothing more to do with Belle.

The situation deteriorated so badly that when Frank came home in the evening, Belle would begin barking excessively as he pulled into the driveway and she would continue to bark even as he approached the house. When he came in, Belle would move closer to Sandra and stand and bark at him. Once Frank had passed through the doorway on the other side of the kitchen, Belle would approach the door stealthily and follow him to see where in the house he was headed. It was as if she needed to know exactly where he was at all times. She would follow him around the house at a distance, slinking, back lowered, ears folded flat, always alert to his movements. If Belle was eating dinner and Frank entered the room, Belle would run off into another room. The same would happen when he entered the bedroom, though sometimes, if Belle was lying down on the bed next to Sandra as Frank came down the hall, she would start barking or emit a low growl before skulking off with her tail between her legs.

Belle's fear of men was becoming a real problem, and the infrequent male visitors to their home were always intimidated by the now almost full-sized German shepherd, who would stand and bark viciously until restrained or until they withdrew. She would also bark at leaves that were blowing, the wind in the trees, a feather duster, the vacuum cleaner, the ringing of the telephone, and sometimes for no apparent reason at all. Frank built a kennel at the back of the house where Belle spent a good deal of her time exiled from the family.

As things went from bad to worse with Belle, Sandra found herself in trouble, too. Her doctor informed her that she had developed sugar diabetes and would have to inject herself with insulin for the rest of her life. She was later termed a brittle diabetic because she had a particularly difficult time stabilizing her blood sugar. Some evenings Frank would find her behaving oddly an hour or two after an insulin shot and would have to feed her cubes of sugar to stop her from slipping into a coma and possibly convulsing. When Frank wasn't there during the day, Sandra's mother took over the diabetes watch. On more than one occasion she had to bring Sandra back from the brink of disaster.

Initially Sandra had no hypoglycemic attacks at night, but she hoped that if she did Frank would wake up. Unfortunately Frank was known to be a sound sleeper, and this caused Sandra some concern. She had no alternative but to rely on her husband, so she just had to take her chances. Then the first nighttime attack occurred. Sandra had what she described as "a very bad insulin reaction" in which she barely knew what she was doing, was hallucinating vividly, and was in desperate need of sugar. She couldn't help herself and probably would have convulsed if it were not for Belle, who awoke Frank by nudging, pawing, and barking until he stirred. At first he did not fully waken but just rolled over and tried to pull the blankets over him. But Belle insisted, becoming more frantic as she tried to get the big hulk of a man to stir. When he eventually opened his eyes, he was immediately aware that something really unusual must be going on for Belle to approach him with such persistence. As he turned his head toward Sandra, he recognized, from her pallid appearance, a crisis in the making and headed to the refrigerator for the sugar. Half an hour later Sandra was coherent again, solely because of Belle, who overcame her fear to help her mistress. Belle's nighttime rescues became a regular feature in the management of Sandra's brittle diabetic state. Belle was her sentinel, her lifeline, and her dear close friend.

Sandra's problems mounted over the years. She had a husband who was often moody and withdrawn and who disliked her dog; she had a dog who hated all men and who barked all day; and she had diabetes that she could not get under control. And then things got worse. During one of her routine checkups, her doctor told Sandra that he detected a problem with her kidneys. Some mild breathlessness she had suffered for years turned out to be the tip of the iceberg of a potentially lethal condition—kidney failure. Sandra had been diagnosed with this problem six months before I first saw her, and by that time her doctor was recommending a kidney transplant as the only way to go.

As I learned of all these tribulations I sat there, jaw hanging, stunned by the difficulties she was facing. I found it almost incredible, given the gravity of her own situation, that she had found time to bring Belle to see me to address Belle's behavior problems. But then again, in a way, Belle's problems were her problems. Getting rid of Belle was not an option for Sandra. Not only was Belle her best friend and companion, she had also saved Sandra's life on several occasions. Belle's fear of Frank was, to say the least, irksome, but her aggression toward strangers and habit of barking at everything was becoming intolerable. If these problems could be addressed, at least something would be set right in Sandra's imploding life.

I suggested the usual healthy regimen of regular exercise, a low-protein, all-natural diet, and daily nonconfrontational obedience training sessions for Belle and fitted her with a head halter and training lead to allow Sandra to control her at difficult moments. Bad behavior, like barking, I explained, could be controlled by exerting gentle pressure on the lead, while good behavior, whether spontaneous or ordered, should be amply rewarded. In addition, I suggested that Sandra try once more to talk to her husband about his participation in Belle's rehabilitation, suggesting that he should be the one to feed her and should play with her in an appropriate manner. If Frank refused to comply, I suggested that Sandra attempt to rid Belle of her fear of men by enlisting male volunteers and working on a program of systematic desensitization (see Appendix 3). The latter involved a gradual, onionskin-layer approach to introducing Belle to her nemesis. The use of the head halter would make this process a lot easier and quicker.

Although some dogs are driven by hunger, Belle seemed to be more motivated by ball chasing. Tennis balls would be more effective than food as a tool to condition Belle to new perceptions of unfamiliar men. We talked a little bit about medication before Sandra left, but she wanted to try the behavior modification alone for a while to see how that worked out before taking the plunge with medication.

Sandra called back about a month later, extremely apologetic about her tardiness and eager to explain the reason for it. She deeply regretted that she had not been able to exercise Belle, change her diet, or engage in any obedience training with her, but her own physical condition had suddenly deteriorated, forcing her into the hospital. I felt really sorry for her and inquired after her health, hoping she would be okay, yet the prognosis was alarming. She said that her renal condition was deteriorating rapidly. "Luckily," she said, "they've managed to stabilize my kidney problem for the time being and I think I will be able to work with Belle in the weeks to come." Her dedication to Belle's cause touched me deeply. I wondered how she could be concerned about her dog when she herself was at risk of dying.

"Let's wait until you are completely back to normal before we start trying to rehabilitate Belle. Until then, would Frank be prepared to help out?"

"No, he refuses to do anything. He doesn't even want to accept that I'm ill. I think he's in denial. Don't worry, I'll get something done and I feel sure that the advice you gave me will help. I'll call you back in a couple of weeks and I promise I will have changed Belle's diet and tried out that head halter by then." Still positive about the future, Sandra hung up the phone and returned to the nightmare that was her life.

I really hoped that things would improve for Sandra and waited to hear better news about her health the next time we spoke, though somehow I feared the worst. What good news could there be? That she had a new kidney? That her diabetes was now under control? That Belle was a new dog? Not likely. Eventually she did get back in touch with me and I listened with interest and amazement as she reported the latest developments. The bad news was that she had to go back into the hospital because of further deterioration in her renal condition. Not only that, but while in the hospital the doctors told her that her diabetes was so unstable, involving so many complications, that a kidney transplant was now out of the question. This, she explained, would mean that she would probably be in and out of the hospital for the rest of her life as her condition fluctuated. She went on to tell me that her husband had left her "because he just couldn't come to grips with my physical condition." Although this possibility had certainly existed, considering his attitude and seeming indifference to Sandra's physical and mental woes, this news still came as a shock.

"What?" I gasped. "How could he leave you when you need him most?"

"Well, he's very confused himself," she said understandingly. "He's never been able to face illness and has always buried his head in the sand when it comes to medical matters. That got much worse after he was electrocuted."

"Electrocuted," I exclaimed. "How did he get electrocuted?"

"Well, it was a while ago," Sandra said calmly. "About five weeks after we got married, in fact. He was working in one of those little buckets on an extension arm doing some wiring work when a strong wind blew him right into the power cables. Thirty-five thousand volts went through his left ear, down his left arm, and out of his left hand. He was lucky that the electricity didn't go across his body, otherwise he would have been dead. Anyway, he didn't even lose consciousness. When somebody came out of their house to see why all the lights in the neighborhood had gone out, they found him sitting on the tailboard of his truck eating a cheese sandwich. He was badly burned and really out of it. Sort of dazed, you know."

I was amazed that someone could survive what was, in effect, high-voltage electroconvulsive therapy and live to tell the tale. Perhaps the jolt to his brain explained his aloofness after the electrical incident.

"What about the burns?" I asked. "Were they bad?"

"Oh yes, he ended up losing a quarter of his hand and a big section of his forearm. He spent days in the hospital afterwards and did lose consciousness for quite a while after he was admitted. His parents came to see him but lost patience and walked out on him before he regained consciousness. When he did regain consciousness, he asked where they were and I had to tell him that they had gone. They didn't even wait to see whether he would recover and be normal. I've never forgiven them for that and I think it had a serious effect on him too."

"That's terrible," I said. "Talk about adding insult to injury."

"It was bad all right," she agreed. "I know it really got to him, and then, almost as soon as he had recovered to the point of getting back to work, his father became very sick and suffered for months before eventually dying. That affected Frank badly, too. He pretended that there was nothing going on but I knew he was hurting inside."

"And now you're ill," I said.

"Precisely. He's just trying to put some distance between himself and me so that when the moment comes it won't be so painful for him."

"But what about you?" I said.

"He can't help me the way he is. I'll manage on my own . . . somehow."

"But what happens if you have a diabetic crisis? Is your mom still there to help you?"

"No, she moved out, but my brother's here a lot of the time. He comes to visit my mother, who's now in a nursing home nearby."

"But when he's not there what happens if you have a problem?" I pressed. "If Belle wants to wake someone up, there's no one there to help."

"Oh, that's not really a problem," she said. "I think Belle would probably create such a disturbance that Frank would come running."

"How would Frank hear? He moved out, didn't he?"

"Well, he did move out for a while, but then I moved into the adjoining apartment, and he moved back into the house. I think if Belle barked her head off in the apartment, he'd probably hear from the house and come running."

"I certainly hope so," I said. "It sounds like an iffy arrangement to me, though. Perhaps you should speak with your doctor about getting a night nurse or social worker to help out. It's really odd that Frank is happy to live in the house as long as you're not there."

"I agree," she said. "He's okay just as long as he doesn't have to witness my deterioration.

"But there is a bright note, Dr. Dodman," she added. "I've been using that head halter on Belle and it really seems to work to stop her barking. I'm not always strong enough to use it—it depends on the day—but if she starts barking at something like a squirrel outside, I can tell her "Cut it out" and put a little tension on the lead and she stops right away. If I take the head halter off, however, she may start barking again, but I just call her over and put it back on again. I think it's going to take a while for her to get the message, but at least we're heading in the right direction. My brother's helping me with it, too."

"I think that under the circumstances it would be helpful to put Belle on some medication to calm her down," I suggested, "because in your condition, you really can't do all the things you're supposed to with Belle because she is such a handful. I think you need that 'unfair' advantage."

"Okay. I think I'm ready for that approach now. What type of medication would you recommend?"

I thought for a second and then suggested an antidepressant, Elavil, to stabilize Belle's mood. That seemed fine with Sandra, so I made a note to call the prescription in later.

"Tell me," I asked her, "how is it that you can remain so calm when things are so bleak? How can you focus on Belle's problems when you've got so many of your own?"

"Belle means everything to me, Dr. Dodman. I've loved her from the moment I first saw her. We're extremely close and we need each other. Belle's the best medicine that I've got. I would never let her down."

"You're amazing," I said. "An inspiration. I wish I could do more for you, but trying to help you with Belle is all I can do. I'll give that my all."

"I know you will, Dr. Dodman," she said. "I know you're trying to help and you *are* helping. The head halter works so I can keep her quiet when I need to. I don't have to worry about her being frightened of Frank anymore. He solved that problem for me." I had to smile at that comment.

Sandra's diabetes stabilized somewhat over time, although she had to be in and out of the hospital to have her kidney condition monitored. She continued to live apart from Frank and got by with some help from her brother. Belle was much better behaved on the medication, which I told Sandra should probably be continued more or less indefinitely. If Belle did start barking at something outside, all Sandra had to say was "Cut" and show Belle the head halter. Belle would then quiet down immediately and slink off to a corner where she would sit with a hangdog expression until Sandra called her over and forgave her. Sandra's position was still far from enviable, but at least she seemed relatively cheerful and had a now somewhat reformed Belle to keep her company.

You have to marvel at the healing power of relationships with pets, even ones with behavior problems. They provide a focus for people who might otherwise be overwhelmed by life's adversities. It has been shown that owning a dog reduces high blood pressure by about ten points, reduces the risk of heart attack, and actually increases life span. These benefits do not come about simply because owners are forced to take more exercise when they walk their dogs. They are attributable to stress reduction. By focusing some of our attention on pets, we're able to cast off some of our own anxieties. I sometimes wonder, though, whether our own neediness doesn't add to our pets' burdens. It seems quite possible that troubled and neurotic owners might unwittingly adversely affect their pets' well-being. Perhaps Belle's problems were compounded in this way. Her dislike of Frank may have been a reflection of Sandra's own lack of confidence in him. We may never know precisely the full impact we have on our animals' perceptions of us and the world around them, but it is interesting to note that the most frequent quotes on the Web site Quoteland.com relate to women's dislike of men; and the most prevalent animate fear in dogs is a fear of men. Men are generally more aggressive than women, so there's often good reason for dogs to end up hating them, but maybe their female caretakers sometimes contribute by fanning the flames of discontent.

Postscript

Two years after Sandra first came to see me, and after a year or more of lost contact, it was with some trepidation that I called her to see how life had been treating her and Belle. She was alive and indeed well, I was delighted to hear, though she'd been in and out of the hospital for periodic fine-tuning management of her kidney condition.

"Your call is so timely," she said. "I have been thinking a lot about you in the last few days."

"How so?" I asked.

"My brother Harry was killed in a car accident last week and I have been spending a lot of time thinking about how he helped me so much with Belle's retraining. It was so sad at the funeral. I will really miss him."

"I'm so sorry. So you are really on your own now without Harry," I sympathized.

"No, I have Frank. We got back together again and life goes on."

I heaved a hopeful sigh of relief. "And Belle? How is she?" I asked.

I heard barking in the background.

"Well, she's still Belle, but I do have a better handle on how to control her now, thanks to you."

"Did she ever bury the hatchet with Frank?"

"Actually, she's much better with him now. Still a little suspicious at times, especially if he moves too quickly, but nothing like as bad as before. The situation is quite livable. Frank even plays with her sometimes now—and plays properly, I might add."

"How about strangers? Are they still a problem for her?"

"Oh yes, especially if they are men. She really hates men. Luckily we don't have too many visitors."

On that note we ended our conversation, until the next recheck appointment, but now, at least, I felt there was some reason for optimism.

6

MIDLIFE CRISIS

Until one has loved an animal, a part of one's soul remains unawakened. —*Anatole France*

The stereotype of a devoted pet owner is a person who, from childhood, has been raised in the company of animals and has developed a strong bond with them. Typically, these people find it difficult to imagine a family as complete without a pet or two around. To them a home without a pet is like life without a soul, livable but without much purpose. But not everyone acquires a deep appreciation of animals at an early age. Some late bloomers come to discover the full richness of the human/companion animal bond only as a result of a chance encounter in later life. Such was the case with Bertha Schuster of Wellesley, Massachusetts, and to some extent her husband, David.

The Schusters followed the course that many of us do in life, leapfrogging from education to career, then courtship, marriage, homemaking, and so on. Their twenty-five years together had slipped by quickly and effortlessly, and their only son had left home some years earlier to pursue his own career. David worked in Boston but Bertha's bookkeeping work allowed her to spend the day at home. Bertha kept herself busy most of the day, but there were times when her attention would wander and she would simply gaze out the window reflecting on her lot in life. On the whole, she was content with her life and her marriage, though since her son's departure she had begun to feel a little lost. When these empty moments arrived, as they did with increasing frequency, she often headed for the phone in search of human company and found herself adopting her friends' interests.

One day Bertha was talking with a woman friend from the local community whose ancillary mission in life was to rescue small dogs from shelters. Bertha listened, wide-eyed, as the friend told her a horror story about a little poodle/bichon frise cross who had been dropped off at the shelter by the dog's former owner with the lame excuse that she just couldn't keep her anymore. Bertha's friend gushed about this little white dog, saying how wonderful she was, and wondered if Bertha might know somebody who would take her. Bertha thought for a minute and then an idea occurred to her. Perhaps this little orphan might find sanctuary with a neighbor of hers who already owned a small dog, a Maltese.

"How old is the dog at the shelter and what's her name?" asked Bertha. "I'm going to run this by my neighbor and see if she might be willing to take her on."

"Her name's Ginger," the friend replied, "and we think she's about seven years old. If you could mention it to your neighbor I would really appreciate it because otherwise you know what will happen to her."

They were silent for a while after this remark, each considering the dog's last moments. For Bertha, this final solution brought to mind images of the Holocaust, and for hours after the conversation with her friend she found herself agonizing over the dog's predicament and the heartlessness that had led to it. How could anybody drop off a seven-year-old dog at a shelter for no good reason? It just didn't make sense. Even though she was not an animal lover herself, she just couldn't understand the mentality of somebody who would live with a pet for several years, presumably developing some kind of relationship with it, and then simply dump it when a problem arose. The very fact that the owner hadn't given a real reason for the dog's surrender, she felt, was an indication of the owner's guilt over what appeared to her to be an inhumane act. Driven to right this wrong, she immediately set off for the home of her neighbor, to whom she explained the situation. Fortunately the neighbor was quite receptive to the idea and suggested that they go to the shelter together to look at Ginger with a view to one of them adopting her.

It was Bertha's first time in a shelter, and almost in disbelief, she walked past rows of distraught-looking dogs confined in what appeared to be prison cells before coming upon Ginger. The noise of dogs barking and whining and the clanking of metal doors and food bowls made it hard to concentrate. In the background, the faint sickly smell of urine, feces, dog food, and disinfectant made Bertha nauseous. Some of the dogs cringed or slunk away; some just lay there with languishing looks; others hurled themselves against the walls of their wire enclosures. In complete contrast, Ginger danced up to the front of her cage wiggling, her tail tucked low and to the side, and looked up longingly at her surprise visitors.

Both ladies peered down at the little inmate and what they saw captivated them. This tiny dog with its dark brown eyes and apricot-colored coat seemed to be signaling to them to take her. It never took its eyes off them and went through numerous charades: "play bow," rolling onto one side, approaching the front of the cage with its tail wagging feverishly, and so on. The body language had the desired effect.

"Oh, she's so cute!" both ladies exclaimed simultaneously.

"You'll have to take her, Margaret," Bertha said to her neighbor.

"I would," the neighbor replied. "I think she's absolutely gorgeous—but what about you, Bertha? Wouldn't you like to have her?"

"Sure, I think she's really sweet, but I've never owned a dog before. I wouldn't even know what to do."

"Oh, don't be silly. It's easy. All you have to do is feed them and take them out for walks. I know, why don't we both own her? She can stay with me in the evenings and she can stay with you during the day while I'm at work. That way you could have some company when David is gone during the day and I can have the pleasure of her company in the evening."

"Well, that does sound like a good compromise," Bertha said, warming to the idea. "Let's do it." After a quick phone call to David to make sure he was on board with the idea, Bertha filled out the paperwork and the deal was done.

Bertha took to Ginger more quickly and more profoundly than she ever thought possible, and even husband David was delighted with their new acquisition. The phenomenon of a couple taking on a pet after their children have left home is sometimes referred to as part of the "empty-nest syndrome." The rationale behind this syndrome is that parents have become so used to having children to take care of that their children's eventual departure leaves a void to be filled. Something of this nature appeared to be going on with Bertha and David.

One of the first things Bertha did after bringing Ginger back from the pound was to take her to the vet for a full physical examination. The vet was reasonably impressed with Ginger's health status at first but did remark on her easily excitable temperament. Ginger just would not stay still on the examination table and squirmed and whined as if being tortured when she was touched. In fact, her distress in the vet's office was so extreme that she began to cough and retch and seemed to be having some difficulty breathing, wheezing like an asthmatic. The vet's attention was thus drawn to her respiratory system, and he was finally able to confirm that Ginger was suffering from what is called a collapsing trachea (windpipe), a fairly common affliction among toy breeds. Things would be fine, he assured Bertha, as long as Ginger was not stressed too much. He gave her two types of medication to help with the problem, one to reduce anxiety and one, a bronchodilator, to help Bertha manage any future crises.

Medical matters aside, the Schusters couldn't have been happier with Ginger. Ginger became Bertha's consummate daytime buddy. With her laughing face and affectionate nature, Ginger added a warmth and sense of mission to Bertha's life which she had not experienced since her son was a child. The way she described her perfect relationship with Ginger made me think of a suitor's words in *Far from the Madding Crowd* as he contemplated married life with his lover: "When I look down, there ye shall be, and when thou looks up, there will I be." It was just that simple for Bertha. In between stints on the computer, she would enjoy tender moments with the ever-watchful Ginger, who, in turn, would revel in her company.

This seemingly utomonan situation continued for a couple of years until Ginger was about nine. At that time, Ginger developed an annoying little habit of urinating on the neighbor's carpet at night. This was making her a *canis non grata* in that household. Bertha, who by this time adored the aging Ginger to the point of obsession, was only too happy to oblige her neighbor and assume nocturnal duties as well. Ginger became the Schusters' pet exclusively. With close attention, it was possible to prevent the nighttime accidents, largely due to the heroic efforts of David, who would get up several times a night to walk Ginger outside. The Schusters mentioned this inconvenience at one of Ginger's annual examinations, and the vet suggested they check for medical conditions that might underlie this type of behavior. In time, the vet came up with a diagnosis of Cushing's syndrome, a disease affecting the adrenal glands that causes increased thirst and urine output, hair loss, liver problems, and muscle wasting. Ginger, by this time, was showing a bit of each. Treatment for this condition was with O,p'-DDD, a drug related to DDT that shrinks the overactive parts of the adrenal gland. The vet also informed Bertha that Ginger's condition was likely a result of a slow-growing pituitary tumor, and could be progressive. Undeterred by this disturbing medical revelation, Bertha and David brought Ginger home and started giving her the medicine, as directed, in hopes that her condition would improve.

Over time, the Schusters thought that some of Ginger's physical problems seemed to abate slightly, but she continued to need to be taken out at night and, if anything, this nocturnal incontinence seemed to be getting worse. In addition, she now seemed to have difficulty hearing and seeing. The vet concluded that she had lost seventy-five percent of her hearing and suspected that she was developing cataracts in both eyes. Old age seemed to be overtaking Ginger at a rapid rate.

When Ginger hit nine and a half years of age, the Schusters noticed that she slept a lot during the day and became very restless, even anxious, in the early evening, pacing around the house and constantly whining for attention. During this time she needed two or three trips outside to completely empty her bladder. Each trip seemed to satisfy her, but only for a short while. She would finally settle down only when the Schusters went to their second-floor bedroom, taking her with them. Then, as they turned in, she would fall asleep immediately, seemingly secure in the knowledge that the three of them were safely in the fold. Ginger would not sleep downstairs and would not sleep upstairs alone. These idiosyncrasies became quite a problem for the Schusters, whose lives were now beginning to be consumed by discussions of how best to manage Ginger's problems. As if the early-evening anxiety were not enough, Ginger would continue to wake them up throughout the night insisting that David take her outside. As a result of the increasingly frequent nocturnal upheavals, David and Bertha were beginning to suffer from sleep deprivation. In fact, when the couple came to see me, one of their primary complaints was not being able to sleep through the night.

At the time of the Schusters' first visit with me, Ginger was ten years old and by now was receiving a veritable pharmacopoeia of medications, including theophylline (for her cough), O,p'-DDD (for Cushing's), estrogen (for incontinence), Valium (for nerves), a tranquilizer (to help her travel and sleep), Frontline (for flea and tick prevention), and a routine heartworm treatment. The Schusters had designed an elaborate cross-reference chart so that they wouldn't forget any one of her many medications. Despite the fact that this little dog practically rattled as she walked, the Schusters still loved her, and Bertha Schuster in particular was utterly devoted to Ginger, who she believed to have a truly unique personality. During the course of the previous year and a half they had visited their vet on numerous occasions and had also been sent to see a specialist at a referral hospital nearby, but there was still no resolution of Ginger's nocturnal anxiety or elimination problems.

The first thing I was able to ascertain was that Ginger suffered from separation anxiety, pacing back and forth between the kitchen and the office whenever the Schusters were not in the house. As she paced she would cry and howl, though she never actually barked. This particular problem, which was something of a side issue to them, was so severe that the Schusters had canceled vacations and never left Ginger alone for more than three to four hours. Even when they left her for this short time they had tremendous pangs of conscience because they knew they would return to find Ginger in a state of near panic. One time they tried to leave her in a veterinary clinic to see if that would ease her separation distress, but no such luck. Ginger worked herself up into such a frenzy there that she started wheezing and turned blue, eventually ending up in an oxygen kennel at the veterinary hospital nearby.

I looked at the Schusters across the consulting desk and pondered the wide array of problems they were facing with Ginger. Ginger sat perched on Bertha's lap, following the conversation like a tennis umpire, occasionally looking to Bertha or David for reassurance. I had a natural affinity for this couple and for their little dog. They had prefaced all their remarks by saying, "Please excuse us, Dr. Dodman, but we are Jewish and, well, you know, very emotional. We're extremely attached to Ginger." Bertha reminded me a little bit of George Costanza's mother in *Seinfeld*—similar appearance, strawberry blondish curly hair, a pretty face, and wearing a constantly surprised expression. David was a largish, slightly overweight, bespectacled business type and wore the traditional pinstriped suit. He was one of those very intense yet highly compassionate people who follow every detail of a conversation, and he clearly loved his easily adorable wife. They were so in tune with each other's feelings that it was almost like talking to a brother and sister. They told me right from the start that they would go to any lengths to help Ginger, with David pragmatically noting that any improvement in Ginger's behavior would also be of great benefit to him and Bertha, as they were both seriously sleep-deprived. David, ever the realist, admitted that on more than one occasion they had considered the unthinkable solution of euthanasia. However, neither of them could bring themselves to go through with it, even though things seemed to be heading that way.

"Is there anything you can do for Ginger?" Bertha pleaded. "David's right, if we can't solve this problem, I don't know what we'll do. Ginger means so much to both of us." David nodded. Then it was my turn to speak. My job was to attempt to resolve this crisis for both the dog and the humans.

Needless to say, I started out on a medical note because there were medical issues involved. "Has Ginger been to the vet recently?" I asked. Indeed she had. "Do you have any recent reports of physical examinations or laboratory tests that have been completed on Ginger?" The answer was affirmative, and David slid the requisite documents across the table for my perusal. A quick glance at the reports indicated that a thorough medical workup had been performed and that Ginger's condition was far from in check. Her liver function, in particular, appeared to be deteriorating. On physical examination Ginger's eyes showed some changes associated with aging and she was partly deaf. Although the O,p'-DDD had caused her hair to regrow, the new hair was of the wispy, undercoat variety, giving her coat the silky, springy texture of a Wheaten terrier's. There wasn't much more I was going to be able to do to check Ginger's advancing physical problems, and there was certainly no point in putting her through a rigid independence training program to address her separation anxiety. The late onset of her anxious behavior and disorientation was undoubtedly the result of her deteriorating health, perhaps accompanied by some old dog-cognitive changes, too. At that time canine Alzheimer's disease was not well documented and there was no treatment available for it, but even with hindsight, the Alzheimer's explanation did not account for all of Ginger's problems, or the ones that would later transpire.

The only road open to me was to try to make Ginger's life more pleasant by helping her sleep through the night and making her less anxious. I thought I could achieve this using a combination of natural and pharmacological treatments. I recommended a microscopic dose of the sleep-promoting hormone melatonin, to be given about thirty minutes before bedtime, to see if this would help Ginger sleep through the night. If the low dose failed, I recommended doubling and then tripling the dose, but asked David to report to me at each stage. In addition, I suggested treating Ginger with a low dose of the mood-stabilizing antidepressant Prozac, which I thought might decrease her separation anxiety and early-evening anxiety. I explained that although Prozac can sometimes affect liver function, I felt that in Ginger's case the likely benefits outweighed slim risks. All was agreed, and the Schusters set off on a somewhat uncertain course of treatment designed to make Ginger feel more at ease and help them all sleep better.

Four days later, Bertha called me back to tell me that the melatonin treatment was working. In an excited voice, she related Ginger's progress to date, and the news was better than I dared hope for. Ginger's internal clock seemed to have been reset by the nightly melatonin and she had slept through the night every night since the appointment. Bertha also reported that on a few occasions Ginger had followed instructions to sit or lie down during her evening pacing sessions. This implied a little more focus on Ginger's part and therefore a little less anxiety. Bertha and David were extremely encouraged by this early success and were optimistic about the future.

One week later, it was David who checked in to say that Ginger continued to do well but he felt there was still room for improvement. In the early part of the evening, Ginger would sit in the family room with the Schusters and simply look at them, instead of pacing to and fro and acting anxiously. Also, David reported that Ginger had slept through the night for three nights that week and would sometimes lie down and go back to sleep when instructed. These changes represented a major behavioral breakthrough, though Ginger would still pace and become anxious and howl when left alone, so the separation anxiety was still present. Struggling for perfection, David had upped the dose of melatonin to the maximum level, and observed a further improvement. To help with the daytime separation anxiety, the Schusters found a pet-sitter to stay with Ginger when they had to be away for extended periods, and Ginger seemed quite happy with her new chaperone.

The week after these early optimistic reports, David reported that Ginger's condition had deteriorated after he'd been away on a business trip for a whole weekend. When he returned, he found that Ginger had reverted to her previous state of high anxiety, pacing in the evening and not sleeping through the night. David asked whether he could increase the dose of melatonin above the normal range, and I told him he could, though I wasn't sure that increasing the dose at this stage was going to get the behavior under control. This turned out to be the case, and Ginger continued to suffer at night, becoming more restless and distressed as the days went by. At the time of the initial appointment, I had mentioned to David that if the melatonin failed to work we could try a more powerful medicine, Xanax, to help Ginger sleep. David and Bertha were now getting pretty desperate and were back in their sleep deprivation mode, so he reminded me of my earlier suggestion and practically pleaded with me for the prescription. I obliged, and recommended at first a low dose and then a higher dose of the medication.

Unfortunately, even at the high dose, the new medication didn't help Ginger, who was by this time in dire straits, coughing more than usual, pacing before bedtime, and moaning and crying more or less continuously. It had been about a month since we started working together to try to improve Ginger's condition, and we were pretty much back to where we started. Perhaps continued growth of the supposed brain tumor was responsible for Ginger's refractory condition? I pondered further diagnostic tests and therapy.

Meanwhile the Schusters were close to the breaking point. This delightful couple, who had barely disagreed or had a cross word in twenty-five years, now found themselves on opposite sides of the fence when it came to what to do about Ginger. David was opting for putting Ginger to sleep because he could barely stay awake at work and because Bertha spent a lot of the day crying as a result of stress and sleep deprivation. Bertha, on the other hand, wanted to give Ginger every last chance and pressed David to increase the dose of Ginger's medication above the recommended amounts in an attempt to resolve the problem. One night Ginger had been coughing a great deal so David, following Bertha's wishes, gave Ginger a large dose of a powerful opioid cough suppressant medicine, Torbutrol, which the local vet had added to their pharmacological war chest. A couple of hours later, at bedtime, David gave twice the maximum recommended dose of Xanax that I had prescribed, not realizing that these two medications may have a synergistic effect. About half an hour after being given the sedative, Ginger became very disoriented and started stumbling around the bedroom floor. Bertha picked her up and put her on the bed to comfort her, but Ginger became very excited and lurched away from her, losing her balance and falling awkwardly onto the bedroom floor. Following the fall, Ginger began to bark and whimper and was in a semihysterical state as she lurched around the bedroom floor, bumping into furniture and occasionally falling over on her side. A second attempt to bring her to the bed and calm her down met with the same result. More excitement, more lurching and lunging, and finally Ginger again rolled off the bed onto the floor. Bertha was beside herself and David was perplexed, wondering what he could do to calm Ginger down so that all three of them could get some sleep. After half an hour or more of unsuccessfully trying to placate Ginger, David decided to bring her downstairs to the kitchen to allow her to sleep it off. He watched her wobble a few steps before turning out the light and closing the door, hoping against hope that the quiet dark environment would help her settle down.

David and Bertha lay in bed listening to Ginger barking from about midnight until 2 A.M. Finally David felt he had to check on her. He put on his dressing gown and went downstairs to the kitchen, where he found Ginger lying on her side, paddling and barking as if she was having a seizure. He didn't know what to do so he returned to bed, where he lay awake until six in the morning, listening to the commotion in horror. Bertha awoke to find that the nightmare was continuing. She and David went downstairs and tried to comfort Ginger, but to no avail. Eventually David decided to call the vet. "Bring her in right away," said the voice at the other end of the phone. "I think we better keep her in the hospital for a while." David wrapped Ginger in a blanket and drove her to the vet's office while Bertha stayed behind and tried to contact me.

I didn't get Bertha's message for a couple of hours but eventually called her back late midmorning and she informed me of the previous night's heartbreaking events. She was obviously distraught and had been sobbing as she agonized over Ginger's condition. By the time I called, David had already conferred with their local vet and between them had decided that it was time to put Ginger to sleep. Bertha was aware of this decision but was still having terrible trouble accepting it.

"What happened last night, Dr. Dodman? Did we give her too much medication? Is that what happened?"

"I think her problem is physical, Mrs. Schuster," I said. "The drugs you gave her probably made her disoriented, and perhaps that's why she fell off the bed, but there's something more sinister going on. The medications should have worn off hours ago, but I hear she's still in quite a state. I wonder if she could have hurt herself falling from the bed or perhaps her current condition is the culmination of everything that's been going on over the last few months."

"Do you think there's any hope, Dr. Dodman? David and our vet both say that I should put her down. But I want you to tell me whether you think that's necessary."

I thought for a moment and truthfully could not see too many options for Ginger. Eventually I decided that we should give Ginger twenty-four more hours—just to see which direction she was heading in. For humane reasons, I ventured the opinion that the local vet should give Ginger something to calm her down and should give her intravenous fluids. Then, if she was better the following morning, we should proceed as before, or hopefully better. However, if Ginger's condition deteriorated or remained the same, I told Bertha, putting her to sleep was the only option. Bertha was grateful for the overnight reprieve. Maybe I was procrastinating, buying time, but I had to see whether Ginger would turn the corner, and at least get back to the way she was before the accident.

As it turned out, we didn't have to wait until the next day for the saga to conclude. The supportive therapy I had called for only gave Ginger some relief for two or three hours, whereupon she reverted to the hysterical, frenzied state she'd been in the night before. David gave the vet the nod and Ginger was peacefully put to sleep by the slow injection of barbiturate. David made the decision that Bertha and I had tried in vain to stave off.

I was stunned when Bertha called me to tell me the news, and spent a long while with her on the phone going over every facet of the case to see if there was anything more we could have done. For what it was worth, I told Bertha that I thought David had made the right decision because the seizure-like state that afflicted Ginger terminally probably had organic underpinnings. I mentioned, for example, that Ginger's pituitary tumor may have slowly expanded to cause some of the problems, including the disorientation, anxiety, and finally the nocturnal terrors that Ginger had endured. I also raised the possibility of a stroke or cerebral hemorrhage. Unfortunately a postmortem was not performed to confirm any of these hypotheses, but, as Bertha pointed out, probably nothing we could have done would have altered the final course of events. Discussing the possible medical factors in Ginger's demise seemed to help Bertha see through the fog of her own despair and begin to think more rationally. I listened patiently as she recalled the memorable times she had shared with Ginger. Ginger had opened her eyes to a new world, the world of animals. "It's amazing," she said. "I never thought an animal could be so dear to me, and there I was with this special friend from another species. After I adopted Ginger from the shelter I started to get mail from the shelter asking for donations to help stray and unwanted pets. It was because of Ginger that I sent them money, and I did so gladly. Ginger helped me to understand more about my own life—who I really was, what was important to me, and that I cared. Of course, as soon as I gave money I found myself on everyone's mailing list and I started to get all sorts of mail from all sorts of humane organizations. I gave each of them a little bit. When I thought about what I had become and what I was, I realized that Ginger had a profound effect on my life. I changed from a person who had no particular experience with or affection for animals to a total devotee, which I remain. Dr. Dodman, I still love Ginger even though I know she's gone. As a gesture to her, I would like to do something to help animals like her to overcome their problems. Is there anything I could do for you at Tufts? Could I join in your Expo next year and perhaps help to spread the word?"

"Of course you can," I said. "I'll mention it to the appropriate people."

The conversation ended on this bittersweet note, with Bertha somewhat revived but with me constantly turning over the details in my mind to see what more, or what else, I could have done. In addition, I was concerned for Bertha because I worried that she might slip back into her old pre-Ginger mode and forget all the joy Ginger had brought her.

I called Bertha a few weeks later to ask her if I might write this story about Ginger. "Please do," she said. "I would be so delighted to have other people appreciate the understanding that a pet can bring to a person's life. They should know that by giving help to an animal they will be enriching their own lives and the rewards are unimaginable. Please *do* tell people about Ginger."

"Consider it done," I said.

"Oh, there's one more thing," Bertha said before signing off. "I have some good news."

"Good news?" I said, somewhat surprised. "We can both do with some good news. Pray tell."

"David brought me back a puppy to take my mind off things. I have been crying practically every day since Ginger was put to sleep. I always cry myself to sleep. David couldn't stand to see me hurting that way and decided that a puppy would help. You should see it, Dr. Dodman, it's darling."

"What kind of dog is it?" I asked.

"A poodle, apricot-colored. A little girl."

"That's fantastic," I said. "I bet you're thrilled."

"I am," she said, her tone changing slightly. "But you know, as much as I love the pup, no dog will ever replace Ginger. Ginger was very special. She meant the world to me."

"I know she did," I replied, "but the little one needs you now."

7

MÉNAGE À TROIS

Far in the stillness a cat languishes loudly.

—William Ernest Henley

It's often very difficult for a pet who has been the subject of a person's undivided attention to learn to share that attention when family circumstances change. Sometimes the disturbing event is the arrival of a new baby or a new pet, or the development of an amorous relationship between the owner and another individual. "Yuppie puppies," for example, may have their noses put out of joint when their owners' carefully planned, long-awaited progeny finally arrives, and may act out with displays of aggression or urine marking. Overly attached cats sometimes have conniptions when their owner strikes up a long-term relationship with a member of the opposite sex. Again, territorial urine marking is often the way in which these pets express their displeasure. But one of the most prolonged insults a sensitive, formerly single-owner pet can suffer is that brought about by its owner's marriage. Dogs and cats alike may react adversely to the arrival of certain unwanted better halves and may express their feelings by exhibiting any of the aforementioned behaviors, plus or minus various degrees of sulkiness, social withdrawal, or rebellion. Some of these miffed animals are just plain unfriendly when the usurper is around. Other manifestations range from moping to aggravated attention seeking as the displaced creature attempts to recoup its loss. Although in many instances a whole constellation of rebellious behaviors may be expressed right from the start, sometimes a pet's initial aloofness and displeasure may give way to more proactive protests in time. Such was the case with Susan Gale's cat, D.G., an eleven-and-a-half-year-old spayed female Burmese affectionately known as Honey.

It is often the case that when a strong bond develops between an owner and a pet, one or both parties were experiencing an emotional void in their lives at the time. The close relationship that developed between Susan and D.G. was no exception to this general rule. For Susan, an intelligent, attractive woman in her late thirties with blond hair and a lovely smile, the void was a result of her upwardly mobile, highly energetic, and demanding professional career. As a buyer for a major furniture chain, she had spent the first ten years of her professional life on the road, cutting important deals with sweaty-palmed sales executives in remote warehouse offices. The pay was good but the cutthroat nature of the business kept her extremely busy. After cross-country trips, she would return to her apartment for microwave dinners, TV, and a few phone calls before retiring, only to rise again a few hours later and repeat the whole cycle all over again. She did have a close friend, Deirdre, with whom she spent some time on weekends, and occasionally she would date men, though few had much patience with her hectic lifestyle.

As the years went by, Susan began to reflect on her hermitlike existence and decided that some relatively self-sufficient yet affectionate and reliable companion would put some color into her life. On Deirdre's advice she decided to get a cat. In her usual methodical manner, she researched the subject carefully before making her decision. Abyssinians, she read, were too active; Persians too dull; Siamese were quirky, and the short-legged Munchkin cats far too odd. Then it occurred to her: a Burmese cat, that's what she wanted—a handsome brown- or sable-colored, yellow-eyed Burmese to welcome her home, share her bed, and be her soul mate. Her reference book, *The Wonderful World of Cats*, said, "Every Burmese will have its own definite personality, will make a delightful companion, and indeed is to be taken seriously as a member of the family." She did not know, at the time, how apt that description would turn out to be.

Susan found a reputable Burmese breeder on the Internet and set off to visit her and a four-week-old litter of kittens who were coming up for adoption. The journey took her from her home in Massachusetts to the neighboring state of Rhode Island, where she found the breeder's home without much trouble. The house itself was a largish, run-down three-decker that looked like something out of a Hitchcock movie. She knocked lightly on the door and waited patiently. A full minute later, a schoolmarmish woman wearing half-frame spectacles and with her hair in a bun opened the door and announced herself as the breeder. With barely a word spoken she led Susan through the otherwise uninhabited house to the kitchen, where an attractive mom cat and four of her kittens were engaging in family life as usual. The kittens' silky brown fur, flat faces, and large yellow eyes appealed to Susan instantly. The whole scene was like a picture on a chocolate box. She knew she had come to the right place. Two of the kittens were female and two were males, though it was hard to tell them apart.

"You can't have that one," the woman said, pointing to one of the kittens, "I'm going to use her for breeding, but any of the others are all right."

Susan dropped to one knee close to the litter and was immediately approached by both male kittens, who greeted her in a friendly manner. The female kitten who was to be bred stayed close to her mum while the other one ran and hid, apparently intimidated by Susan's Gulliverian presence.

"Did you say you wanted one cat or two?" the breeder asked brusquely, taking off her spectacles and cleaning them on the scarf she was wearing.

"Just one," Susan said without looking up, barely able to take her eyes off the kittens.

"Well, if it's one you want," the breeder pressed, "you should take the female. Females are much easier to keep as single pets because they adapt more easily to being alone."

"But she seems so scared," Susan answered, "and the males seem to have taken to me already."

"She's only scared because she's young. When you come back in two or three weeks' time, you'll find that all the kittens are as confident as can be. That's about the right time for adoption, you know."

Susan didn't know this but now she had time to ponder the matter. She was actually relieved that she didn't have to make up her mind at that instant because for the life of her she couldn't decide which of the three kittens to take home.

Three weeks later she returned to the breeder's home to make her final selection. The experience was practically a case of déjà vu, except that all the kittens were now considerably larger. As before, the males approached her and were friendly. As before, one female stayed close to mum while the other ran for shelter.

"I know you said a female might be better for me, but these males seem so friendly that I think I'll take one of them," Susan said, hoping not to offend the woman.

"Whatever you like, this is the best one," she said holding one of the males high in the air and turning it around like a pie on a pastry stand. The kitten's limbs hung limply like noodles, and it blinked in astonishment as it surveyed the world rotating below from its new, elevated platform.

"Okay," said Susan, "I'll take that one. So what do we do now? What's the procedure?"

"I fill out the paperwork, you pay me, and then you're on your way," the breeder said. "Make the check payable to me if you don't mind."

Susan sat there as the woman scratched some information on a piece of paper: age—seven weeks, sex—M (indicating male). . . . Susan sat there waiting patiently with her new acquisition in her lap. Suddenly the hitherto timorous female darted across the room, jumped onto Susan's lap, knocked her sibling onto the floor, and, purring loudly, started playing with Susan's necklace. It appeared that the female had chosen Susan and ousted her brother. Susan was so touched by the mite's display of courage and affection that she decided to change her adoption plans. There was something really special about this plucky little cat. A warmth, a welling feeling from deep within, began to spread through her body. It was inexplicable but she knew she was experiencing immediate bonding; it was as palpable as the thrill of blood coursing through her veins. With three strokes of a pen a capital F was placed in front of the M, indicating female (FM) on the cat's papers, and she was now the proud owner of a small brown cat.

The breeder herself also sensed something unique about the interaction between Susan and the kitten, and her attitude softened ever so slightly as she escorted Susan to the door.

"You know, I've never heard her purr before. She was always so frightened of everything. I think you two will be good for each other," she said, with a glimmer of goodwill.

Susan didn't even put the kitten into the carrier for the journey, allowing it to sit on the passenger seat next to her where the contented creature purred the whole way home. Susan pondered the question of what to call her new friend. She ran through a host of possibilities in her mind but eventually came up with the idea of making a hybrid of her best friend's first name, Deirdre (Deirdre had been instrumental in suggesting she acquire the kitten in the first place), and her own name, Gale. No combination of these two names seemed right—Dale, Geirdre, Galdre, etc.—so in the end she settled for the initials D.G. D.G.'s nickname, Honey, came years later, courtesy of Susan's local vet, "So how's Honey doing?" he would say. "Time for Honey's vaccinations again," and so on. No doubt every cat in this vet's practice was referred to as Honey, but to Susan this nickname seemed particularly appropriate, so it stuck.

When Susan got the kitten, still named D.G., home from the breeder's, it wasn't long before she was reminded of the more anxious, nervous side of her disposition. D.G. was afraid of everything and everyone apart from her. When Susan had visitors around, D.G. would be found hiding under a bed or in the back of a closet. Sometimes she would hide in a laundry room on the second floor or wedge herself up in the rafters. When Susan went away on trips she had a pet-sitter take care of D.G., but the pet-sitter never saw D.G. at all. The only way she could tell there was a cat in the house was that the food disappeared and the litter box was used. The pet-sitter commented, "It was like taking care of a ghost cat." It slowly dawned on Susan that, though D.G. doted on her, her dear cat was otherwise a recluse, a social misfit.

When at home alone with Susan, D.G. was reasonably comfortable unless there were any loud noises, which would invariably make her tense and afraid. Susan became very much aware of D.G.'s high-strung and antisocial nature but found herself becoming more strongly attached to her misanthropic soul mate as the months slipped by. It was, in a way, extremely flattering to be the only human being in the world on the receiving end of this timorous creature's trust.

The time came, some years later, when the bond between Susan and D.G. strengthened to the point of virtual inseparability. Of course, Susan still had to travel, but much less than in the earlier part of her career. The temporary separation necessitated by such trips was clearly painful for D.G. When Susan returned, the pet-sitter invariably reported not only that D.G. vanished for the duration of the trip but also that she could be heard crying in some remote corner of the house.

Then a new phenomenon began to emerge, apparently signaling D.G.'s mortification at being left. When Susan returned home after a trip of any length, ranging from overnight to several days, D.G. would stand and wail at her, Siamese-style, for up to twenty minutes without stopping. D.G.'s mouth was wide open during these wailing bouts, displaying her raspy pink tongue and giving a view down her throat practically as far as her tonsils. Her chest would heave accordion-style during the effort as she pumped out volley after volley of grating, throaty sounds. Susan interpreted this hypervocalization as a serious token of D.G.'s displeasure at her desertion, and nothing she did could appease D.G. during these episodes. Then Susan began to notice that D.G. would vocalize at other times, particularly before eating and sometimes early in the morning. It was as if D.G. was trying to tell her something extremely important and became frustrated because she couldn't understand. Susan sought to comfort her by picking her up and putting her on her lap or by moving her food to a preferred location (upstairs). Although these strategies sometimes worked for a short time, there was often a recurrence of the caterwauling a short while later. Nevertheless, the frequency of D.G.'s yelling was sufficiently low at this point (twice a day during the week, slightly more frequently on the weekends) that Susan could tolerate it. Tending to her disturbed pet's apparently angry distress calls fostered the nurturing side of Susan's character and kept her on her toes. It was as if she had a newborn baby to take care of.

Life went on like this for seven or eight years, and Susan never looked back with regret on her decision to adopt D.G., now affectionately renamed Honey. With additional years of work experience, Susan had now become a vice president in the company she worked for and was shouldering considerable responsibility. Her reflections on life resumed with renewed intensity as she turned forty. Was the exchange of family life for a successful career worthwhile in terms of the quality of her existence? Did a substantial salary and an expense account compensate for the children she never had? What would have happened if the serious relationship she had enjoyed in her late twenties had run the gamut? She didn't have any of the answers. It was while in this frame of mind, during the course of her work, that Susan found herself in the company of an attractive male executive. He wasn't like the others, his palms weren't sweaty, he didn't wear loud suits or ties, and he didn't smell of cigar smoke. He was tallish, handsome in a rugged sort of way, and well spoken. His expression when he first saw her told her that the admiration was mutual. They began to talk and found they had a lot in common: for example, Peter (which was his name) was a career bachelor who was also beginning to have second thoughts.

Susan dated Peter for the best part of a year before the two of them were married. It was a fulfilling event for both, and the two of them were, and still are, in love. During the year-long courtship period Peter visited Susan regularly, much to Honey's quite obvious disgust. Honey would sulk off when Peter and Susan were together and would brood for quite a while after he had left. But little did Honey know, there was worse to come. Upon marrying, Susan moved from her apartment into Peter's more spacious home a few towns over. Of course Honey had to go along, too. Susan's suspicions that Honey would not take kindly to this new situation turned out to be well founded. Cats don't take well to geographical moves in the best of times, but for a cat like Honey, the stress proved almost overwhelming. Add to this the ultimate insult of having to share her owner with a live-in stranger, and here was a recipe for total disaster. Even in the old days, anyone who deflected Susan's attention away from Honey was persona non grata to this self-centered cat. Under the new, challenging conditions resulting from the move, Honey's negative feelings toward Peter became progressively more profound and her mood darker.

As Susan later succinctly put it, "She hates my husband." "Hate" might have been too strong a word, but Honey certainly didn't appreciate Peter's presence and shunned all interaction with him, her attitude seemingly veering from aloof or antisocial to frankly disdainful. Honey wasn't scared of Peter because he always treated her very kindly and with respect. The problem was more one of Honey's jealousy, contempt, and stubborn refusal to accept the new circumstances. The ever so patient Peter must have considered Susan's feelings profoundly as he attempted to build bridges of mutual understanding with Honey.

Susan and Peter soldiered on against a backdrop of Honey's demanding cries and complaints. Honey even took to waking Peter up in bed by screaming at him nose-to-nose like a baseball manager yelling at an umpire after an iffy call against a player. Long-suffering Peter would respond by swinging his legs out of bed and shuffling around to start the day, whereupon her nibs would jump into the warm spot he had vacated and snuggle with her beloved Susan. Peter was also obliged to tolerate being screamed at by Honey whenever he approached the little princess's favorite resting place on the cable box on their dresser. Despite his best attempts to pet and interact with her, she would always shy away. The only time Honey showed any affection at all for Peter was after he had had hip replacement surgery and was flat on his back in bed. During this period of incapacitation she would crawl up on his chest and purr as if he were her best friend. You could interpret this as empathy, as an attempt to console him, but Susan said she thought Honey was finally happy because she figured that Peter was dying. Unfortunately the cupboard love, or whatever it was, only lasted as long as Peter's illness, and following that it was business as usual for Honey.

In this family triad, Peter loved Susan, Susan loved Peter, Susan loved Honey, and Honey loved Susan (though in a rather demanding sort of way). Peter even had some affection for Honey despite her constant rebuffs, but the affection was not reciprocated. You might think that Honey's refusal to accept Peter would have been the main problem in the household, but it was not. Honey's negative attitude toward Peter was something the couple had learned to live with. The last straw was the increasingly demanding behavior that Honey directed toward Susan. This demanding behavior took the form of incessant caterwauling, guttural at times, which was like an auditory Chinese water torture. Intimate moments between Peter and Susan were rudely framed by Honey's irritated response. She would either sit on the cable box and stare in total disbelief as if betrayed by Susan or would turn her back in apparent disgust and sulk for hours. Susan was beginning to wilt under the strain. The increased frequency and intensity of Honey's demands seemed to be associated with Peter's presence. Honey was working harder and harder to restore the status quo. Susan clearly needed help.

It was at this time that a slightly frazzled Susan beat a track to the door of the Behavior Clinic at Tufts Veterinary School, and that was where we first met. We introduced ourselves at the front desk in the reception area of the Small Animal Hospital and proceeded directly to the consulting room. Susan had Honey secured inside a carrier. My assistant, Gina, an elegant, well-spoken, young Hispanic woman in her twenties, was waiting for us in the room. We arranged ourselves in the consulting room with me across a desk from Susan and I asked her to gingerly open the door to Honey's carrier. This she did, and, to her great surprise, Honey stepped out warily and began to slink around the consulting room until she found a safe place beneath my desk. Susan swept her wayward bangs back from her face and I found myself gazing into the steady stare of her lightly mascaraed blue eyes. She laughed out loud as she told me Honey's story, but I thought I could see tears welling in her eyes as she spoke and sometimes she appeared to be choking on her words. It didn't take me long to figure out that she was trying to put on a brave face for me, and to report things accurately and unemotionally. It was evident that there were deep emotions connected with what she was relating.

My suspicions about the impact of Honey's behavior on her well-being were confirmed when on more than one occasion during her narrative she dropped her head and covered her eyes, taking a deep breath before she was able to resume.

"I'm sorry," she would say on each of these occasions, "I can't help it," and she would wipe a tear away.

Eventually her monologue drew to a close. As my assistant wildly scribbled notes in the chart, I started to run through some possible explanations for Honey's behavior and to ponder what we could do to free Susan from her predicament. As usual, I was the last resort. The tension Susan was under was almost palpable. I really hoped that I could turn things around for her, and for Honey, who was also obviously very confused. Before addressing the issue of treatment, I had to confirm my suspicions about the cause of Honey's vocalization by asking some more detailed questions. Most importantly, I wanted to know exactly what triggered the behavior and what caused it to stop. Surely the cacophony could not be incessant, as Susan had first indicated. I already knew of some of the triggers for the behavior, but I needed more specifics to fill in gaps in my knowledge of Honey.

Susan said she didn't really know what set Honey off but that she often started to meow loudly early in the morning at around 5:30 A.M. Knowing that the racket would continue until she or Peter got up, Susan would usually get up and remove Honey from the bedroom, shutting her in the family room downstairs. Peter arose only if Honey got in his face because he had a higher tolerance for the din. When Susan went downstairs later to let Honey out, she would find her perched atop her large kitty condo and glowering at her. Another high-risk period for excessive vocalization was at feeding time, when Honey, who spent most of her time upstairs, would appear at the head of the stairs and howl continuously, even though her food had been set out for her downstairs. The food was only a flight of stairs away but Honey wasn't prepared to make the trip. Honey's third most frequent occasion for vocalization was whenever she wanted to go outside, in which case, she would stand at the door and howl until Susan opened it.

Susan admitted that it had been her practice, prior to her marriage to Peter, to allow Honey to snuggle next to her first thing in the morning. Apparently Honey found this formerly regular, now intermittent experience so rewarding that she would use whatever ploy was necessary to make it happen. By trial and error she learned that screaming in Peter's face and generally disturbing the peace caused the couple to respond in ways that at least occasionally achieved the desired effect. Intermittent reinforcement of the behavior, such as this, is a powerful way of ensuring that the behavior will continue. It's the slot machine principle, the same one that keeps people pulling the levers on those "one-armed bandits" in Las Vegas. Susan would sometimes respond to Honey's cries by bringing the food bowl up to her, while sometimes she would ignore her. Eating upstairs was preferred by the nervous cat, who would do whatever it took to get what she wanted. What worked best was howling. It was a similar story at the back door. Honey cried by the door because this *sometimes* caused Susan to open the door. Honey was so determined to achieve her goal that she would continue shrieking to the point of shaking, and breathed so hard that she looked like she was going to keel over. And sometimes she got her way.

Honey's screaming at Peter either got him out of bed or made him go away. Screaming at Susan led to attention, snuggles, a preferred dining location, or freedom. Curious about the attention-seeking components of Honey's behavior, I asked Susan whether Honey ever vocalized excessively while she was away, that is, when she was alone with Peter. The answer was a resounding no. While I felt sorry for Honey because of her ingrained fear of strangers and general skittishness, neither of these was the direct cause of the problem at hand. In the peace and sanctuary of her own home, Honey was a manipulator of people, a crybaby, even a bully, who would scream for anything she wanted—and often get it. There was no reason to scream at Peter when Susan was away because Peter didn't respond the same way. He might get out of bed in the morning after a bout of screaming into his face, but then there was no Susan lying there to snuggle up with. Also, by extension, I figured that Peter wasn't quite as active in his attempts to appease Honey when Susan was away. The minute Susan returned to the house, Honey started all over again. Susan's touching devotion to meeting Honey's needs and her compliance with her demands were instrumental in perpetuating the demanding behavior.

I was once consulted about a cat exhibiting behavior almost identical to Honey's. In that case, the problem was solved when the owners acquired a second cat. The new cat diverted attention away from the beleaguered owners, resulting in an immediate cessation of the attention-seeking behavior. I asked Susan whether she'd thought of getting another kitten to occupy Honey's attention. Tears brimmed in her eyes again and she pressed her lips tight together as she tried to compose herself. She then related a hitherto unknown component of the unfolding plot. She said that she had once brought a shelter kitten, a tiny tiger-striped tabby, into her apartment five years earlier, and that Honey, in Queen Victoria's words, was "not amused." Actually, in true Honey style, she was mortified and didn't purr for a year. She did, however, continue to vocalize and insist on having her own way, but only when the kitten was out of sight. Bad turned to worse as the kitten, a formerly angelic white powder puff of a cat named Sugarfoot, grew up to be an eighteen-pound juggernaut. Sugarfoot started to attack Honey on a routine basis and also began to deposit urine and feces on the rug instead of in the litter box. Honey became a silent recluse, often seeking sanctuary on top of the cable box in Susan's bedroom. All this was too much for Susan, who returned Sugarfoot to the shelter, Strays in Need, because it seemed that neither cat was happy with the situation. A tragic twist was that Sugarfoot refused to eat in the shelter, developed a serious liver problem as a result, and died two or three weeks later. Susan, clearly a highly emotional person, was weeping openly by the time she finished relating this tale, and confessed her guilt over Sugarfoot's premature demise.

Although during Sugarfoot's reign of terror Honey had been sufficiently intimidated to quiet down, it didn't take her long to regain her self-confidence and resume incessant wailing once she realized that Sugarfoot was permanently out of the picture. Gone were Honey's days of sequestration on top of the cable box in the master bedroom. Back came her bullying and controlling ways. The Sugarfoot experiment had been a disaster and Susan was in no mood to try anything remotely similar again.

This led me to Plan B: hoping to interrupt the cycle of reward, I instructed Susan not, under any circumstances, to respond to Honey's defiant cries. In this context, I told her that each time Honey began to shriek and complain, she should make a "neutral" sound, such as that made by a duck call or tuning fork, and then turn her back on Honey and walk away. A neutral sound is one that has no positive or negative connotations and is used merely as a signal. It is used not to punish the animal but rather to focus its attention on a particular point in time: namely, the moments leading up to the owner's departure. When used in this way, the neutral sound is referred to as a bridging stimulus. Susan elected to use a low note on her monano to signal withdrawal of her presence and attention. The flip side of this plan was that when Honey was behaving well she should receive the attention she craved in the form of petting and praise, or be fed food treats or given access to the garden. I warned Susan that Honey's caterwauling would probably get worse before it got better as Honey tested her resolve, and I encouraged her to stick with the program.

In addition, I asked Susan to switch Honey's feeding from free choice to two meals a day so that Peter could become a food provider. Any brand of kibble or canned food would do—just no human food, which is not healthful for cats. Susan wasn't happy with this scheme, because Honey had always been able to eat whenever she chose, and worried that the change might upset her. But I managed to convince her that preventing Honey's "manna from heaven" (or from Susan) approach to life and encouraging her dependence on Peter was the point of the exercise. I needed Susan's compliance on this one.

For good measure I also prescribed some mild antianxiety medicine for Honey to alleviate her fear and help foster the new relationship I planned for her. The medication, buspirone (BuSpar), boosts confidence and encourages affection and playfulness—and that's just what I wanted for Honey.

There wasn't much more to do or say after this, although we did listen to a tape recording that Susan had brought of Honey's vocalizations. She was right, the noise was hideous, both extremely loud and grating. After a while, Honey, who was looking perplexed, joined in, creating a horrid, discordant racket. The tension in the room subsided and we laughed as we pushed our chairs back and sauntered outside into the waiting room. I could tell that Susan was feeling much more at ease for having shared her burden. The hour or so of consultation seemed to have had a cathartic effect, causing her to express feelings and call up memories that she had been repressing. It would be several days before we would talk again, but I felt positive about the outcome and thought that she was encouraged, too.

While I waited to hear back from Susan I gave her predicament more thought. It was hard for me to imagine that a cat was responsible for driving this successful and happily married woman to the brink. Indeed, I didn't believe that Honey's behavior alone accounted for her mental state. Sometimes, to understand the nature of an individual's predicament, you have to take a step back from the problem and take a wider view. I am no human psychologist but it was clear to me that Susan, like Honey, was emotionally overwrought, perhaps at least in part because of her nature. Personally, I prefer emotional people to so-called thinking people, but being overly emotional has its downside. It's tough to have feelings that are so intense. Perhaps for this reason Susan had chosen to lose herself in work when a more personal social world was at her fingertips.

For whatever reason, the world did not seem to be Susan's oyster and she chose to withdraw from it, at least until she chose to share her life with Honey, and then with Peter. Honey was there to nurture and care for, to provide company and affection. Peter, I thought, symbolized stability, trust, and love. Together the three of them would have lived in perfect bliss if only Honey had welcomed her new parent and appreciated her enviable lot. But Honey, like Susan, was trapped within her own anxious, reclusive skin, trusting no one and finding it difficult if not impossible to see past her fear. This situation was, if anything, perpetuated by Susan's doting, well-meaning, but misguided nurturing behavior toward Honey. It is said that cats think of us humans as maternal facsimiles because we feed and groom them. If true, this means that we can easily fall into a mothering role with cats if biology and necessity so directs us. Why else would it be that when behaviorists address groups of cat owners the audience is 85 percent female? The nurturing potential offered by a small, cuddly, and sometimes doting dependent might explain the phenomenon.

I believe that a quasi-parental attachment possibly explained the dynamic between Susan and Honey—but this couple went a stage further, becoming codependent and thus inseparable. Both cat and owner found themselves caught up in some kind of symbiotic bonding process in which they both identified some unique need in each other. Susan knew this when Honey chose to approach her at the breeder's home, and I think Honey must have sensed it too. Susan gained a dependent and Honey a mom. The only problem was that, as with some real moms, Susan did not set proper limits for Honey, because, prior to Peter, she had no need for them. Honey was raised as a spoiled child, demanding this and that and getting it. This was fulfilling for both parties until Peter came along. The intellectual side of Susan must have said, "This is Peter, he's my partner. Together we can sustain a lifelong relationship that will bring pleasure to both of us." But the emotional side of her might have fretted, "But what about poor Honey? How will she feel?" The same thoughts often go through the mind of a divorcée when she meets a potential second match. "What about the children?" But in the same breath: "What about me?" It's the same old story but with a pet in the middle instead of a child. The animal, like the child, if so inclined, knows how to play both ends against the middle. There have been divorce cases recently in which the parties have sued each other for custody of their pets. In fact, 80 percent of spouses say that if forced to choose between their partner and their pet, the pet would win. Pet power is alive and well in the United States.

My behavioral advice was aimed at teaching Susan to set limits for

Honey, to reward acceptable behaviors and to ignore the rest. The same advice might help parents who have remarried cope with the integration of their children into the new family unit. Children, like pets, will sometimes act out in such situations, and while our instinct is to nurture them, it is important that we not inadvertently reinforce unwanted behaviors. In the situation that Susan found herself, it was as if a demanding offspring had decided to undermine her attempts to establish a new relationship by means of attention seeking and disrespect. She had to work to change this dynamic or her whole domestic situation would be in jeopardy. I think that's why she was crying.

My first follow-up communication with Susan came one month after her initial visit, and I think she was beginning to understand Honey's role in her predicament. Her leadoff words were, "Dr. Dodman, you know, Honey is probably the most willful being I have ever seen in my entire life."

I smiled at the way she phrased this but knew from the sentiment that she must be having continuing difficulties. That was hardly surprising considering the limited time she had been working with Honey, but I had hoped for some good news. Happily there was some. Honey, she thought, was much calmer and had not gotten into her crazy-eyed panting mode for the entire month, despite having had her demands denied. Also, the shrieking episodes were less frequent (in her own words there was "less shouting"), though some hypervocalization did still occur. Other positive news was that striking the monano key and leaving the room was having a positive effect, though Honey usually started up again a few minutes later. Finally Honey was showing more affection and had taken to spending quality "calm time" on Susan's lap in the evenings.

On the negative side, Honey was still acting out too often for comfort and the feeding strategy was not working well. I asked Susan to elaborate on this and she said that Honey would not eat her food, or even food treats, if the victuals were offered by Peter. She had shown no acceptance of him whatsoever. I inquired whether Honey simply went hungry following her refusal to eat, and Susan then admitted something that explained the failure of our plan. If Honey didn't eat when Peter offered her food, and then wailed long and hard enough, Susan took over and put the food down herself—because she felt sorry for Honey. Patiently I reexplained to Susan the rationale of not giving in to Honey's demands, and this time I felt somewhat more confident that she would follow directions. She had been concerned about Honey missing meals, but when I told her that missing a meal or two wouldn't harm her, she finally agreed to try again. I emphasized that Peter should be the one to offer all meals until Honey caved in and accepted him. There was to be no alternative for Honey.

Considerable time passed before I heard back from Susan, and this time I had to call her.

"How's Honey? I asked cheerily, hoping for good news.

"Dr. Dodman," she sighed, "I wish I could tell you that she's a wonderful cat, but she's still as horrible as ever. We're still victims and I have given up on ever being able to change her. I know it's my fault, that's why I didn't call you. She was doing well for a while on the BuSpar, but our pet-sitter messed up when we went away for four days. Obviously the girl couldn't give Honey the medicine, so that treatment lapsed. Also, I told the girl that she was supposed to meal-feed Honey and pick up the food if she didn't eat it. Well, she took this request far too literally and Honey, who always hid from her, didn't eat for days. Honey was in a terrible state when we returned—practically out of her mind. I just couldn't stand it so I went back to feeding her free choice and whenever she was hungry. I'm afraid I've caved in on all your recommendations. I'm such a bad client."

"So you see no residual improvement at all?" I asked.

"Well, maybe a little," Susan said, perhaps trying to spare my feelings. "She is always happy when she's sitting on my lap, and she will occasionally sit on Peter's lap, too. Peter says it's only when she thinks he is ill, but I really believe there has been some improvement in their relationship."

Hallelujah, I said under my breath. "And the vocalizing . . . ?"

"Pretty much all the time when she's not sleeping," came the immediate reply. "She has a noise for everything, and the sounds are really unpleasant. The worst noises still occur when I come home from traveling. Sometimes Peter and I just have to shut her away to get a moment's peace."

I paused and thought for a second.

"Honey must have some redeeming feature that allows you to continue this way. Most people would have given up by now."

"It goes way back, Dr. Dodman. She and I have had this incredible bond since she was a kitten. We both need each other; I suppose that's because she came into my life at a time that wasn't good for either of us. Just to see her contented look when she's with me and to see her looking up into my eyes adoringly makes it all worthwhile. Oh sure, it would be nice to have her behave better, and God knows together we tried. The bottom line is that I'm prepared to tolerate her not-so-good side, and Peter is, too. You do understand, don't you? You see, she's my little girl and she's beautiful."

I did understand. I hear statements like this all the time and never get tired of hearing them. There's something almost indescribable about the bond that can develop between a person and a pet. I did wish I could have helped Susan more with her problem, but it wasn't to be. Maybe someday some new treatment will come along and I'll be able to call her and offer my help once more. I am always painfully aware, as Susan's story reveals, that endings are not always perfect and that sacrifices have to be made and compromises reached in order to maintain a relationship with any living creature. Susan and Peter had to make more sacrifices than most, but they were prepared to accept what they had to accept and they should be respected for that.

8

THE PIT BULL FROM HELL

For the soul of every living thing is in the hand of God.—
Job 12:10

Both pit bulls and their owners have come in for some pretty bad press recently, and not entirely without cause. Originally bred for aggression and tenacity, pit bulls, if provoked, will bite hard and hang on, making them as potentially dangerous as a handgun without a safety lock. However, if properly socialized in the first few months of their lives and if looked after properly by a kind but no-nonsense owner, they can become quite civilized, developing into loyal and entertaining companions. But the *potential* for trouble is always lurking somewhere, as a result of their genes and breeding.

I remember a story told to me by a friend of mine, Stewart Bragg, who owned an independent but playful pit bull for five years, without incident, before he learned an important lesson. His dog, Henry, was sitting next to him on the couch one day when Stewart, in good humor, blew into Henry's ear—just for fun. As it turned out, this was something Henry really didn't appreciate. As Winston Churchill put it when corrected after ending a sentence with a preposition: this was something "up with which he would not put." Henry let out a bloodcurdling roar and lunged toward Stewart's face, missing his target by a mere quarter inch. The hair on the back of Stewart's neck prickled as he realized what could have happened. He will never forget the feeling of the rush of air and the clack of Henry's teeth snapping shut right up next to his ear. Stewart now appreciated that there were limits beyond which Henry could not be pushed.

In contrast to Henry, some pit bulls are selected and trained for aggression by unscrupulous owners. I remember one such dog named Hitler by his skinhead owner, who no doubt acquired the dog to enhance his own fascistic image. Some owners of this ilk actually torture their dogs to make them meaner and revel in the ferocity that results. "Gunpowdering"—literally putting gunpowder inside the dog's rectum—is one of the horrendous forms of torture they employ. There's also isolation, starvation, water deprivation, taunting, goading, yelling, and hitting. Bad owners make good dogs bad and bad dogs intolerable. Probably in part due to the irresponsibility of such owners, pit bulls have been banned in Great Britain as too dangerous to have around. They are not banned in the United States, but they do head the list of breeds causing human dog-bite-related fatalities and are blacklisted by several home insurance companies.

Beyond their tenacity and potential for aggression, pit bulls also have extremely high prey drive and, through nature rather than nurture, will hone in on and kill small rapidly moving prey. They do so with speed and confidence, and they're very good at it. Unfortunately their predatory tendencies are not confined to vermin and sometimes are directed toward less acceptable targets, such as chipmunks, squirrels, rabbits, neighborhood cats, and even small dogs. Even more of a problem occurs when a misdirected prey drive causes them to attack rapidly moving children, whether running or on bikes or skateboards. This variation on the theme of predatory aggression is even more likely when dogs with high prey drive, such as pit bulls, are running free in a small group. This dynamic arouses a pack mentality, leading to what has been dubbed pack or group aggression. The unwelcome awakening of this primordial response is the result of a phenomenon known as social facilitation. Of course, pit bulls aren't the only dogs with high prey drive, but the combination of enhanced prey drive plus tenacity, strength, and fierce bite makes them a lethal weapon under some circumstances.

All pit bull owners should be aware of the nature of their charge and should be on guard to prevent accidents from occurring. Prevention is always the best strategy when the consequences are so severe. Responsible and caring pit bull owners do exist, especially among those who have rescued unwanted pit bulls, and many well-behaved pit bulls live in harmony with their environment under the watchful eye of such owners. In this best-case scenario, the good qualities of well-bred pit bulls can be fully appreciated.

Nigel Darling of Springfield, Massachusetts, was not even thinking "pit bull" when he decided to get his first dog. He had lived at home with his parents for all of his young life and they had forbidden him to get a dog. At the age of eighteen, this tall, slim, well-groomed youth left home and got his own apartment, stepping out into the wide world of self-sufficiency for the first time. Perhaps because of his parents' taboo or perhaps because of some inner voice, Nigel decided that one of the first things he would do was to get the dog he had yearned for so long. He had read in books about boxers and seen pictures of them, and so, on the very first day of his independence, he set off to the local pound to see if they might have one. Not being particularly savvy about dogs, he identified two or more dogs he thought were boxers only to be informed they were pit bulls. He liked these dogs because of their playfulness and character but was told they were not adoptable (the pound manager muttered something about aggression). Nigel was pointed in the direction of a local breeder instead. With a shrug of his shoulders, he went on his way with the image of these playful pit bulls hovering in his mind.

A couple of days later, Nigel went down to the breeder's kennel and bought himself a pit bull pup, his dream pal to be. Good guy and gentleman that he was, Nigel took on the pup for only the best reasons. He was not a villain in need of a vicarious extension of his own aggressive personality but an upright citizen with a responsible job and nothing particular to prove. He was both personable and well liked at work and in his neighborhood. Although kind, Nigel was no weakling. He would not cave in to pressure but neither did he lose his cool. In fact, he was almost ideal for the pup except for one thing: he lacked experience as the owner of any dog, let alone a pit bull. And heaven knows, a pit bull is not a dog for a novice.

It didn't take Nigel long to come up with a name for the pup. Tucker was the name he chose for the seven-and-a-half-week-old brown and white male, who reminded him of another dog of the same name. Tucker and Nigel spent long hours together as they got to know each other. Nigel was thrilled with his new roommate. All was well in the apartment for a few weeks. Nigel enjoyed looking after and reading about the care and management of his little buddy. Tucker grew quickly. By three months of age, he was already beginning to bulk up and looked more like a small dog than a pup. Nigel took him to the vet's office for all the usual vaccinations and deworming. He spared no expense in caring for his new pal.

Nigel's friends were all curious about Tucker, and Nigel must have been proud as he introduced him to them.

I can almost imagine the conversation:

"Oh, he's terrific, so cute. What breed is he?"

"He's a pit bull."

"Oh, aren't they dangerous?"

"No, not really, not if you look after them right."

But his pride in ownership would not last long. Tucker was only about five months old when the sinister side of his personality began to emerge. The first disturbing incident occurred while Nigel was visiting his parents. In that early carefree period of life with Tucker, Nigel brought him along for the ride. Nigel's mother had bought a ham to celebrate the return of her prodigal son, and the family dined in style while Tucker lurked in the wings, pacing along the periphery of the dining room and shooting occasional glances at the feast. Following the meal, the family kicked back and Nigel's mother suggested that it might be fun to have Tucker do some tricks in return for an opportunity to gain access to the ham bone. As Mrs. Darling commanded him, "Tucker sit, Tucker down, come on Tucker, be a good boy now," Tucker's body began to tense up and his muscles bulged as he underwent a Jekyll-and-Hyde transformation. His eyes appeared glazed as he fixed her with a deadly stare, and began to walk slowly toward her in a threatening manner. If Nigel's mom didn't immediately grasp what was going on, she certainly got the message when Tucker started to emit a low, menacing growl. The room fell silent and Mrs. Darling retreated into a corner as Tucker continued to approach her menacingly. This was the first time that Nigel, or anyone for that matter, had witnessed Tucker's dangerous side.

"Tucker no!" Nigel yelled as he raced toward the crazed dog. "Mom, throw the bone away, quick!" he screamed. Mom didn't need to be told twice and hurled the bone across the room. As Tucker hesitated, Nigel grabbed him by the collar and dragged him toward the bone. "Go get it, Tucker," he said as enthusiastically as he could. Tucker trotted forward to enjoy his ill-gotten gains, knowing that he had won the battle. He then lay down demurely and started gnawing on what was, from that time forth, forbidden fruit. Everyone was shaken by the event and no one knew exactly what to make of it. Their solution to the problem—to ban Tucker from having ham bones—produced a false sense of security among the family members, who overoptimistically interpreted Tucker's reaction as a onetime event.

A second incident took place about a month later, when Tucker was six months old. Nigel was once again visiting his parents when the next unfortunate event transpired. This time it was Nigel's father who was the object of Tucker's aggression. Nigel had brought around a bag of dog food so that some could be kept at his parents' house in preparation for future visits. Nigel's father was transferring the food from the feed bag into a metal container. Tucker stood motionless watching the performance, his ire slowly rising as it dawned on him that this man was messing with his rations. Unaware of Tucker's changing mood, Mr. Darling allowed Tucker to approach as, crouched on one knee, he paused between scoopfuls. Tucker came to a halt with his muzzle about one inch from Mr. Darling's face and sniffed him for a moment before baring his teeth and emitting an ominous low growl. Nigel heard this from the next room and came running. He grabbed Tucker by the collar and yelled at him to stop. Once again disaster was narrowly averted by his timely intervention. No one was in any doubt as to what would have transpired if Nigel had not been there, and Mr. Darling for one didn't want anything like this to happen again, ever.

"Get that dog out of my house and keep him out," he said, clearly shaken by the experience. "He's no good, Nigel, you should have him put to sleep." Nigel was stunned. Confused thoughts raced through his mind as he clipped on Tucker's lead and frog-marched him out to his truck. He knew his father was serious about banning Tucker from the house but he was determined not to have Tucker put to sleep. There must be some explanation for Tucker's bad behavior, he thought. Surely something could be done. Nigel vowed to do whatever he needed to do to make Tucker less aggressive.

In the process of making numerous inquiries about what might be going on, Nigel learned that neutering Tucker might reduce his aggression. It's true that neutering can help, but it only reduces aggression toward family members in about 30 percent of cases. However, Nigel wasn't interested in odds, only results, so he took Tucker to the vet's and had the operation performed, hoping against hope that this would put an end to Tucker's aggression. It didn't. For a while, Nigel's new life continued much as it had before. His office job at the Department of Public Works kept him busy all day, and in the evenings he would return to his apartment to hang out with Tucker. Tucker's greetings were never very enthusiastic, and Nigel began to suspect that Tucker was only pleased to see him because his arrival signaled the prospect of food and bladder relief. On coming home, Nigel would take him out on lead to a designated bathroom area, feed him, and finally let him out to play in a large field behind the building. As time went by, Nigel noticed Tucker becoming more distant and self-sufficient, seemingly needing little from his devoted master other than the bare necessities. Tucker would occasionally solicit petting, but the way he went about it was more demanding than affectionate. Nigel usually obliged anyway because this was one of the few intimate moments the two of them shared.

When Nigel's friends came over, Tucker usually remained aloof or indifferent. But if they came anywhere near any of his resources or attempted any physical interaction with him, he would growl menacingly and curl his lip. Several times he actually snapped at people when they approached his food while he was eating it, and once he bit one of Nigel's friends who foolishly reached down to grab him by the collar. You could argue that to approach or interfere with Tucker's food while he was eating it, or to suddenly grab him by the collar, were affronts that he had every right to resist. Personally, I think that such behavior is intolerable and, in the extreme, potentially dangerous. Apparently Nigel's friends agreed, because one by one they refused to come around to the apartment while Tucker was there. Nobody wanted to be on the receiving end of Tucker's aggression when it finally erupted full force.

After a while, only two people were not the target of Tucker's threats: Nigel and his best friend, Andrew. Neither of these boys had ever experienced the feeling of having the hair on their necks stand up on becoming the object of pit bull aggression. There's something unforgettable about the intense stare, the glint of sharklike teeth, and the ominous low rumble of a belly growl that precedes an attack. All Nigel's friends except Andrew had received this emphatic message. Andrew didn't understand the reason for his immunity, but was grateful for it. Nigel felt safe because he believed he had earned Tucker's trust and respect. As unwelcome as Tucker's aggression was, the kinship that developed among this gang of three must have been somewhat uplifting. To be the only members of the human race never to be challenged by a dog who put the fear of God into everybody else was something of an achievement, an esteem builder. Even just walking down the sidewalk with Tucker in tow, fearing no one, must have been a bit of a thrill.

The months passed and Tucker reached his first birthday. Only Andrew came to the party. Now technically an adult, Tucker was even more confident and willful than before, and even the two boys began to tread warily around him, especially when he was eating. It was food that triggered Tucker's first act of aggression against Nigel. The food in question was a highly appealing canned dog food that Nigel had bought him as a special treat. Tucker was hunched over it, scoffing away greedily, as Nigel passed by a bit too close for comfort. Tucker stood stiffly, staring at him, hackles raised, emitting the now familiar low belly growl. The growl continued for at least thirty seconds, following which Tucker lunged at Nigel and only just missed biting him. Fearing for his safety, Nigel kicked Tucker away, acting more out of self-defense than fear. It was animal against animal, a matter of survival. Deflecting Tucker with one more well-placed kick, Nigel managed to slip out into the next room, shut the door, and slump on a chair, ghost white, trembling uncontrollably. He didn't like to think what would have happened if he hadn't escaped. It took him several minutes to compose himself, but when he finally did he went to the door, opened it a crack, and peered in. Tucker, who had now finished his food, was cruising around on the opposite side of the room. Nigel steeled himself and stepped in. Tucker looked at him for a second, blinked, and then approached in a friendly manner, seemingly back to his happy-go-lucky, tail-wagging self. "What did you expect?" he seemed to say. "It was my food." This is a typical response of a dominant dog following an attack. Do they remember what happened? Sure. Are they sorry? Some are, some aren't. While some dogs appear contrite or remorseful for temporarily losing control, others, like Tucker, seem indifferent or satisfied that their actions were fully justified.

After this incident Nigel was really perplexed and he decided to take Tucker to a trainer to see if schooling might help. Tucker did passably well in the class and didn't really pose a problem for any of the people or dogs around him. He appeared a little bored at times but would sit and lie down on command and sometimes seemed to be enjoying the food treats and extra attention he received. Leash corrections produced the desired effect of making him respond to commands when he was drifting a bit, but nothing really fazed him. Sometimes he would obey a "down" command sufficiently quickly to avoid a leash correction, but he would never respond with alacrity. It was one elbow down and then the other, leaving his butt sticking up in the air until he would finally drop to the ground for a second before springing up again. It was a trying experience for Nigel with Tucker constantly straining Nigel's tolerance.

In the British army this type of behavior is referred to as "dumb insolence," when troops obey a command but only in a desultory manner.

For example, a sergeant might say, "When I say good morning to you I want you to say good morning to me. Do you understand me, Corporal?"

"Yes, Sergeant."

"Good morning, Corporal" (said deliberately and without hesitation).

The corporal takes a breath and after a short but obvious lag responds in a sarcastic tone, "Good morning . . . *Sergeant.*"

"Three days in the barracks on potato-peeling duty," the sergeant retorts sharply.

"But why? That's not fair," the corporal complains, "I did what you told me. What's the charge?"

"Dumb insolence is the charge," comes the reply.

Just as the sergeant knew that the corporal was behaving disrespectfully, so Nigel knew that Tucker followed directions grudgingly and not in good spirit. This silent rebellion against direction by others is actually a leadership quality that I believe reflects above normal intelligence. Dominant dogs in general do seem to be the smartest ones and are quick studies at obedience class. The problem is that their propensity for independent thought often makes them resistant to the will of others around them. They might know a particular command very well but choose to obey only when it suits them.

A few weeks passed and Nigel still felt that Tucker posed a danger, even though no further incidents had occurred. His awareness of Tucker's hair-trigger temper and concern for his own safety led him to give Tucker a wide berth, especially at mealtimes, and to avoid any challenging interactions. Nigel was living in constant fear of the next attack. It was at this point in the history of his relationship with Tucker that Nigel first heard about the Behavior Clinic at Tufts.

"Why don't you go and see Dr. Dodman?" a friend said. "He deals with pet behavior problems for a living and should be able to tell you what's going on. Maybe he can help you and Tucker. It's got to be worth a visit."

Nigel pondered this suggestion for a few days as he mentally wrestled with the daunting prospect, and expense, of paying a visit to a "pet shrink." What would his friends say? How could the appointment help? What did the future hold for him and Tucker? In the end he decided that he really needed to know what was going on, so he plucked up his courage and scheduled an appointment. Nigel knew that without help he would be in serious trouble, though he wasn't sure that anything he could do would help Tucker. In any event, he needed to know what the situation was and how it might progress. Andrew kindly agreed to accompany Nigel to Tufts for moral support, and the two of them duly arrived one April day with Tucker in tow.

They walked into the consulting room, heads bowed, and I ushered them over to two blue padded seats on the opposite side of my desk. Both boys looked at me intently as Tucker ignored us all and confidently explored the four corners of the office, apparently without a care in the world. Nigel spoke slowly and deliberately. I sat and listened to the tale and had no doubt about the diagnosis of dominance aggression. The aggression was shown particularly in connection with what Tucker perceived as valued resources, especially food, and also in response to threatening postures and gestures and when he was disturbed while resting. I explained that dominance was a natural canine characteristic designed to stabilize the pack order but admitted that Tucker had more than his fair share of dominance. He was a tough dog, and to make him fit to live with was going to be a tough project.

I had terrific respect for Nigel as he sat there listening thoughtfully, all of twenty years old. He was, I thought, a bit of a philosopher, a committed dog owner, and a person of great sincerity. Despite the events of the past, he insisted on trying to help Tucker, at least for a while, because he didn't want to give up on him before he had done everything possible. I told him that the likelihood that we could turn Tucker around completely was slim, but that we might be able to improve him considerably, if we were lucky. I pointed out the physical, legal, and emotional liability Nigel faced in proceeding and advised him to protect himself and others at all times by avoiding all known aggression-promoting circumstances. This he agreed to do, and so I launched into what turned out to be a lengthy explanation of the dominance modification program known as the "12-Step Leadership Program for Dominant Dogs" (see Appendix 2). I told Nigel to make Tucker work for all necessities and luxuries in life, including food, petting, exercise, attention, and freedom. Tucker would, in effect, be working for his living, never again to receive something for nothing. In addition to this behavior modification program I felt that Tucker's condition was so severe that he should receive antiaggression medication right from the start. Accordingly, I prescribed a mood-stabilizing antidepressant, clomipramine.

As the weeks slipped by, I stayed in close contact with Nigel. The news was quite good initially, with Tucker much less threatening by about the three-week mark. He seemed to accept that there was now no free lunch, was a little less pushy and demanding, and seemed to be more aware of Nigel's presence and authority. But Tucker's improvement plateaued and then he began to backslide, appearing testy and anxious, particularly around feeding time. One dreadful evening about five weeks after I first saw him, Tucker really "spazzed out" (Nigel's words) and attacked Andrew. As usual, food was involved. Both boys were in the kitchen talking while Tucker was eating his evening meal of kibble plus half a can of wet dog food. Neither of the boys was looking Tucker's way or encroaching on his precious meal. They knew better than to do that, but it didn't prevent what followed. First they heard a low growl, and just as they turned to see what was going on, Tucker hurled himself at Andrew, grabbing him by the hand and hanging on. Andrew struggled and managed to pull his hand from Tucker's mouth, but Tucker immediately latched on again at the level of Andrew's forearm, easily penetrating his thick sweater and denim work shirt. Andrew again struggled free, raining blows on Tucker's head, but Tucker lunged at Andrew one more time, grabbing hold of his sweater and snarling viciously in a demented rage.

Nigel was momentarily frozen to the spot, the whole scene appearing to unfold as if in slow motion. He knew he had to do something but he didn't know what. Instinct directed his hand toward a large glass-bottomed table lamp sitting on a countertop. He grabbed it and hurled it with all his might against the wall on the opposite side of the room while screaming Tucker's name at the top of his lungs. The glass shattered into dozens of pieces with an almighty crash. Distracted, Tucker let go of Andrew's shirt and raced over to where the remains of the lamp lay strewn across the floor. After puzzling over the debris for a few seconds, he slowly lifted and turned his head, looking over his shoulder at the boys who were dreading his next move. But there was no next move. Instead Tucker seemed to snap out of his aggressive mood and to realize what he had done. Nigel and Andrew looked at each other in disbelief as Tucker sheepishly slunk away into the next room, apparently embarrassed by his outburst.

As Andrew left that day he informed Nigel that he had never been so scared in his life and that he wouldn't be coming back to the apartment while Tucker was there. He also warned Nigel to look out for his own safety, thereby joining the ranks of others who had no faith that this situation could be managed. Alone at last, Nigel and Tucker lived together for another three days while Nigel considered his options. During this time Tucker was his usual "bad-ass" self, if not worse, and growled at Nigel whenever food was around or if Nigel walked too close to him while he was resting. Nigel called me and informed me of the latest turn of events, winding up by confiding that he could no longer see himself keeping Tucker. In fact, he had already made an appointment to have him put to sleep the following day. Needless to say, I was deeply disappointed that the treatment hadn't worked, but I agreed with Nigel's decision in light of what had transpired. Miracles do happen, but by this time I felt pretty sure that one was not coming Tucker's way. I empathized with Nigel as he wrestled with his tough decision and tried to cheer him up a little by telling him what an outstanding effort he had made. Many people, I said, would not have had as much patience as he did, and at least he provided Tucker every possible chance to reform. Nigel took into account his own experiences with Tucker and the enormous and building pressure from his friends and family to have Tucker put to sleep. Eventually he came to the conclusion that the latter course was the only one open to him.

Tucker was only fifteen months of age at the time of Nigel's painful decision to have him euthanized. I had done my best for the poor creature but it wasn't enough. My only consolation was that I knew Nigel had tried his best and felt sure that he had made the right decision. If he had continued with Tucker I believe the future would have been grim. I had become extremely concerned about the possibility that Tucker would seriously injure someone toward the conclusion of this tragic saga. Even Nigel, Tucker's last friend, had eventually lost faith and was at risk. At this very difficult time, Nigel shared his view of events. His conclusions were, to my mind, both profound and accurate. He said that although many people think that extreme aggression is created or cultivated by ignorant or malicious owners, his experiences with Tucker led him to a different conclusion. He knew that he had done everything possible to help and support Tucker, and now believed that genetic influences play a considerable role in shaping behavior, with breed and individual influences instrumental in the final reckoning. Prior to owning Tucker, he would never have believed that such extreme aggression could be an inevitable consequence of owning a dog whom nature had slated as dominant. He used to think that a responsible dog owner who interacted and cared for his dog properly would never end up with a hound from hell. He now knew better and swore that he would never own another pit bull. Despite his realization that faulty genetic wiring underlay Tucker's aggression, Nigel was still extremely attached to his dog, and it was with a sorrowful heart that he brought him to the vet's office the following day.

Apparently the "procedure" went smoothly. Nigel held Tucker tightly in his arms as the vet adeptly and painlessly inserted a needle into one of Baxter's forearm veins and slowly injected the viscous blue euthanasia fluid from the attached syringe. One milliliter, then two, five, ten. Tucker didn't flinch but looked stoically and trustingly into Nigel's eyes. Eventually, after ten to twenty seconds, Tucker's eyelids began to flutter, his eyes rotated downward, and his breathing slowed. He heaved one last sigh, and then his tormented soul left his now limp body. Tucker was at peace with the world.

When I heard nothing from Nigel for an entire twenty-four-hour cycle, I realized that he had been true to his word and that Tucker had been returned to his maker—whoever that was. I let a discreet period of time go by before calling him to ask him how he was doing. When I did finally make contact with him, Nigel informed me that the week after the tragic event was one of the most difficult weeks he'd had to endure in his entire life. A grayness came over his life and things that normally interested him were unexciting—yet he found it difficult to sit and do nothing. The empty apartment constantly reminded him of Tucker and he didn't know where to turn. He reflected on how, at one time, he used to think that Tucker was at least a devil he knew and could trust. Finally he acknowledged that Tucker had undergone a profound transformation into a devil he didn't know, and one he could no longer depend on. If only he could have communicated to Tucker that he didn't have to be possessive. If only he could have conveyed to Tucker that he could have anything he wanted, perhaps Tucker would have seen the error in his ways. But, alas, dogs of this disposition do not display such profound thoughts and many protect the darnedest things because of their insufferable paranoia.

Nigel had always wanted a dog and he got Tucker. What an experience that turned out to be. I did ask Nigel one last question during this postmortem conversation.

"Would you ever consider getting yourself another dog?" I asked.

"Not right now," he replied. "Perhaps someday, but, you know, if and when I do, it won't be a pit bull."

I often wonder how Nigel is getting on in his apartment and whether his friends have regrouped and are back to visiting him. I imagine so. I sincerely hope so. He was a really great client to work with, caring, compassionate, and dedicated. These qualities indicate a better type of human being, the thoughtful unselfish type. I wrote to Nigel sometime after our last telephone contact to tell him that if ever he decided to get another dog he should bring it to me to evaluate before committing to own it. I told him I didn't want him to go through this sobering experience ever again, and I'm sure he didn't. Despite the problems he had endured, I thought Nigel would one day get another dog, but I haven't heard from him yet. Perhaps he's still healing—it was a severe wound. I look forward to the day that the phone rings and it's Nigel asking me to check out his next dog. If this happens, I will do all within my power to make sure that this particular type of lightning does not strike twice.

9

SOMERSET FARM

Loving dogs goes along, more or less, with despairing of humans.—*Roger Grenier*

As usual, the reception area at Tufts's Foster Hospital for Small Animals was positively hopping with people and animals. An assortment of folk from all walks of life sat around the perimeter of a tiled waiting room with their nervous-looking pets beside them. That day there were giant dogs, wary-looking terriers, lapdogs, a spaniel or two, and even a couple of cats pressed tightly against the back of their carriers. An informational videotape droned on from an overhead monitor, but nobody was paying much attention to it.

"Dr. Dodman, your next appointment is here," prompted the receptionist at the front desk as she slid a case record a couple of inches closer toward me.

"Thank you, Gina," I replied, glancing at the owner's and dog's name on the outside of the manila file.

Gina swept a few wayward strands of her long dark hair away from her indigo eyes and flashed me an impish smile. "Have fun with this one," she said.

"I always do," I replied with a grin.

It had been a tough day, or at least it seemed that way, and this was my last patient on a long list. The cases I had seen earlier had all been unusually taxing, requiring me to draw on those deep reserves that must be tapped when owners are lukewarm about a treatment plan or when a diagnosis of the behavior problem is intricate or involved. I gazed out into the sea of faces in the waiting room and called out the owner's name.

"Sanders, Carol Sanders."

No one answered, so I tried using the dog's name.

"Osaka Sanders."

That did it. A slim blond woman rose slowly from her seat in the corner of the room and signaled to me with a wave before stooping to secure her dog. Osaka was initially hidden from my view by a group of people discussing a sad-looking spaniel sporting a plaster cast. Ms. Sanders circumnavigated the group and stepped into the corridor leading to the reception desk, her dog trailing behind her. As she rounded the corner, Osaka came into full view. He was an Akita, a large one at that, and it was clear from the start that he had a mind of his own. Although Ms. Sanders was heading directly toward me with her hand outstretched, Osaka was tugging at his lead and attempting to go at right angles to the direction she was going. He seemed completely transfixed by the activity in the waiting room and intent on investigating all the other animals around him. More than once he got too close to another dog for its comfort and I saw a series of near "scenes" start to materialize in front of my very eyes. Watching Ms. Sanders and Osaka proceed toward me was like watching a three-legged race where the runners are out of sync. The pair finally reached me without serious incident, and Ms. Sanders and I introduced ourselves and exchanged brief pleasantries before heading into the consulting room. She continued to struggle with "Ossie" while I herded the student accompanying me in the right direction. Once we were all ensconced in the "behavior room," the consultation proper began.

I observed Osaka closely as he confidently explored the room, apparently lost in his own world as he learned something about my former patients from the olfactory signals they'd left behind. Ms. Sanders led off by inviting me to call her Carol and then plowed into an extraordinary tale of joy and grief. The joyful part was about the close relationship she and Ossie shared. At home, Ossie was a veritable angel, showing no aggression and no fear of anything or anyone, and appreciating the bountiful life Carol had provided for him. Outside, his behavior was also impeccable—except when they met other dogs on walks. Off lead, Ossie would charge any other dog appearing on the horizon, and calamities had been only narrowly avoided thanks to the heroic efforts of the other dogs' owners. On lead, things weren't much better, as Ossie lunged at perceived opponents, sometimes almost dislocating Carol's shoulder and, on more than one occasion, dragging her to the ground. For a lightweight like Carol, this made walking Ossie something of a cross between Russian roulette and bungee jumping. Had Carol been built like Lou Ferrigno and Ossie like Lassie, the on-lead problem would not have posed such a physical challenge, though Ossie's deep mistrust of canine-kind would still have been cause for concern.

As I looked at Carol I saw a free spirited, successful and intelligent woman who was well aware of her strengths as well as her weaknesses. I gathered from her outspoken and opinionated views that she likened to be in control. When she told me about Ossie's aggression toward other dogs, it was not in a pathetic "help me" tone but rather in an authoritative "what are you going to do about this" attitude. She spent quite a while telling me about all the other experts whose opinions she had sought before coming to see me, and the list was impressive, featuring some of the Northeast's top guns. She had spared no expense and no effort on Ossie's behalf, but no one had had more than fleeting success regarding his nibs' behavior. Instead of feeling in charge of the interview with Carol, I found myself the subject of what seemed like third-degree interrogation. Carol was the kind of client who assumed that any information she received was wrong unless the information provider could convince her otherwise. She did, however, acknowledge that she approved of my philosophy outlined in *The Dog Who Loved Too Much*, and wanted this approach to be extended to treat and cure Nin's problem. I saw the student wince more than once as Carol made her wishes patently clear. As she spoke, Ossie approached me a couple of times, checking me out, perhaps seeking acknowledgment or possibly looking to be petted. I obliged both requests.

My assessment of Ossie was that he was a rather pleasant teddy bear of a dog who loved people. He was a smart dog who had been spoiled without becoming spoiled. Dominant, yes, but not aggressive, and generally respectful of people, including his owner. Did I think that Carol could have better control of him? Of course. When other dogs came along, he completely disregarded her and followed his own misguided agenda. The question was, was his aggression toward other dogs a result of him wanting to protect his most valued asset, Carol, from their unwelcome advances, or was he a tad anxious, as well as overly controlling, when around members of his own species? It could have been a bit of both. One thing was certain: in either case, dominance, a powerful leadership trait found in abundance in Akitas, was probably contributing to the problem.

I gave Carol my read on the situation, but (no great surprise) she did not immediately embrace the interpretation.

"Are you suggesting that if I had more respect from Ossie he would be better behaved around other dogs?"

"Yes, I am," I responded.

"That's absurd. I have total control over Ossie. Watch."

So saying, she called Ossie to her and proceeded to roll him on his back and scratch his belly. The teddy bear clearly enjoyed this indulgence and groaned in pleasure as he relaxed, his head lolling from side to side, his eyes half closed.

"Now tell me that's not control. He totally submits to me whenever I demand it of him."

"Not when he sees another dog," I replied. "Many dominant dogs do what they're told when they want to, usually when there's a reward at stake, but when they have their own agenda they just don't listen. Also, you have to remember that when dominant dogs roll over in order to be petted, they're just saying 'yes' to a 'front rub,' not signaling submission."

"I don't believe that," Carol responded. "Ossie listens to everything I say and usually obeys. He's never aggressive toward me and he knows that I am his leader. I've insisted on that since he was a pup."

"I'm not saying that you're not his leader," I said, defending my position, "just that you need more authority. I'm going to suggest a leadership program for you."

As I said this and saw Carol wrinkle her nose, I realized that this was not going to work for her. She lived on her own and Ossie was her buddy as well as her dog. To expect her to engage in a hard-nosed, toe-the-line behavior program with her "one and only" just wasn't realistic. I had to try another approach.

"Let's start with some basics," I said, changing the subject in hopes of picking up some therapeutic momentum. "We can disagree about the exact motivation for his behavior, but what is important is that we get it under control."

"Agreed," Carol said, giving me airspace for the first time in thirty minutes. "Fire away."

"First of all, I would try and get Ossie some regular aerobic exercise. Some twenty to thirty minutes per day of running around off lead is a bare minimum. This will be difficult for you, because Ossie cannot be trusted off lead around other dogs, so you will have to find a fenced-in area, such as a tennis court."

"Okay, I can do that," Carol replied, "I have a tennis court nearby, but I can't see how that is going to help."

I continued with the next suggestion. "And I would change his diet. You are currently feeding him a premium ration designed for performance dogs. I think you would be better off feeding him a low-protein, all-natural diet to try to help curb his aggression." I carefully avoided mention of the word dominance, though this was the behavior I was trying to control. "Finally, daily obedience training will help in time, but it will take a few months to achieve the level of control that you need. You will have to start this training on lead, training in a quiet, undisturbed setting. Later you can progress to noisier, busier environments—perhaps with other dogs in view." Carol generally agreed, although I did detect a sort of "we'll see" attitude. As far as specifics were concerned, I strongly recommended a head halter for better control of Ossie on walks, and advised Carol not to let him off lead in the presence of other dogs. Finally I got around to discussing behavioral medication.

"Like what?" Carol bristled.

"Like Prozac," I replied in a matter-of-fact tone. I had some confidence in Prozac based on studies we had recently conducted using the drug to treat dominance-related aggression in dogs.

"Okay, I'll try it," Carol responded cautiously. "It won't cause him any problems, will it?"

"It shouldn't," I replied. "Prozac is one of the safest drugs around. If a person wanted to kill himself with Prozac, he would have to swallow the bottle as well and hope for an intestinal obstruction. It seems to be just as safe in dogs."

"But are there side effects in dogs that I should watch for?" Carol asked.

"There can be," I replied. "Side effects like sedation, reduced appetite, and vomiting do occur in some dogs, but the vast majority show no adverse effects whatsoever. In fact, you wouldn't know they were on Prozac except for the specific effect on behavior that you are seeking. It's the same for people," I added. "Odds are, with over four billion dollars each year spent on Prozac, that some people in the waiting room are taking Prozac but you can't tell which ones."

"I do know something about Prozac," Carol ventured sheepishly. "I have been given several different antidepressants over the course of my life, including Prozac. They helped in a way, so I know what you're saying. I don't take any of them now, though."

"Great," I said. "So you appreciate that if we get Ossie's dose right, neither you nor anyone else will be able to see any obvious signs of him receiving this treatment. Not that it's a big secret, but neither of us would want him to become lethargic. That's not behavior modification to me, it's sedation."

"So when do we start?" Carol asked.

"Now's as good a time as any," I replied.

The appointment drew to a close and Carol lugged Ossie to the reception desk to check out, with a head halter and a prescription for Prozac clasped in her hand. As the bill was prepared we chatted for a short while. I learned that she was an expert portrait photographer, an artist, who had once worked in her own studio in Manhattan. After years of great success in what was a cutthroat business, she had withdrawn to a farm in New Hampshire called Somerset Farm, a name that I thought might have had some relevance in this case. What with her energy and need to control, I wouldn't have been surprised if she hadn't been under considerable pressure at some point in her life. It occurred to me that Ossie's behavior was, in many ways, a reflection of his owner's own personality, and that, like his owner, he was perhaps in need of purposeful direction.

A few days after the appointment I received an e-mail from Carol. Predictably, she pulled no punches.

"When I came to see you," she wrote, "I expected to find the dynamic and witty person I had come to recognize through your books. Instead, to my great disappointment, I found you a shadow of the person I thought you to be. You seemed tired and uninterested, anxious and distracted, barely able to raise a smile. What on earth is wrong? I am sure people impose on you now that you have your newfound recognition and that you are severely overworked, but that is no great comfort or justification to me. Furthermore, you did not even take time to address Ossie directly during the appointment. In fact, you didn't interact with him at all. I want to remind you that Ossie is the patient here and he deserves your undivided attention. I believe you hurt his feelings because of your indifference, and I would like to set up another appointment in which you actually take the time to interact with him."

I cracked my knuckles and took a deep breath before responding. First, I honestly acknowledged the fact that I had been feeling somewhat burned out at the end of what had been a long day and apologized for my lackluster performance. What I didn't tell Carol was that she may have contributed to my seemingly apathetic manner through her constant belligerence and automatic rejection of anything I tried to say. The advice I had given her, I said, was good as long as she was able to follow it and sought help when difficulties arose. On the second issue, I explained that having a conversation with a dog about its behavior problems was not what I did for a living, and that observation of the dog and consultation with the owner was my usual modus operandi. Finally I reminded her that I had interacted with Ossie, calling him to me, petting him, and giving him food treats on more than one occasion. But to make up, I said I would be happy to arrange a follow-up appointment at some point in the future, at which time I would try to be brighter and more cheery, though the recommendations would remain essentially the same.

A couple of e-mails later, I had straightened Carol out about my role in the consultation and follow-up process, though I was sure she saw me as an emotionally detached, Spock-like scientist, rather than the animal lover I am. Carol's perceptions aside, I had my work cut out with Ossie and had to plod on with the treatment program despite the volleys of criticism. The next week Carol was on the phone again, this time delighted to slam-dunk me with the news that Ossie had reacted badly to the Prozac. Within a couple of days of starting the Prozac, he had apparently become extremely lethargic and had difficulty walking without swaying and bumping into things. As this was the first (and last) time I had ever heard of such profound side effects with Prozac, my initial thought was that she was exaggerating. I questioned her in some detail about Ossie's response, but Carol remained unswayed in her belief that Prozac was to blame. Treading carefully, I recommended that she take Ossie to her vet to make sure that there was nothing else going on that could have caused him to experience such a disturbance, but meanwhile advised her to discontinue the drug. Initially she resisted my suggestion that she take Ossie to see her veterinarian, but when I told her that should anything more serious develop she might be sorry later, she reluctantly agreed. A couple of days later she called me back, ecstatic that the vet had found Ossie to be in perfect health, and reported that, following the discontinuation of the Prozac, Ossie had reverted to his normal alert self within twenty-four hours. This was proof positive, she declared, that my recommendations were suspect and my conclusions invalid. I wondered whether anything that I advised was going to work out for Carol and Ossie.

Metaphorically picking myself up off the floor and dusting myself off, I pondered the next plan. It was time for another clinic appointment to help straighten things out and find a treatment for Ossie that worked. Carol and Ossie duly arrived at the clinic, and once again we trudged into the consulting room, with me expecting the worst. But the consultation started out on a happier and less formal note than before. Ossie had arrived wearing aviator goggles because he liked to stick his head out of the car window and Carol was worried about his eyes. I tried on Ossie's goggles for fun and Carol was delighted at the attention I was paying to Ossie and his paraphernalia. Carol whipped out a mini camera and snapped a couple of quick shots of me wearing the goggles and with my arm around Ossie. I saw the pictures sometime later and they were excellent—fit for a book cover.

Carol and I chatted for a while about Ossie's joy of riding in the car with the windows down, and she told me that she had recently bought him a classic (black) 1950s Bel Air convertible so that he could really indulge himself on rides. Lucky dog! I thought. The extra attention I gave to Ossie broke the ice between Carol and myself, and the rest of the consultation went much more smoothly than before. Carol even seemed to be listening to what I was trying to tell her. Bearing in mind Ossie's needs and Carol's concerns, I felt that a holistic approach might be more acceptable to her at this time, so I suggested tryptophan as an alternative to the "evil" Prozac. Carol leapt at this suggestion, pumping me for more information about this neutraceutical substance.

"Tryptophan," I explained, "is an amino acid building block of serotonin that is an essential part of every dog's diet. By increasing its concentration we can increase Ossie's serotonin level, stabilize his mood, and reduce his aggression, in pretty much the same way as we would have with Prozac. Adding tryptophan to the diet, however," I pointed out, "is a somewhat milder, more natural approach."

Carol seemed happy with this plan and signed off with the promise to report back in a week or two. I went back to my office in a more relaxed frame of mind and hoped for the best.

My next conversation with Carol was extremely cordial as she reported great success following the incorporation of additional tryptophan into Ossie's diet. Apparently he had encountered several dogs while out walking with Carol and had displayed atypical composure and self-restraint in their presence. Carol was thrilled by this breakthrough. I must admit I was relieved that at last something was going right. I cautioned her that Ossie's change of heart might be nothing more than a fluke and advised her to continue to keep him under control and observe him closely over the next few weeks.

As time passed, Carol's reports continued to be positive and she began to comply with every aspect of the behavior modification program. She didn't take unnecessary risks with him, kept him under control with the head halter at all high-risk times, and continued to feed him the dietary supplement. At last, everything in the garden appeared rosy for Carol and Ossie.

A short while after the apparent success of Ossie's treatment, I received a mysterious package in the mail. It was a midsized brown cardboard box bearing a New Hampshire postmark, delivered to the hospital to my attention. I carefully undid the package, fighting my way through a heap of polystyrene chips, to find at the center of the package a large-sized opalescent blue glass with a scroll inside it. I read the scroll and the inscription went as follows:

"Fill the glass with water, drink slowly, then proceed into the gale."

I knew Carol had sent the glass, but the meaning of her cryptic message was lost on me. I found out later that the process of filling and drinking from the glass equated with entering some Zen-like state, and that walking into the gale was symbolic of reengaging a turbulent life. The more I thought about the message, the more I liked it, and although I never followed the instructions to a T, I knew that her wishes were well meant. Once adversaries, we had become friends, with me looking out for Ossie and Carol looking out for me.

When I phoned Carol to thank her for the glass, she told me how concerned she was about my hectic existence. Her advice was to take a day off and retreat into the small enclosed space of a converted cupola on top of her barn, where she wanted me listen to music through headphones and read prescribed literature for relaxation. My only contact with the outside world would be food and water delivered through a crack in the floor. As compelling as this plan sounded, I decided to pass on it for logistical reasons. A few weeks later I received another package from Carol, this time a large box containing about one cubic yard of polystyrene beads and a dozen broken eggs. I really could not figure out the significance of this gift and wondered for a while whether I had said or done something to anger her. Not so. The eggs were fresh and whole when they were posted, and were intended as a gift from the country, purely for consumption and appreciation.

Several months passed before I heard from Carol again, and this time it was about a new problem, or at least a potential problem. She determined that Ossie needed a soulmate and decided to buy a young Akita pup she hoped would grow up to become his friend. Although Ossie's behavior continued to be good, she wasn't sure she could trust him with the youngster and asked how best to introduce the pair. She wasn't asking me whether she should get a friend for Ossie, just how to introduce them and what difficulties she might experience. The new puppy was already on order from a breeder in California and would be flown into Boston within a couple of weeks.

I discussed all the usual safety measures, such as introducing the two dogs on neutral territory and with both under control, with Ossie wearing his head halter and the pup on lead and under someone else's control. I also suggested that the circumstances be made as pleasant and entertaining as possible and inquired about Ossie's favorite pastimes.

"Swimming and tennis," Carol was quick to respond. "That's what he likes best. Do you think it would be a good idea to introduce them down by the lake near my house? Ossie usually has a blast down there and he's always in his best mood."

"That's sounds like a good idea," I responded.

"Oh, and I can try the tennis court," she said. "Would it be possible to introduce them on the tennis court and have a few tennis balls around? Would that be a good idea?"

"That might work too," I acknowledged. "Though they should probably be at opposite ends of the court and not walk too close unless Ossie seems entirely relaxed and comfortable in the pup's presence."

"Okay, that's what I'll do," said Carol. "That's what my trainer said I should do, too. I just wanted to check if you agreed."

With that backhanded compliment still ringing in my ears, I wished her luck and continued with my day.

Again I heard nothing from Carol for a long while, and eventually, out of curiosity, decided to call her up to see how the introduction had gone.

"It's doubly good news," she said. "Not only is Ossie still behaving himself with other dogs, he absolutely adores the puppy. They're just the best of friends and they have terrific fun cavorting around the house. Oh, of course I always take some precautions. I always feed Ossie first and make sure he gets plenty of attention so he doesn't become jealous, but other than that this is just plain sailing."

"Oh, so the introduction went well, I gather?"

"Yes, it did," Carol said. "But I didn't take anyone else's advice. I just followed my own instincts. I just threw them together in a room and waited to see what would happen. Ossie growled a bit at first and I had to reassure him, but eventually he accepted the fact that the pup was here to stay and completely warmed to him.

"Oh," I said, happy that the meeting had been a success, but trying to hide my disappointment at not being able to take even a little credit for it.

By now Carol and I were thoroughly good e-mail and telephone friends. In one follow-up telephone conversation sometime later, I asked Carol how she came to be living in New Hampshire, on her own, with Ossie and the puppy, now named Sapporo, her only true friends. In the process, I informed her that I might like to write about her and her relationship with her dogs. Apparently unfazed, she told me that it was a very long story, that began with her being the youngest of six children in a large and successful family who argued all the time and never got along.

"We're just all too bright," she said. "My father was a high-powered scientist, my mother a lawyer, all my siblings have excelled in their fields, but no one's talking to anybody. My sister and I don't get along all that well. And then there's the New York bit, the celebrity photographs, the glitz and the glamour, the ups and the downs. I don't know, it all became too much for me, so I decided to withdraw to the country. As John Lennon said, I just had to let it go. Ossie's my best buddy, my companion, a true friend, and he's really intelligent and fun to be with."

"So the good thing about Ossie is his unconditional and reliable affection?" I asked.

"No, that's not it. Dogs aren't that dumb. They choose whom they like and whom they want to spend time with and whom they respect. They don't just like you because you're there."

There was obviously some truth in what she was saying, but in my final analysis, I felt certain that the humans in her life, whether family or friends, must have seriously disapointed her. Perhaps they were put off by her aggressive intelligence and her opinionated and frank expression of her views. But Carol was a brilliant and compassionate artist who was almost too intelligent to tolerate the tedium of modern life without stirring it up a little for her own amusement. Fortunately, she found great solace and purpose in her life with Ossie. He interpreted her actions rather than her words, was neither perverse nor corruptible, and was a simple soul with a noble if not elementary Don Quixote attitude. As disturbing as it had been when Ossie went off to fight his windmills, it provided an intense focus for Carol's life, as did the acquisition of the new puppy. Both were wholesome country pursuits, far away from the madding crowd. Her interest in the dogs had rescued her from what I assumed to be the emotional wreckage of a former life.

The only question I was left with was what would be her next adventure? Carol was a woman who needed a challenge, and Ossie had provided this while he was acting out. Now something would have to fill the vacuum created by his trouble-free behavior. I wondered what her next adventure would be.

Postscript

Two years later Osaka had settled into his new, more peaceful lifestyle and was continuing to behave himself. Sapporo was now mature and also a joy to have around. The two dogs still adored each other and enjoyed each other's company, cavorting and playing together daily. All was well at Somerset Farm, except for one little wrinkle. When both dogs were at home, there were no problems. When they were out walking on lead, ditto. But if other dogs ran up to them too quickly, they could be in for trouble. I advised Carol to resume using head halters for both dogs (she had lapsed in this regard), to correct some marginal thyroid deficiency that both dogs were showing, and to modify her routes. She did all of the above *and* invented a deterrent spray to put off unwelcome canine socializers on walks. The latter consisted of a spray bottle containing lemon juice, garlic, cayenne pepper, etc. Carol found it so effective that she even wanted to market it as Dr. Dodman's Vamoose Juice. I said I was flattered, but took a rain check on the endorsement. Astringent sprays were not exactly my cup of tea. Carol seemed to understand. In closing our most recent dialogue, she added that she was once more taking on photographic assignments. I gathered from that that the pack at Somerset Farm was finally at peace with the world.

10

ROMEO AND JULIE

Once he ceased hunting and became man's platelicker, the Rubicon was crossed.—*Robert Louis Davidnson*

As marketing director of special events for an ultra-chic catering company, Julie Smythe was always on the run and constantly rubbing shoulders with the rich and celebrated. She was clearly dynamic, passionate about her work, a tad compulsive, and sometimes even a little hysterical. Basically, a normal New Yorker. She lived alone, in an apartment in Times Square, rose at the decadent hour of 11 A.M. each day, and often worked until 2 A.M., when she finished up her paperwork. Somewhere in the middle of all this frenzy, she found time to entertain a boyfriend in an on-again, off-again relationship of a few years' standing. I can only surmise that this boyfriend must have been fairly good-looking because, by all accounts, he did not have very many other redeeming features. He had no patience with children, did not like old people, and positively hated pets.

One day Julie was sitting by her window sipping her midmorning latte and watching the traffic flow fifteen floors below when a thought entered her head. It was one that she could not shake. For years she had felt that there was something missing in her fast-paced, highly successful life. She knew that most people would be envious of her job, her financial success, her apartment, her (presumably) handsome boyfriend, but wondered to herself, Is this as good as it gets, or is there something more? She briefly considered adopting a child, but really didn't like children much, and besides, caring properly for one would take too much time and would interfere with her job.

Wouldn't it be nice, she thought, if I had a dog to keep me company? A little canine companion with whom to share my life.

After all, she reasoned, I always had dogs when I was growing up and really enjoyed them. So now that I can afford one and have my own apartment, why not get another one just for me?

The idea took firm root in her mind and gradually inched toward reality. There was only one potential obstacle: her boyfriend. There was also research to do to find out what type of dog would be right for her given her particular situation, but telling the boyfriend came first.

A couple of days later, when she had his undivided attention, she made her pitch. "Victor," she said, with the unwavering look of somebody who's already made up their mind, "I'm going to get a dog."

There was a brief silence before Victor replied. "If the dog comes, I go."

And so he did.

Julie spent the next few weeks conscientiously researching the ideal breed for her—one who would be well suited to apartment life as well as being low key enough to tolerate the bustling crosstown traffic. She had in her mind's eye a picture of what she described as a lazy dog, one who would lie around and decorate the place without requiring much exercise and attention. The yellow brick road of her research brought to her attention the cavalier King Charles spaniel, otherwise known as the comforter or the spaniel gentle. She remembered seeing King Charles spaniels adorning fine paintings and needlepoint from yesteryear, and in all cases the dogs sat upright or lay curled at the feet of their owners radiating calmness and composure. In today's world, the King Charles spaniel is described as a city dog, a nine-to-five dog—a breed that is "so darned cute that it is difficult not to overindulge them (but you must steel yourself not to)." Indeed, this would be the breed for her.

Before too long, Julie had located a woman breeder of King Charles pups in Kentucky. After being carefully "vetted" by the woman on the telephone for her suitability as an owner of celebrated King Charles stock, Julie flew to Kentucky to check out the dogs and found them every bit as appealing as she had imagined. King Charles spaniels, with their black, tan, and white markings, long floppy ears, and curly coats are handsome as adults, but as pups, with their large saucer eyes and flat faces, they're totally irresistible. There were no spare pups there at the time, but the breeder was about to arrange another mating of her best brood bitch. Julie made a snap decision to take one of this bitch's pups once they had reached an appropriate age and flew back to New York with butterflies of anticipation in her stomach.

Back in New York the days passed rapidly, as usual. Then one day, while she was daydreaming about a new promotion, Julie received a call from the breeder in Kentucky. "She's pregnant," were the breeder's first words. Julie's emotions surged and she covered the mouthpiece of the phone to whisper to a colleague, "We're pregnant, we're going to have a puppy." Confused, the friend offered her congratulations on the happy news and left the office, slowly shaking her head. Julie pushed for a female pup, but the breeder said she had already made some promises and would just have to see how the composition of the litter turned out.

The months went by with Julie calling the breeder almost every day. Eventually the happy day arrived and the bitch delivered three pups, one female and two males. Julie was going to have to be content with a male. She agreed and the clock was ticking until his arrival in New York.

Eight weeks later, Julie strode excitedly into LaGuardia Airport to pick up the new arrival. Almost as soon as she had crossed the threshold into the airport, she heard plaintive barking from the arrivals area.

She started crying with emotion as she ran toward the sound. On reaching its source, an airline kennel, she saw inside a tiny black, tan, and white pup with long floppy ears. It was *her* boy. She took him out and hugged him and he responded by licking her face. A passerby said, "What a great pup you have there. What do you call him?"

Julie hadn't thought about a name and hesitated for a moment, thinking. "Romeo," she replied. "His name is Romeo because he's a heartthrob."

All was well for the first eight months Julie owned Romeo. The affection between dog and owner was mutual and Romeo found himself pampered and adored. He certainly had all the attention, food, and fun that any dog could wish for, though he had no opportunity to socialize with his own kind, got insufficient exercise, and basically spent the day sequestered in the apartment with Julie. Toward the end of Romeo's first year of life, he began to display one mildly disturbing behavior whenever she took him to the park. From humble beginnings of whining just before she brought him into Central Park, Romeo's apparent excitement in anticipation of his parkside experiences eventually evolved to the point where he would go practically berserk, spinning in tight circles and screaming and wailing hysterically. His behavior on many occasions caused passersby to ask Julie, "What on earth is wrong with that dog?" Though slightly perturbed, Julie explained away the behavior to herself as a manifestation of his extreme joy and excitement at what he was about to experience. Little did she know that Romeo's spinning and screaming indicated anxiety, a displacement of pent-up energy, and heralded a likelihood of other compulsive behaviors developing in the future.

Whatever she had experienced to that date, nothing prepared Julie for what transpired after she brought Romeo to a groomer for a haircut. Sparing no expense, she took him to an upscale dog-grooming salon in Manhattan where she sat patiently as skillful hands combed, clipped, and manicured her pampered boy. Adding the finishing touches to the job, the groomer took a pair of electric clippers to trim the long hairs on Romeo's prepuce. During this procedure Romeo let out a sharp yelp and began to struggle, so much so that they decided to call it a day and returned him forthwith to the open arms of his doting owner. After settling the bill, Julie took Romeo home and prepared him a feast fit for a King Charles spaniel. But instead of eating his food, Romeo began licking his prepuce continuously. Julie rolled him onto his side and inspected the site of his intense focus. Her eyes immediately fell upon a series of narrow cuts toward the end of his prepuce—cuts presumably made by the clipper blades.

"My poor boy!" she exclaimed out loud to Romeo, who paid her no attention and seemed unaware of her concern. Julie was not sure what to do but managed to find some kind of salve in the bathroom cabinet, which she applied to the lesion in hopes that it would provide some relief from what she presumed would be an uncomfortable or stinging sensation. The salve was gone in no more than three seconds as Romeo continued to lick incessantly. At bedtime Romeo was still licking, and he continued to do so the next morning and throughout the next day. After several days of this aberrant behavior, Julie became so concerned that she took Romeo to see her local vet. Various balms and lotions and an injection of cortisone failed to suppress Romeo's continuous licking. Long after any wounds should have healed Romeo was still licking and the whole underside of his prepuce became red and raw and was weeping.

Now Julie was becoming angry. Every time she thought about what had happened at the grooming salon, she felt her pulse start to race and her face would become flushed. Nothing the vet did made life any easier for Romeo, and Julie was convinced that he was suffering dreadfully and was in considerable pain. In desperation she sought the help of first one and then another behaviorist in New York City. Each of them advised various measures, such as attention withdrawal when he was engaged in the behavior, frequent exercise, the use of a head halter to divert him from the behavior, and one ever advised antidepressant medication. As before, nothing worked, and to cap it off, Romeo became extremely anxious, almost paranoid, following treatment with the medication and practically refused to leave the apartment. By this time, Julie was not only distraught, she was furious at the people in the grooming salon for all the pain and misery they had caused Romeo, to say nothing of the expense to which she had been put (her vet bills had now reached nearly two thousand dollars).

Prevention of Romeo's licking was now the only solution, so on the vet's advice Julie fitted Romeo with a plastic Elizabethan collar that kept him from reaching the affected area, and, as a belt-and-suspenders strategy, the vet had Julie fit him with sani-pants to protect his prepuce. Expanding her search for help beyond the New York City area, Julie found experts in Boston and at Cornell University in Ithaca who tried to help her resolve the problem. One dermatologist suggested that Romeo now had a deformed penis because of his continued licking. This was never confirmed, but one thing was certain: the whole area was inflamed, scarified, and infected. Another expert diagnosed a compulsive licking disorder, in effect, a lick granuloma of the prepuce, and concluded that he would either have to endure it or be put to sleep. At her lowest ebb, Julie seriously considered the latter option, though it pained her to do so.

As Julie worked ceaselessly to find a solution for Romeo's problem, she wrote an angry letter to the grooming salon demanding reimbursement for the medical expenses she had incurred. The letter read:

Dear Gentlemen,
In January of this year, after a letter and numerous phone calls to your shop, you agreed to refund the cost of the grooming and the veterinary bill for the damage that was done to my puppy Romeo on Saturday, December 20, 1997, while he was a client at Midtown Canine Coiffeurs. After an overdue time, you did in fact refund those costs.

Enclosed you will find a current photograph of Romeo outfitted with a collar and sani-pants to protect himself from the damage that he has done to his genitalia stemming from the cuts incurred during that grooming. Also enclosed is a reminder photograph that was taken shortly after he was groomed at Midtown Canine Coiffeurs.

Although the cuts that he received from your groomer have now healed, the psychological wounds intensify by the day. If you are not familiar with animal behavior problems, let me take this opportunity to inform you that if an animal is wounded, as he was in your shop, and although the wound may have healed, the animal may continue to lick and gnaw at the location of the problem, thus leading to a destructive habit. This is what has happened to my puppy Romeo.

From the moment that he was returned to me from your shop, crying in pain from the cuts on his prepuce, he has continued to lick and fuss with the wounded area. Numerous visits to various veterinarians and animal behaviorists here in New York and Boston were helpful, but even the experts could not determine a cause for the hysterical itching of his genitalia. His distress was so great the Animal Medical Center suggested that I have him put to sleep. That not being the route I was ready to take, and as there is not one canine dermatologist in New York City, I took Romeo to Cornell University in Ithaca, New York, to meet with such a doctor.

At Cornell, I met with Dr. Miller, the canine dermatologist, and Dr. Flanders, a canine reproductive surgeon. Also in the consultation were Drs. Virga and Houpt from the behavioral department. After a lengthy examination, it was determined that Romeo, because of his continued licking to the wounded area, has developed an abnormal penis. He also has inflamed tissue, scar tissue, and a yeast infection. Upon their advisement I am now treating him with a steroid and a panalog cream that each evening I need to massage into his prepuce before I diaper him for the evening. In consultation with Dr. Virga, I am now weaning him off the behavior drug clomipramine and onto amitriptyline. This medication is to continue for at least one year.

Need I tell you that he has constantly barked and whined from the stress and frustration caused by all this. Need I tell you that this has also caused my landlord, my neighbors, and myself undue stress and months of sleepless nights. His distress was so great that this summer I could barely take him outside. At one point, the police pulled me over and questioned my care for him as his hysteria was so severe that it warranted their asking questions.

It is my deepest hope that with proper treatment Romeo will return to normal. In the meantime, and at all future times, I am holding you responsible for all bills inclusive of medications and therapy stemming from the damage done to Romeo by your groomer.

Enclosed you will find the current bills that amount to $1,717.08. If I do not hear from you with a check within five days of this letter, I will take legal action not only for the bills enclosed but for an amount for emotional damage done, to be determined in court.

Sincerely,
Julie Smythe

Needless to say, no further monies were forthcoming, and Julie had to settle for disparaging the groomer to all dog owners that she contacted. However, she was also smart enough to send a copy of her letter to eighteen specialists in the New York and Boston areas, sharing with them the physical and psychological hardships that Romeo and she were now forced to endure, and soliciting input.

I was one of the recipients of Julie's copied letter and read the story with both interest and concern. Could it be that Romeo did indeed have a compulsive licking disorder? If so, it certainly was an unusual manifestation, but I thought I might be able to help. I wrote back to her and suggested that she sign up for our PetFax remote consultation service. Through this service we could supply her with recommendations, both behavioral and pharmacological, which she could share with her vet. This was the beginning of a correspondence between Julie and myself; in effect, we became pen pals.

When Julie sent the original PetFax forms back to me, I noted that Romeo, who was almost two years old by this time, had developed some ancillary behavior problems. He had begun barking excessively and whining apparently as a result of the stress and frustration associated with his problem. His crying had caused Julie's landlord, neighbors, and Julie herself considerable stress and months of sleepless nights.

Romeo's distress seemed to be most marked whenever there was any change in the status quo, for example, when he was moving from room to room, leaving the house, or meeting new people. At these times he would begin to whine and scream, spin in circles, and scoot his rear end along the floor. Although the vet checked his anal glands, there was no physical explanation for this behavior. In addition, Romeo became something of a recluse, and when dog friends came over to play he was totally uninterested. His typical behavior toward them was to scream and hide in his box, following which he would frenetically suck the threads of his blanket. Julie would usually hold him to comfort him and tell him to stop barking until he calmed down. This very often worked. Romeo did not have a social life with anyone except Julie, and he became so attached to her that he displayed most of the usual signs of separation anxiety when, albeit only occasionally, he was apart from her. This was another indication of his underlying nervous disposition. Fortunately for Romeo, his separation anxiety did not present much of a problem now as he was practically always with Julie, both at home and at work. When she brought him to work, he would immediately drink water and then gravitate toward his favorite pillow close to Julie's desk. His routine was always the same and he seemed much happier when he was following it.

I told Julie that I thought the most likely diagnosis was that of obsessive compulsive disorder, triggered by the physical injury inflicted by the groomer. I explained that physical events, such as the trauma he sustained, often set the pendulum of compulsive disorder swinging, and that in many cases, the compulsive behavior problem persists even after the original lesion has healed. Though compulsive licking was the primary diagnosis, Romeo's hysterical screaming, blanket sucking, and spinning also appeared to have some compulsive properties. I warned Julie that other compulsive behaviors might develop later, whether Romeo was treated or not. The cornerstone of the treatment I recommended was to avoid all conflicts that would exacerbate his licking or hysterical behavior. He was, for example, not to receive any canine visitors at home as his tolerance of other dogs was practically nonexistent. I advised Julie to avoid loud verbal corrections while Romeo was licking or sucking blankets, as such tactics frequently increase a dog's anxiety and thus the OCD. I also told her to remember that Romeo was not engaging in the repetitive behavior to annoy her, and that he probably could not help himself at this stage. It was better, I told her, to ignore him or to intervene in a positive way by giving him something different to do. I advised continued daily obedience training, regular exercise, and environmental enrichment in the form of food puzzles and other distractions.

Though these recommendations were sound, I also strongly advised her to consult her local vet to get Romeo treated with Prozac, which works as an antiobsessional and antipruritic agent. That, I thought, would likely decrease both Romeo's licking and irritation. Though antidepressant therapy had not worked before, I told Julie that Prozac was a much more specific treatment than the antidepressants Romeo had been prescribed earlier.

Julie agreed to give the treatment program a try, including the recommendation of putting Romeo on Prozac. Romeo became a little agitated initially on the Prozac, but after a few weeks was licking noticeably less. By six weeks Julie was convinced that there had been a major improvement, and by three and four months he was so much better that the raw area on his prepuce had begun to heal. So dramatic was the improvement that Romeo now no longer had to wear his Elizabethan collar and the sani-pants became unnecessary. There was no question that a huge transformation, a change for the better, had occurred that allowed Romeo, and therefore Julie, to lead a much more normal life. But had the licking ceased completely? The answer was no. But it had been significantly reduced and now was only occasional and desultory, allowing the injured area to heal. That is success.

Over the next few months I had several interesting packages from Julie as a token of her appreciation. The first was the published script for a Broadway play, *Sylvia*, about a man who adopts a stray dog, whose role is played by a woman. I eagerly read the script from cover to cover during one long flight across the United States and laughed so hard that I actually cried. The second gift was a delectable assortment of animal-shaped cookies that unfortunately arrived somewhat broken but nevertheless tasted superb. Finally she sent numerous packages of follow-up information and photographs of Romeo that I enjoyed immensely.

On the one-year anniversary of the original PetFax inquiry, I called Julie to see how things were progressing. I was relieved to hear that Romeo's improvement had been sustained. Although he was still not cured and was still occasionally licking his prepuce, he was much less anxious. This was great news and Julie was still very pleased about the results we had achieved together, but she did report that one of my earlier predictions was coming to pass. Despite the fact that he was still on Prozac, he had developed a new obsession, this time with cracks in the sidewalks. When walking down the street he wanted to push his nose into every crack and to eat every bit of gravel he encountered. Also, he would eat cigarette butts, discarded chewing gum, and other street items that he came across in the course of his daily walks, and had even begun to lick the pavement. In addition, Julie reported that he continued to display a fondness for rituals, including sniffing, barking, and twirling at transitional times during the day. Her description made me think very much of the human disorder Tourette's syndrome, which is also often associated with obsessive-compulsive disorder. In the morning, as she prepared to leave, he would immediately sense the transition, and as she opened the door he would descend two levels, start running in circles, barking excitedly, and then scoot along the ground on his derriere. When they reached the lobby, he would retire to the far end of the corridor furthest from the door and would wait for Julie to approach him and get behind him before he would even consider moving. Once she was in position, he would jog jauntily toward the door in anticipation of the sniffing, licking excursion that was to come. In the house, he would insist on accompanying Julie to the bathroom but had to do so in a certain way. He would always enter the bathroom, loop around the back of the toilet, and then sit by the bath or shower, where he remained motionless until she stepped out. If his usual route was blocked by some box or other obstacle, he would immediately begin a shrieking, circling, and rear-end-dragging session until human hands came to the rescue. When Julie went to turn off the lights or the power supply to various gadgets, Romeo would immediately bark, spin, and run into the next room whimpering. He would then jump onto the bed and take a few licks of his prepuce before settling down. He could barely contain himself when there was any excitement in the offing, showing signs of impatience bordering on attention deficit/hyperactivity disorder. So my treatment was not exactly what you would call an absolute cure; nevertheless, Romeo's condition was sufficiently improved that he could lead a normal life, and he was now well clear of death row.

I said to Julie, "You know, a lot of people wouldn't have toughed this saga out, but you did. Can you tell me why?"

"I believe I can," Julie replied. "Despite his many idiosyncrasies, his rituals, his need for routine, and his peculiar twirling and scooting, he is the sweetest dog I have ever come across and he has the deepest heart."

"So you like him a lot?"

"No, I don't like him, Dr. Dodman," Julie replied, "I love this dog. A lot of my friends have told me that I should have given up on him, but I couldn't bring myself to do that. Although I wavered at one point, I have discovered that that isn't the kind of person I am—one who gives up, that is. If I had a child with birth defects, I would love that child and stay with him. If I wanted a drink and only had lemons, I'd make lemonade. Well, I have Romeo and he's here to stay."

"You mention children. Do you think of Romeo as a child?"

"Yes, Dr. Dodman, I suppose I do. When his mom was carrying him, I felt as if we were both pregnant and told my friends exactly that. Also, I mentally went thorough the birthing process with his mom and, well, he's my baby."

"No regrets about the loss of your long-standing boyfriend when you first decided to get a dog?" I asked.

"Dr. Dodman, I always made such a bad job of choosing boyfriends. At least, I think it was my fault. Before Victor, I had a string of boyfriends who were all losers. I went out with married men, and guess what, that didn't work either. Then there were some that were clearly the wrong men for me, creeps, you know. Victor was a handsome but rough Italian guy who just wasn't warm. I don't know why I stuck with him for so long. I knew he would leave me eventually anyway. I tell you I've had more love from my dog than I've ever had from a boyfriend. Romeo's always there for me, always concerned, always right there wanting to know what I'm going to do next. I've never had that much love and attention from a man."

I mused on this honest admission and thought long and hard about how dogs, with their unconditional acceptance and total dependency, can sometimes make pretty good substitutes for human company—especially when nurtural voids exist or when a person's experiences with other people have been less than overwhelmingly positive. Both were factors in Julie's love affair with Romeo, and she never looked back.

11

FOR THE LOVE OF SETH

Cats are rather delicate creatures and they are subject to a good many ailments.—*Joseph Wood Krutch*

The bond that can develop between humans and animals is sometimes so profound as to almost defy comprehension. This is often a very good arrangement for the person and the pet, and there are often medical and physical health benefits for both parties. Such an intense bond causes people to tolerate the otherwise intolerable on behalf of their pets and to refuse to give up even when things go terribly wrong. Although some behaviors that the pets develop arise from stubbornness or boredom, others have an organic basis and are caused by functional disturbances of the pets' hormonal systems or brain chemistry. The difference between these two types of problems, normal nuisance behavior and the veterinary equivalent of psychological or even psychiatric problems, is not always immediately evident to the owner, and sometimes not even to a veterinary health professional. Seth, a castrated male Siamese–Maine coon cross cat owned by Arlene Levite of Northampton, Massachusetts, provides a good example of a cat exhibiting truly aberrant behavior whose cause took some time to fathom.

Arlene, a single woman in her early forties, acquired Seth at eight weeks of age from a private breeder in Maine. Heaven knows why a pedigree Siamese cat would be crossed with a Maine coon, but the result was rather spectacular—a handsome, grayish, longhaired cat with lynxy tufts on his ears—and Arlene was thrilled with her find. Arlene and Seth bonded immediately, and as soon as she got him home she began to indulge him right away. Life was pretty fine for Seth, who, as an only cat, had the undivided attention of Arlene and her gentleman friend, Howard Weiss, a computer company executive, who spent his weeks working in Boston and joined Arlene in her magnificent two-hundred-year-old antique colonial home on weekends. Seth would wake Arlene or Howard up at 5:30 to 6 A.M. and ask to be fed. His requests were never denied. As Arlene showered at around 7 A.M., Seth would wait patiently for his turn in the tub. Almost as soon as she stepped out of the steaming shower and tub, Seth would hop in and play in the bathtub until it cooled down. Depending on the day of the week and who was there, he might play for a while and then sleep for an hour or two at midmorning or shadow either Arlene or Howard around the house. His favorite game was chasing toys that were thrown for him at least three times a day. Sometimes he would retrieve the toys only to deposit them in his food bowl or water bowl. Another curious habit he had was of playing with water that dripped from the tap. If any tap was inadvertently left dripping, Arlene and Howard could be sure that Seth would be found in the sink or tub beneath the dripping tap batting the water with his paws. After a busy day of doing nothing in particular, Seth would receive his evening meal between five-thirty and seven o'clock and would then curl up on his owners' bed, on the sofa, or sometimes in one of the hall closets.

Seth displayed no alarming behavior problems at all for the first two years or more of his life. He was a tad on the anxious, nervous side, and might hiss on occasion if stroked the wrong way, but in general he was affectionate, playful, and a fine family friend. This almost utopian situation came to an end one June evening when Seth, then just two years and three months old, became completely unglued. Arlene was sitting out on a screened porch with Howard enjoying a glass of wine by candlelight. At precisely 11 P.M., they decided to turn in and packed up shop to move back into the house. Arlene was last in and, in the process, as she tried to balance a tray in her hands, was a little slow closing the door behind her. Seth slipped out onto the porch through a three-inch gap and disappeared into the shadows. Arlene raised her eyes heavenward and continued on her way to the kitchen to deposit the tray before returning to apprehend the escapee. When she came back, the candle on the porch was still burning and by its flickering light she caught sight of Seth crouched in a corner, his attention riveted on something she could not see. Arlene slowly approached to see what he was looking at. On seeing her, he stared up at her with a menacing expression and hissed like a scalded snake. Arlene slowly stood up, turned, and quietly walked away toward the opposite side of the porch. In a split second, she heard the muffled drumming of soft feet on the floor and then felt a searing pain down her back, arms, and legs as Seth savagely attacked her, clawing and biting her body. She fled for the door to the house, trying to sweep Seth off her back by flailing her arms, and just managed to escape to security on the opposite side of the door. Howard heard the rumpus and came running.

"My god, Arlene," he gasped as they both surveyed the damage. Arlene's arms, legs, and back were covered in deep scratches and blood was trickling from the deepest wounds. There were bites and bruises, scratches and puncture marks, all over her back, and her shirt was torn in several places. Seth had lunged at her with full force in an uninhibited attack designed to inflict injury and pain, and presumably to drive her away.

Arlene and Howard left Seth on the porch that night and retired to the bedroom to take care of Arlene's wounds. The conversation revolved around what could have triggered such a terrible assault. Perhaps Seth had been hurt. Perhaps he was unwell. Perhaps he didn't recognize her. The possibilities were endless but none seemed to account for what they had just witnessed. Sleep came slowly that night. Eventually Arlene and Howard nodded off in the "wee hours" only to wake up to the realization of what had happened the night before. Nine hours after Seth's meltdown, at eight o'clock the next morning they crept downstairs and peeked out onto the porch to see whether Seth had calmed down. He hadn't. He still seemed highly agitated and was most definitely not himself. Fearing for their own safety, they slipped some food and water around the door and left him there for a few more hours before checking him again. At around lunchtime he did seem much calmer, though he was still very wary and remained in a high-strung, seemingly apprehensive mode for the rest of the day.

When Arlene and Howard tentatively looked out on the porch the next day, Seth came toward them, head lowered and tail curved like a question mark, apparently wanting affection. Though still shaken and far from ready to offer this affection wholeheartedly, Arlene did consider the situation safe enough to allow Seth back in the house. She and Howard were delighted that he seemed to be back to normal. The day passed uneventfully with Seth basically being himself. He did a little fetching when they threw objects for him, slept for a while, and then woke to have some fun in the warm tub after Arlene took a late shower. It was one of those "now you see it, now you don't" situations, leading Arlene to believe she had imagined the whole catastrophic affair. But she had only to look at her wounds to be reminded of reality.

Days passed and Arlene and Howard got back into their usual routine and began to regain some confidence in Seth. They continued to talk about the event of that fateful night but never came to any firm conclusion about what had gotten into Seth. Their best guess was that something must have aroused him to such a degree that he lost all control. This was a not unreasonable speculation, but it may not have been the whole story, as we later discovered.

About a month after the first incident, Seth struck again. It was eleven o'clock in the evening and the environment was a little noisier than usual, with ceiling fans whirring and the air conditioner in the window droning incessantly. Against this backdrop, a plastic bag fell from the kitchen counter onto the floor, making a rustling sound as it became caught in a draft from the fan and moved a few inches across the floor as if it had a life of its own. Seth immediately began his transformation: he became very agitated, his pupils were dilated, his hackles raised, and he started moaning like a Halloween cat. At the height of his metamorphosis, he flew at Arlene and her mother, who was visiting at the time. The two ladies ran to the front door in terror and managed to escape to the front yard, slamming the door behind them. Arlene's mother, a spry sixty-five-year-old with a Betty Crocker look and graying hair, pressed her back to the wall, rolled her eyes at Arlene, and sighed.

"Arlene, is there something you haven't told me about Seth?" she quizzed with a wry smile. Arlene proceeded to give her an abbreviated version of the story from the month before. Knowing how long Seth could remain in his agitated state, Arlene concluded that "discretion was the better part of valor" and went to stay at her mother's house that night.

The next morning the women returned and made a cautious inspection of the kitchen area via the window to determine whether it was safe to enter the house. Seth hadn't quite reverted to normal and was still wary, but he certainly was calmer than he'd been the night before. The two of them braced themselves and entered the house. Arlene went over to raise the shade, but unfortunately it fell off the window, metal bracket and all, and hit the wooden floor with a clatter. Seth became incensed again and started to moan exactly as he had done the previous night. Slowly and menacingly, he walked toward Arlene, failing to respond to her attempts to calm him by speaking to him gently. As he approached, Arlene and her mother backed away, closing the storm door behind them. Just as the door snapped shut there was a thud against the other side as Seth launched himself at it.

The two ladies looked at each other in total disbelief. As they turned to peer back through the storm door, he attacked it again, before standing back a few feet, hissing and growling. Arlene made an attempt to get back in the house an hour and a half later, but upon touching the handle of the storm door, which she opened one inch, she heard growling nearby. Still concerned about his welfare, she left food and water inside the door a few hours later but did not reenter the house until the following morning. When she went back in, Seth was initially extremely wary, even scared, but within a half hour of her return he wanted attention.

All this was beginning to get to Arlene, who by now had lost faith that Seth would remain on an even keel. He came in for some close scrutiny over the next few days. Arlene did notice the following week that he suddenly became very sensitive to sounds, even sounds as subtle as the movement of paper. He was also easily alarmed by sudden movements, such as someone walking toward him with arms swinging. She felt that in this state he was likely to reerupt at any moment, and sought out the advice of her vet and cat owner friends concerning what she could do to identify and permanently cure this problem. A veterinary technician suggested that Arlene confine Seth in a large dog crate for her own safety and Howard's. This she willingly did as the discussions about Seth continued. Somewhere in the midst of the sea of advice, the name of Tufts University School of Veterinary Medicine came up and she called to make an appointment at the Behavior Clinic. Although the waiting list for appointments is normally six to eight weeks, Seth's appointment was scheduled as an emergency and he was brought to the hospital within a couple of days of Arlene's call. In the meantime he remained anxious, aloof, and on edge. I was receiving cases the day Seth was brought to the hospital. It was my duty to diagnose and treat his problem. I had no idea what was in store for me, but it didn't take long for Arlene to fill me in on all the hair-raising details of the preceding weeks of terror.

As I listened to the story, I glanced at the scribbled notes Arlene had brought with her and was intrigued by the fact that she had described two problems, not one. The first most obvious problem was aggression, but then she had described Seth's extreme fearfulness and anxious behavior as a separate problem. I found this categorization quite useful and feasted on her detailed description of each affective state. It seemed to me that the two problems might have been inextricably linked. The fearfulness initially surfaced at the time of the first attack. It subsequently disappeared but returned coincident with the second attack. Since that time Seth's fearfulness had been more or less constant. In her description of the fearful component, Arlene used the term "hyperesthesia" in connection with Seth's apparent overreaction to various noises or sudden movements. She also noted that his pupils were consistently enlarged, making his eyes look like large black pools, and that the tip of his tail had started twitching constantly. The hyperesthesia, as she called it, was less marked during the day, when Seth, though still easily frightened, could be very affectionate. However, as evening approached he appeared haunted and had bouts of extreme anxiety occurring in clusters with little respite in between. Then Arlene told me about the most recent oddity, which had happened the evening before when Seth was resting peacefully in his carrier. All of a sudden, without provocation, he bolted from the carrier and tore around the apartment like one possessed. This was the first time Arlene had ever witnessed this peculiar manifestation.

By about this time I was beginning to get a clearer picture of what was going on with Seth. My diagnosis was one of feline hyperesthesia syndrome, a bizarre manic condition that primarily affects young adult Siamese or Siamese-crossbred cats. Arlene was accurate when she used the term "hyperesthesia" to describe his mental state. Seth had all the cardinal signs of this condition: dilated pupils, twitching, and sudden bizarre fluctuations of mood ranging from mania to extreme fear and even to affection. It is quite typical for such cats to suddenly look alarmed and then tear around the house looking over their shoulder as if pursued by a ghost. In the altered state of mind that accompanies these episodic attacks, affected cats may become quite aggressive, as Seth did, and inflict serious injury on innocent bystanders. It is by no means clear that cats actually know what they're doing when in such a state. Some even appear to be hallucinating.

I explained the signs of feline hyperesthesia syndrome to Arlene and she was stunned to learn of this condition.

"So what do you think he was looking at out on the porch?" she asked.

"It could have been anything," I replied, "or nothing. Maybe he sensed a wild animal moving around under the porch and his emotions were triggered to the point where he couldn't contain them anymore and redirected his hostility toward you. Then again, maybe there was no precipitating cause, maybe he just erupted."

"I see," Arlene said. "So he may have just blindly attacked the first thing in front of him, which happened to be me."

"Something like that," I replied.

"But why would he remain so worked up and for so long?"

"Cats, even normal cats, often do take a few hours to calm down after a conflagration. There is a condition called redirected aggression where typically cats see something they don't like out of a window and, in their frustration, turn and redirect their aggression toward a nearby cat or person. Following an attack, affected cats will remain worked up for some time afterwards, but they don't usually display the other signs that Seth is showing and don't normally remain agitated for so long. In Seth's case, I believe that there is some underlying organic problem that causes him to be so mercurial. It may have something to do with seizures. Seizurelike activity is thought to account for the clinical signs of feline hyperesthesia syndrome."

"Seizures?" she gasped. "Can anything be done about this problem or will he be like this forever?"

That was my cue, and I launched into a discussion of treatment. It wasn't a terribly long discussion because medication is the mainstay of therapy for this condition. We discussed the several options that were available, ranging from antidepressants to anticonvulsants, eventually settling on the antidepressant clomipramine as the most reasonable starting point. This medicine, which was to stabilize Seth's mood and reduce his aggression, had to be given once a day, mixed in with Seth's food. I saw Arlene let out a sigh of relief when I mentioned that it could be mixed in with food, because the thought of putting the medicine down his throat each day was not an appealing one to her. The incidents of the past had caused her to lose all confidence in her former buddy, and I think Seth sensed this.

Over the next few days I had several conversations with Arlene about Seth. Most of them centered on her nervousness and my concern for her personal safety. Unfortunately clomipramine's effects take a while to become noticeable, so there was a danger zone within which Seth could conceivably have another attack. Alternatively, perhaps the medication wouldn't work at all, because it is not effective in all cases. As it happened, we were in luck. At about the three-week mark, Arlene reported considerable improvement in Seth's disposition and there had been no further incidents of aggression or any bizarre spooking episodes. I could practically feel Arlene's confidence growing as she began to see signs that the medicine was working.

That could have been the end of the story, and a happy one, but it wasn't. The peace only lasted for about three months, until early November. At this time Arlene and Howard decided to go on vacation to escape the cold dark nights that were encroaching, so they upped and went, leaving Seth with some friends. There is some question of whether Seth was receiving the proper dose of his medication during their absence as the friends admitted some difficulty in getting him to eat it. Arlene and Howard knew something was amiss the moment they stepped back into the house and saw a wide-eyed Seth slowly advancing on them and growling. Once again they narrowly escaped attack by darting behind a door, and once again he took several hours to return to seminormal. I say seminormal because his pupils remained large and that had always been a warning in the past that he was likely to have another attack at any time of the day or night.

Arlene took it upon herself to increase the dose of the antidepressant to make up for what she thought were missed doses during her absence. Three weeks later Seth attacked a friend of hers who was visiting, and this time he remained highly aroused for several days, attacking anybody who entered the room in which he was confined. Seth had to have his food and water passed around the door as if he were a violent psychiatric inpatient—and for good reason. Given the opportunity, he would attack and bite the hand that fed him. Luckily Arlene was so quick that he would wind up clawing or body-checking the door instead. It was time for her to call me again. Arlene spoke with a wavering voice when she called and I knew she was desperate.

"You've got to help me," she said. "Seth's gone berserk again. My own vet won't come out here, won't give him an injection, and won't take him in. I can't live like this, I'm scared. Seth's like a volcano that's going to blow at any moment. What can I do, Dr. Dodman? Can you come out here and take him, please?"

There was no way I was going to be able to get to her house that day because I was fully booked with cases, but I had to do something to help her.

"Couldn't you bring him to us?" I asked.

"I would but I can't get him into the carrier," she replied.

"Couldn't you get him to go inside the carrier by putting food in it?"

"I don't think so, Dr. Dodman. He will attack me as soon as I open the door. Please send someone out here."

Not having an assistant available, I was stymied, but then an idea came to me.

"I know," I said. "Why don't you ask a vet tech at your local vet clinic to come out and bring special equipment, heavy gloves, and so on. They will probably be able to catch Seth and put him in the carrier and then you can bring him to me."

"That's an idea," she said, suddenly sounding more hopeful. "I'll call them and then let you know how I made out. But if no one will come, I don't know what I'm going to do."

I was delighted to learn, later on, that she succeeded in enlisting the help of a wildlife worker who managed to catch Seth by snaring him. The man put Seth into a carrier and Arlene called to say that she was on her way.

"Come on down," I said, and began to prepare for the arrival of the wild one.

Arlene arrived at the hospital at about five o'clock in the afternoon and dropped Seth off with a supply of food, medication, toys, and food treats.

"I can't take him back the way he is, Dr. Dodman. Howard and I are petrified of him but we could never see him put to sleep. We have too much of ourselves invested in him. I do hope you can get him back to normal for us."

I smiled a comforting flicker of a smile but was concerned myself about how things would turn out.

While Seth was in the hospital I decided to switch his medicine. The antidepressant was clearly no longer suppressing the condition, so I decided to go with an old standby, the anticonvulsant drug phenobarbital. In his stainless steel cage, Seth looked the picture of innocence. It was hard to imagine the havoc he had wreaked and the heartbreak he had caused as I saw him sauntering around his new "digs," checking the place out. My resident, Dr. Flannigan, looked after Seth during his stay and the two of them got along really well. Apparently Flannigan could handle Seth without any trouble and even managed to conduct a thorough physical examination. Nothing of note was found and neither was any abnormality evident according to the results of blood tests, but we kept Seth in the hospital anyway to allow Arlene to get her life back together and to give the anticonvulsant time to work. It was imperative that Seth be handed back to Arlene only when his problem was fully under control.

Seth was with us about a week when, in the wake of glowing reports of his in-hospital behavior from Flannigan, Arlene came to visit him just before Thanksgiving with a view to possibly taking him home.

She was impressed with what she saw, as Seth pressed his nose to the bars of the cage, purring and looking like his old affectionate self, so she steeled herself and decided to take him home. In a way it was good that he was going home, where, theoretically, he would be less stressed, but both Arlene and I felt some trepidation as we parted company outside the hospital.

Three weeks elapsed and Seth was doing well, showing no signs of aggression, but then he flipped again. This time his aggression was directed toward a cleaning lady who fled with her sleeves in tatters, never to return. The aftermath of this incident lasted several days, during which Arlene couldn't always get Seth to take the medication. She called us again in desperation and asked if she could bring him back into the hospital for us to stabilize his condition. I agreed to do this. Since a few weeks had elapsed since Seth was started on the phenobarbital, I elected to take a blood sample to check the level and found that it was too low for optimum effect. Consequently, during his stay I increased the dose of the medication and waited to see what would happen. As before, Seth's mood was mellow throughout his stay.

Arlene finally came by to take him back a week or so later. I wondered at her patience. Not many people would live in a house with a cat who terrified them and who had brutally attacked them in the past. Not many people would feel so concerned about such an animal that they would worry about its welfare as they literally nursed their own wounds. The logistics of managing Seth were far from simple, the medical bills far from inexpensive, and the future far from bright, and yet Arlene pressed on, never for a moment considering bringing him to a shelter or asking her vet to put him to sleep. Neither of these things was an option for her and she was absolutely determined to stay the course. In Arlene's case, her perseverance arose from her intensity and commitment. Clearly she was not used to encountering problems she couldn't solve. On the emotional side, she loved Seth for all his failings and felt that, in his heart of hearts, he loved her too.

I must admit the light at the end of the tunnel was little more than a glimmer, but I did my medical best for Seth and hoped for a miracle. Of course, I advised Arlene to be cautious around Seth and to isolate him in the event of a problem, as she had done in the past. But Arlene was not fearless. The incidents with Seth had taken their toll and there were times when I know she was terrified and almost at her wit's end. But if the true definition of bravery is overcoming fear, rather than being fearless, she was certainly brave. As she headed out through the electric doors with Seth, I didn't envy her task of medicating him daily and watching him carefully in case he lost control again. Months went by and I heard not a word from her. No news is good news, I thought to myself, so I wasn't concerned.

I contacted Arlene again after the turn of the year, almost nine months after the initial event, and things had remained peaceful. In fact, things had settled down dramatically since Seth's last visit. It seems that the anticonvulsant had kept him fully in check. His positive response to this medication was further proof that feline hyperesthesia has seizural roots. I always learn something when I treat a difficult case, and Seth's case was no exception. I learn something about the animal and I learn something about people. Seth taught me more about managing feline hyperesthesia, and his case provided another piece of the puzzle regarding the etiology of this condition. Arlene was one of the most determined, brave, and caring clients I have ever encountered. To this day I don't know what kept her going. Whether her concern was innate or learned from her parents I will never know. What I do know is that Arlene was one of the few people who would have seen Seth's problem through. Her patience and perseverance paid off and she really deserved the final victory.

Postscript

Seth has continued to do well for years since his last appointment here at Tufts. Arlene and I remain in contact and regularly discuss his continued mellow mood. Sometimes I have her vet check his blood phenobarbital level, just to make sure it remains in the therapeutic range, and sometimes I have his liver function checked. So far all is well. It seems likely that Seth will have to remain on medication indefinitely, but that is by far preferable to the fate he once faced. The fact is that medication saved his life, so in a way he has nothing to lose by continuing on with it. Anyway, Arlene shudders at the mention of trying to reduce or eliminate Seth's medication, and my instincts tell me that she is right.

12

LIFE WITH LENNY

There is honor in being a dog.—*Aristotle*

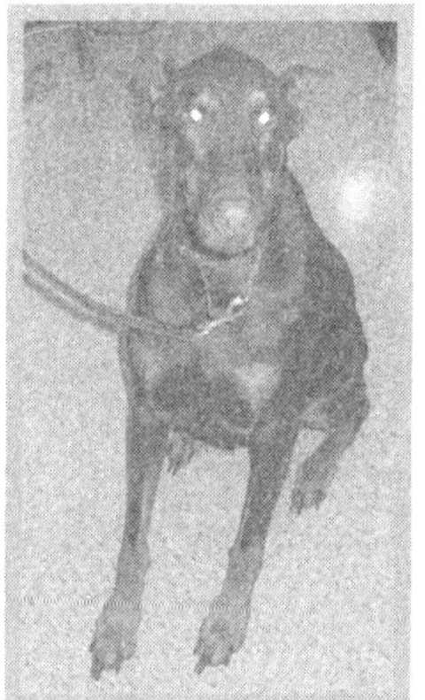

John Davenport of York, Maine, arrived at the Behavior Clinic one January afternoon along with his 80-pound neutered male Doberman, Lenny. John was seeking my help in addressing a particularly irksome habit of Lenny's, that of territorial urine marking around the house. At the time of the visit, Lenny was four years old, and I noticed from the record that John had owned him for about three and a half of those four years. As we settled into the sparsely appointed consulting room, I surveyed the awkward pair in front of me and wondered who and what I was dealing with. They didn't seem to have much in common. John was a heavyset, somewhat overweight linebacker type with an orthopedic problem that caused him obvious difficulty getting around. Lenny, on the other hand, was lithe and majestic, and nimble on his feet. John was sullen, if not somewhat depressed, and sighed constantly, while Lenny seemed joyous and ambled carefree around the consulting room, investigating everything and apparently thoroughly enjoying his new surroundings. While Lenny was in perfect physical condition, John clearly was not.

I smiled at John, who had been nervously adjusting the cuffs of his plaid shirt.

"So where did you get him from?" I asked.

"A shelter," John replied. "He had been abused."

"Really," I said, waiting for the other shoe to drop. But no further information was forthcoming.

"Tell me more," I pressed, prompting John to elaborate.

"Oh, I don't know," John replied, taking a deep breath. "The usual, you know, chained outside twenty-four hours a day surrounded by rotten wormy dog food. He was a mess."

"You know something about abused dogs then?" I asked. "When you say 'the usual,' it makes me think that you have some experience in this area."

"Well, yes, I do really," John said, rolling his eyes. "My wife and I have helped the local humane society for several years. You could say we were activists in that respect. We're also intimately involved with the local Doberman Rescue League. We both have a thing for this breed."

"That's commendable," I said. "Do you still work with Doberman Rescue now?"

"No, don't get much chance now," John said, sighing again. "My wife and I have three kids and they take up pretty much all of our time."

"How did you come to get Lenny?" I asked. "Were you on the lookout for a dog for yourself or did he find you?"

"No, we weren't really looking for a dog," John said. "Actually we already had one. Another Dobie, called Shana. We didn't *need* another dog. But the humane society called us up to ask us if we would take care of him. It's very difficult to find a home for Dobermans, especially ones with behavior problems, and there are a lot of them out there that need to be placed."

I saw John's eyes turn a little misty as he looked off into the horizon and I could see he was mustering up strength to continue.

"Part of the problem is jerk owners, you know, the kind of guys who buy a tough, mean-looking dog to chain to their motorbike to guard it. And then there are owners who just can't handle them. Dobermans can be tough dogs. There are a lot of dominant ones around."

"I know," I said quietly, finding common ground with John for the first time. "Do you still have Shana?"

"No, she died a couple of years ago, from cancer."

"What type of cancer?"

"Oh, some kind of fatty tumor on her hip. The vet removed it, but within a few months she started to have seizures and they found the tumor had spread to her brain. She was dead three weeks later. Yeah, Shana was the best dog we ever had. My wife and I adored her."

"But you like Lenny, don't you?"

"Yeah, I suppose so. He's a bit of a pal but this pissing problem is just too much, you know. I don't know if I'm going to be able to keep him."

I glanced over at Lenny, whose hangdog expression seemed to say it all, his eyes glancing to the side and ears flat, at the tone of John's words.

"It would be a real shame if you couldn't keep him. He looks like a pretty good dog."

"Yes, he is a good dog. A very good dog," John acknowledged, shaking his head slowly from side to side. "Other than the marking, that is."

"I see from the record that he's been urine-marking since you first got him. Tell me what you've tried to do about it."

"Oh, practically everything," John replied. "First I sent him to a training school with a six-month follow-up at home. That failed. I tried yelling at him, I tried crating him, and I tried shaming him. Nothing worked."

"How did you shame him?" I asked, frowning slightly.

"I used a shame collar."

"A shame collar? What's that?" I asked.

"Well, what you do is you soak up the piss in some kind of rag and you tie it around his neck until it starts to stink. The idea is that it shames him out of the behavior."

"Listen," I said, "there's no way that would work. If you're going to punish a dog at all, the punishment has to be immediate. But punishment is not the right way to go anyway. Before we go any further I want you to understand the basic premise that we work under in this behavior clinic, that is, no yelling, no hitting, and no chain jerking. In fact, we rarely use punishment at all. Our techniques are directional and reward-based as opposed to being correctional and punishment-based. After all, the opposite of reward is not punishment, it is no reward."

John nodded slowly. "Whatever works, Doc, I'm all ears."

"Now let's start at the beginning. Has your vet done a urine test to check for possible medical problems?"

"Yes, he has. He said Lenny's blood work and urine tests were all fine."

"Good. And Lenny was properly neutered, I trust?"

"What do you mean, properly neutered?"

"What I mean is both testes were removed in an uncomplicated neutering operation."

"Yeah, the neutering was fine. I did check that out with the vet. I know some dogs can have a retained testicle. What do you call that? Cryptorchid, isn't it?"

"That's correct. And if one or both testes are still present, the dog will behave like a male and males do more marking behavior. Neutering is no guarantee that urine marking will not occur, but it does substantially reduce or eliminate the problem in about two out of three cases."

"So Lenny's the one out of three who keeps marking even after he's neutered, right?"

I nodded. "I'm afraid so. Tell me, does he always mark on vertical surfaces by cocking his leg or does he sometimes squat on the floor?"

"Oh, he sometimes squats. It's often just a few drops of urine, but then again, sometimes he lets rip and the piss runs like a river. You never know what he's going to do . . . or when."

"Okay, in that case, there is a possibility that his marking may be intertwined with a good old-fashioned housebreaking problem. I'm going to have you treat him as if he's a puppy again and to train him to go to the bathroom outside."

"I've done that but it didn't work."

"I think you should give it another go, this time under my direction," I said, attempting to keep John on track and thinking positively. "What I'm going to describe to you is a program. If you do all the things I suggest simultaneously, there is a much better chance that it might work."

"Okay, I'll try it. What have I got to lose by following your orders?"

I rattled off the usual house-training protocols, including having John take Lenny outside on lead to a chosen spot, preferably one Lenny had shown some interest in before, and praising him for using that location to urinate. I advised John to do this as often as he could manage, especially morning, noon, and night. Lenny was to be rewarded with a delicious food treat immediately after he'd successfully accomplished a task.

"That's going to be very difficult for me, Doc. I have a bad leg, so taking Lenny out into the yard all the time is going to present a few problems."

"Oh, I'm sorry to hear that. I did notice you were favoring one leg when you came in. Will it get better in the near future?"

"No, it'll be that way forever now," he said, heaving a sigh. "At least unless I have the bone broken and reset."

"What on earth happened?"

John took a deep breath and braced himself to tell me what was obviously a very painful story. "Well, I broke my leg when I was in the Army . . . fell off a tank. They never really fixed the break properly. First they sent me to a civilian hospital where it was plastered until they could find a surgeon to operate, but the leg healed before I ever got proper attention and it healed in the wrong position. I've been battling them in court for years trying to get them to pay for the surgery."

"That's terrible. And here's me asking you to go gallivanting around the yard with 'the boy.' "

"Don't worry about it, Doc. You weren't to know," John replied kindly.

"Could your wife help you, perhaps?" I ventured.

"No, she works. She's never around during the day. I'm always the one looking after Lenny."

"So you don't work?" I asked.

"No, this injury prevents me from getting around. I'm pensioned and disabled. Lousy pension it is, too. I'd rather have my leg back and go to work."

I sympathized and then refocused us on our mission.

"Well, let's see what can be done with Lenny, anyway. Make sure he gets turned out in the garden regularly, on his own if necessary. It would be good if you could go with him sometimes and reward him, as I suggested, so that he can learn what's expected of him. Next on the agenda is cleanup of areas inside the house that he has soiled. It's particularly important to use a proprietary odor neutralizer to clean up urine marks; otherwise he'll be attracted back to the same spot as surely as a heat-seeking missile is attracted to a source of heat. I have a handout on this to help you remember exactly what you should be doing."

"So that's it?" said John incredulously. "That's going to cure him?"

"Ah, no, not exactly," I said. "There are a couple of other things we need to attend to. The first of these is that you should confine him in a crate, or behind a kitty gate, or simply tie him to your belt if you find yourself unable to supervise him during the day."

"So that he doesn't get a chance to sneak off?" John asked.

"Precisely. It's the old yin-yang approach: teaching him to go outside while preventing him from soiling inside. I want you to make sure that he spends as much time as possible in the same room as you so that he can't sneak off and urinate in some other location. If you see him start to sniff around or act suspiciously, immediately turn him out into the garden or, even better, take him outside. If you are too late and catch him in the act, just make a loud noise, creating a distraction that will shut down his sphincters midstream. Never punish him for urinating in front of you. That would be counterproductive. Confine him only when you can't be around to police the situation. He's never had separation anxiety or shown problems when crated, has he?"

"No. He used to be a little anxious when I left him when he was a pup, but he grew out of it. Right after I got him, he chewed up a brand-new couch while I was asleep at night. When I came down the next morning, I found the damage and I was so angry that I picked him up and threw him onto the couch. That didn't help. He urinated all over it as he landed. I suppose I shouldn't have done that, right?"

"Right," I said, as patiently as I could. "That was submissive urination. You came on way too strong."

John looked repentant, dropping his head and inspecting the floor.

The next behavior modification plan that I ran through with John was a dominance control, or leadership, program. I frequently employ this program to help owners assert greater control over their dog. Enactment of the program helps suppress the dog's perceived need to engage in territorial marking duties. The more clearly owners are in charge, the less pressure the dog feels in this respect, goes the rationale.

John seemed to be in favor of this approach and understood what had to be done.

I handed him the "12-Step Leadership Program for Dominant Dogs" (see Appendix 2) and highlighted again some key areas of the program, such as requiring Lenny to sit or lie down before receiving food, praise, exercise, or freedom.

John gazed at the sheet I had handed him for quite some time as my words sank in and then he looked up.

"That's it? All done?"

"Pretty much," I said. "That is what I would suggest we do behaviorally, but there is a possibility that this program alone will not work to suppress Lenny's urine marking, so I suggest that we use some medication to help him along."

"I'm game for that," John replied. "I've already tried a lot of the things you just suggested and nothing has worked. The retraining program that you described is very similar to the one they gave me at the training school. And I believe that I already have pretty good control over Lenny as his leader now. He obeys me whenever I tell him to do something and he's never aggressive to me."

"You have a point," I acknowledged. "This is a tough problem and I expect we will need medication to pull it all together."

"What medication would you give him and how does it work?" John asked.

"I would give him an antidepressant. Antidepressants seem to reduce urine marking for reasons that are not absolutely clear. The modus operandi may involve mood stabilization, or mood elevation, or it may even be that the beneficial effects are related to a side effect."

"I know something about antidepressants," John replied. "Which one are you thinking of using?"

"Oh, I thought I would start with the old tricyclic drug amitriptyline, otherwise known as Elavil. In due course, we could run the gamut right up to drugs like Prozac and Zoloft."

"Yeah, that's the one my sister takes, Zoloft," John announced. "She'd be in bad shape without it. I think that I may have to ask to be put on it, too, if Lenny doesn't stop this crazy pissing problem. It's really getting me down."

It was crystal clear to me just how serious Lenny's problem was to John and the impact that my failure to treat it might have on the whole family's well-being. I really hoped that my treatment strategy and the winds of fate and good fortune would transport them out of the behavior doldrums. Feeling a little less chipper than I had at the beginning of the appointment, I gave John details about dosing Lenny with amitriptyline, and then he and I exited the consulting room. I had to help John circumnavigate the numerous fire doors that lined our route to the outside world and relieved him of the necessity of having to manage Lenny, too. The final obstacle was the double swing doors at the hospital entrance which sometimes present a physical challenge for those in the peak of health.

The next year of treatment with Lenny did not produce extraordinarily successful results, although I did manage to cut down the frequency of Lenny's marking behavior by about half. The road toward this limited success was somewhat bumpy. In most of the telephone conversations I had with John, I found him to be somewhat pessimistic in his approach. For John the glass was always half empty. In various conversations, I urged him to follow the various components of the programs we had talked about and, in particular, to buckle down on cleanup issues and the dominance control program. We seesawed on the drug dosage, going through periods in which Lenny appeared to be somewhat lethargic, necessitating reductions in the dose of amitriptyline, to periods when his urination frequency seemed unchanged, necessitating upward modification of the dose. Throughout our dialogues, I always worried about the possibility that Lenny would permanently revert to his former ways and wind up homeless—or worse. I must admit I worried about John, too. His personal well-being was always at the front of my mind as we spoke.

I only saw John one more time after our original appointment, and that was at the one-year recheck appointment. Lenny romped in beside him, and sat there looking at me with smiling eyes, as John and I talked over other ways to maximize Lenny's improvement. John's concern over Lenny's residual urine-marking behavior was still quite intense, so after performing a thorough examination of Lenny to ensure his continued good health and running some routine blood work, I recommended upping the dose of amitriptyline into the very high range in one last desperate attempt to get the problem under better control.

After the appointment, I was in close contact with John for another few months. Lenny was improving steadily, although his record was still not perfect. Life became more hectic for me around this time, with a trip to Japan and a series of meetings that I had to attend. It was fall before I realized that John and I had not been in contact for months and I had no idea how Lenny was doing. I finally made the long overdue call in November.

"Hi, John. What's going on with our buddy?" I asked in an upbeat way, hoping for the best but prepared for the worst. John sounded genuinely pleased to hear from me.

"He doesn't mark anymore, Dr. Dodman. He seems to be completely cured now on this medication."

"Wow, that's great," I said. "You've made my day."

"I said he doesn't mark anymore, but he does have some other problems, different ones," John added.

"Oh?" I said. "What kind of problems are those?"

"Well, he's got some sort of bowel problem. The vet said his bowel is not in the right place. I've had him in and out of the vet's office several times and have had about $1,200 worth of tests run on him."

"I'm sorry to hear that," I said, genuinely sorry that Lenny was in such dire straits. "So how is he?"

"He seems depressed and doesn't eat well anymore. He's like a sickly old pensioner, nothing like the dog he was when you first saw him."

"But he's only six," I protested. "He should have at least another five or six good years in him. I don't understand why he's gone downhill so fast. Let me talk to your vet and I'll see what we can come up with together."

"That's very kind, Dr. Dodman, I would appreciate that, but I don't know there's anything that can be done. I don't think he's going to live much longer, and the way it is for me right now, I don't think I'd get another dog. Lenny will be the last for me."

"Are you okay?" I added hesitantly. "I know you had some problems with your knee and you were a bit depressed when I saw you but—"

"Oh, yes," he said, "I've had some health problems of my own. Walking out of kilter had put strain on my back and I popped a disk out. I had to go in for back surgery to get things sorted out. I'm lucky I'm still walking at all. Talk about pain."

"Wow, you've really been through the wars. At least it's all over. It should be all downhill from here."

"I certainly hope so. I think I've had my share of misfortune for a while, if you know what I mean."

I winced as I considered what he had been through.

We then reviewed Lenny's case history before finishing our telephone conversation, and I left John with the good thought that at least Lenny was not urinating in the house, and that his medical situation might well be manageable.

Immediately after this call I contacted John's vet, Dr. Blythe, who worked in a small practice, aptly named Treat with Care. Dr. Blythe was most amenable to discussing Lenny's case on the telephone and was able to answer most of my questions. He admitted he wasn't quite sure what was going on with Lenny's intestines but said that the problem was not as drastic as John had made out and disagreed that Lenny looked like an old man of a dog. "Looked fine to me," was the way he put it.

Apparently, all that had happened was that Lenny had had a couple of bouts of diarrhea and had been hospitalized while Dr. Blythe ran "some tests" to shed light on the matter. The results of the tests were unspectacular and not particularly revealing, so the whole medical issue remained something of an enigma. While I had Dr. Blythe on the phone, I suggested that we decrease Lenny's dose of amitriptyline, since the desired effect had now been achieved. In closing, I asked if we could remain in close contact about Lenny over the next few weeks to be sure he was doing better. Dr. Blythe agreed.

Lenny remained in good health and there were no further bouts of diarrhea. Neither did the urine-marking behavior resurface. After a few months, it was possible to wean Lenny off the amitriptyline entirely without any behavioral slippage. Finally John admitted that he had a near perfect dog. In his words, Lenny was now a good dog—a very good dog. As far as John's medical problems were concerned, he was much improved in terms of his disk problem and had lost weight, which helped relieve some stress on his knee. He was even planning to have his leg reoperated on at some time in the future, and I detected refreshing optimism in his voice when we spoke. Somewhere in this equation, even though John was not about to admit it, Lenny figured in as an important component in John's life. Lenny was his only friend; he followed him from room to room and accompanied him on all sorts of errands. The two of them were almost never separated. The amount of time, energy, effort, and money that John had put into caring for Lenny was at least some indication of his deep feelings for the dog. True, John's life had been difficult, but it was better for having Lenny in it, and I think John knew that. I ended up concluding that John would never have gotten rid of Lenny, despite his earlier saber rattling. Lenny may have been part of the reason that John struggled on amidst numerous personal trials.

When Lenny finally passes away, hopefully not until his old age, I feel sure that John will get another dog and that it will be a Doberman. Just as Lenny was not a patch on Shana, John may find the new dog to be not a patch on Lenny. But, completing the cycle of life, the newcomer would find a place in John's life and become indispensable, too. John was a dyed-in-the-wool Doberman owner, and a good one at that. Even though he'd been taught some of the wrong ways to handle dogs in the early days, he could command their respect and affection without resorting to harsh words or punishment, and that's not always an easy feat. Specialist breed that they are, Dobermans always seem to need strong leaders, and John had the ability to deliver that message.

13

THE WILLING PRISONER

Nothing is more fatal than the disaster of too much love.—*D. H. Lawrence*

Nancy Crighton was a career person and a bit of a loner. Shortly after leaving college she discovered the joys of pet ownership when she teamed up with her first dog, Jazz, a stalwart Labrador-Newfoundland mix. The two of them were inseparable, but Jazz developed bone cancer and died prematurely, leaving a huge vacuum in Nancy's life. For months after Jazz's demise she tried to get over her sadness and, at least partly as a form of occupational therapy, took some additional college courses over the summer and fall. So profound was Nancy's grief that she could not consider getting another dog at this stage. She needed time. She recognized there would never be another Jazz.

Nancy's grief lessened as time went by, but her loneliness did not. So, one day in the middle of a seemingly endless New England winter, she set off for the Cocheco Valley Humane Society in New Hampshire in search of another canine companion to replace the inimitable Jazz. Shelter people usually know their business, and good ones know yours, too. In this case, the shelter manager, an older man with a graying beard and a sparkle in his eye, saw Nancy coming and knew right away that he had a special-needs adopter. Even after a brief introductory conversation, he realized that it was not going to be easy to supply Nancy with exactly what she was looking for—a replacement for her old friend Jazz—but he felt certain he could accommodate her in some fashion. Years of experience had equipped him well for the Sergeant Pepper role, and anyway he liked helping people. He spent a while asking questions about Jazz before sizing up Nancy's needs. What was it about Jazz that she liked so much? What kind of dog was he? What activities did they enjoy together? What exactly had she lost that would have to be replaced? It finally came to him that she might be interested in a newcomer to the pound, a desolate soul of a dog named Duncan, who had been found wandering by the side of the road just a few days earlier. When he was found, Duncan had no collar or tags and had frost all over his back. He was shivering and was limping along the road without bearing any weight on one of his hind legs. He was brought to the shelter, where it was discovered that he had a badly broken leg. A vet who was summoned recommended immediate surgery to repair the break. The shelter manager agreed to the surgery, paying for the operation out of a special fund he had at his disposal for just such needy dogs. When Duncan returned from the surgery, he had an external fixation device precariously jutting out of his leg. Because of the delicacy of the device, the manager took Duncan into his own home for rehabilitation, and that's where he was at the time of Nancy's visit. The manager eyed Nancy carefully, wondering if she and Duncan would be a good match. Duncan was a Labrador mix, like Nancy's Jazz, and was largish and black, as was Jazz. Not a bad match as far as appearances went. Duncan also seemed like a gentle dog, like Jazz, and at this particular time in his life certainly needed someone's support. Nancy immediately agreed to pay Duncan a visit, but just to look, she insisted. She still wasn't sure that she was ready for another dog yet, but some mysterious force had drawn her to the pound.

Nancy and the manager set off for his home and they chatted about dogs and dog ownership en route. On entering the home, Nancy peered down a long hallway toward the kitchen, where Duncan was said to spend most of his time. Sure enough, a slender black form appeared silhouetted by the light streaming in through the kitchen window. He limped slowly toward her, favoring his back right leg. It was an eerie experience for Nancy to see this ghostly apparition approach in complete silence. The form was like Jazz; the demeanor and carriage like Jazz. Jazz had even exhibited a similar right hind lameness because of an old knee injury. Nancy said yes to Duncan without hesitation, and Duncan, seemingly sensing the good karma, approached with confidence and allowed Nancy to pet him. It wasn't long before Duncan was in Nancy's car and the two of them were speeding home to spend the rest of their days together.

When Nancy got Duncan home she soon discovered another side to his character which had previously been concealed. Although he adored her right from the outset, he disliked everyone else. He only wanted Nancy in his new life. No one else was welcome. Paranoia seemed to overwhelm him whenever he was faced with what he viewed as a especially threatening outsider—and that was most everyone. He was especially uncomfortable in the presence of unfamiliar men, particularly tall men and men in uniforms. In addition, other dogs easily intimidated Duncan, especially if they approached him quickly or too closely, and he didn't like horses at all. When off lead he would either circle the feared person or animal at a safe distance and bark or, if approached too quickly, would beat a hasty retreat away from the unwelcome presence. Occasionally Duncan would express his displeasure a little more proactively by lunging and baring his teeth at perceived invaders. This he did most emphatically from the safety of Nancy's car or when on lead at Nancy's side. It takes some confidence and a degree of security for a dog to come forward to address his fears, and that's what Nancy's car and her supportive presence provided. After all, a strategy of intimidation may backfire, and fearful dogs in particular don't want to wind up on the receiving end. For this reason they are always a lot braver when they are operating from a safe haven, or if the subject of their fear is even more fearful of them (as is the case with people who are afraid of dogs).

With fear-aggressive dogs, the surge of courage in the face of danger is fueled by a modicum of dominance. Dominance can be thought of as a form of willfulness that propels them to try to control events and circumstances rather than being swayed by them. Without dominance, fearful dogs sheepishly shrink from their adversaries. They cower, back up into corners, collapse in a heap, or urinate submissively to ingratiate themselves with challengers. Duncan was not a complete wimp and would show some assertiveness by challenging strangers when circumstances were conducive to that approach, but it didn't take much of a challenge to bring out his cowardly side. Duncan's fragile dominance displayed itself in certain contexts, including possessive guarding of favorite food and toys, when he was approached by other dogs, or when he was "guarding horse poop on the trail," a curious phenomenon considering his deep mistrust of the beasts themselves. Duncan was, in fact, a bit confused and underconfident, somewhat dysfunctional if you will, probably as a result of earlier adverse experiences, as is often the case with adoptees.

Duncan's Achilles' heel(s) notwithstanding, he made a fine friend for Nancy and in no time won her heart. All was well in the Crighton household, at least for a while. Duncan clearly adored his new, sensitive, hugely attentive, and concerned owner, returning her affection in equal measure. Needy dogs usually do make the most adoring and adorable pets. Duncan was no exception to this general rule.

Over the years, Nancy tried to socialize Duncan to strangers because she hated to have to leave him behind when she went out in public. At one point the retraining seemed to be producing some positive results so Nancy mustered up the courage to take Duncan to work with her to see how well he would cope. To her great joy and surprise he took a shine to her office mates, even the men. They were, of course, previously clued in on Duncan's social phobia and agreed to hold in check any raucous behavior that might unhinge him. To their credit, they took great pains not to invade Duncan's space and plied him with food treats when he came toward them on his own steam. The results were spectacular, with Duncan gaining in confidence almost daily.

Occasional visits to the office led to more regular appearances. Peace reigned in the office and Nancy's colleagues were delighted with their new office mate. But a new problem was surfacing. On days when Nancy did not bring Duncan to work, he started to "complain" about being left alone. As Nancy prepared to leave each morning, Duncan would shadow her, panting and pacing to and fro anxiously. If she sat down, he would sit on her lap, seemingly in an attempt to prevent her from getting up. Or he might sit in front of the door to block her access. If she tried to move him, he would sometimes snap at her, never making contact, of course. Getting out of the house was getting tougher by the day. As Nancy opened the door to get out, Duncan would squeeze past her through the narrowest of cracks like a greased seal. Once out, he was almost impossible to get back in. On one occasion when Nancy won the battle and escaped from home without him, he barked incessantly and scratched and chewed at the door molding. Separation anxiety was beginning to rear its ugly head. Duncan began to show anxiety at other times, such as when Nancy went out in the evening, when she took a shower, put on jewelry, put on her shoes, gathered up her knapsack, or even if she just walked toward the door. It slowly began to dawn on Nancy that she was in a real jam. By this time she had bonded so closely with Duncan that she could not possibly consider returning him to the shelter. Yet in accommodating his needy personality she was fast becoming a prisoner in her own home.

You've probably heard the story about the drowning man who shouts to his dog, "Lassie, get help," and then the next scene is of the dog reclining on a psychiatrist's couch. Well, that's what Nancy did, get help—for Duncan. First she consulted a local trainer/behaviorist named Georgie Wade.

Georgie correctly advised Nancy to:

1. Change her attitude to Duncan so as not to be overly sympathetic to his needs.

2. Increase firmness and discipline in the course of everyday interactions with him.

3. Ration kindness toward him, rewarding independent behavior.

4. Change the order in which she did things before she went out (to prevent Duncan from picking up on her impending departure).

5. Put down a peanut-butter-stuffed bone before leaving the house (to divert and occupy him and to condition him to expect this treat when she left).

6. Avoid making a fuss over him before leaving (make a speedy, unheralded departure).

7. Leave by a different exit each day.

8. Refrain from greeting Duncan on her return home—basically, ignore him until he had settled down.

This was all good advice, but unfortunately it didn't solve Duncan's problem. No program works all the time. Individual dog factors and owner factors sometimes prevent successful resolution of behavior problems even when acceptable behavior modification techniques are employed. Dog factors include the severity of the condition and some dogs' seeming slowness to learn. People factors include failure to understand the gist of the retraining program and failure to comply fully with the recommendations. In Nancy's case, I think a bit of both was operating to thwart the program. In desperation she tried herbal remedies, leaving on the stereo while she was away, and trying to tire Duncan out before she left the house. Nothing worked.

Then Nancy got wind of a veterinary behaviorist, Dr. Brenda DeVore, who, as a veterinarian, was licensed to prescribe behavior-modifying medications. Dr. DeVore reinforced aspects of the previous behavior modification program, teaching Nancy how to get Duncan to sit and stay in place during mock departures. DeVore also prescribed an antianxiety drug, buspirone (BuSpar), to take the edge off Duncan so as to hasten his recovery. The "sit and stay" program worked well for about two weeks, but then one windy day Duncan had a really bad separation attack and subsequently refused to cooperate at all, ignoring Nancy's doorside commands and even turning up his nose at food treats. The medication did, in time, reduce Duncan's predeparture anxiety, but the improvement was minimal. While on medication, Duncan would allow Nancy to leave without body-checking her or doing the greasy-seal impersonation, but he still panicked after she had left.

At about this time, the unthinkable happened: a burglar tried to break in while Duncan was home alone. Undoubtedly Duncan was already somewhat anxious when he heard the unwelcome visitor jimmying his way through the bathroom window.

Oh my god, he must have thought, I've got to get out of here.

And he did, by bolting out of the house through a vinyl-curtained gap between the air conditioner and the window frame. Dogs in this frame of mind do not look before they leap and some hurtle to the ground from great elevations. Luckily the window was at first-floor level so Duncan simply slumped to the ground. The commotion Duncan made must have scared off the burglar, who apparently left hurriedly, his work undone.

Duncan was missing for days after this event, presumably lurking in the bushes as he had that December morning when he was first located by the shelter crew. Nancy finally found him by means of a neighborhood alert and brought the poor dog back to the safety of her home. A day or two later, once Duncan had calmed down, Nancy decided to risk a twenty-minute trip to the store to pick up some groceries. When she returned, she found him breathing heavily, shaking, and more anxious than she had ever seen him. Quick surveillance of the room indicated that he had chewed the plywood Nancy had placed around the air conditioner and, judging from the damage, had also attempted to escape through a different window. Like so many other dogs afflicted with separation anxiety, escape from his miserable circumstances had risen to the top of his lonely agenda.

From this time on, Nancy felt she could not leave Duncan alone at all. Luckily Duncan could be left in the car for up to five minutes at a time, so Nancy was able make quick dashes into stores for food and other provisions. Being able to take Duncan to the office periodically during the week was a blessing for her in an otherwise closeted life, but Nancy didn't want to overtax her work mates' patience. Doggy day care, sometimes a boon in such cases, was an option Nancy was forced to explore, though it proved less than one hundred percent satisfactory. Even in this situation, he would soil his cage out of sheer terror if left alone while the other dogs were taken on walks. Because of this, he had to be chaperoned at all times, making him the highest-maintenance visitor in the place.

It was at about this time that Nancy found her way to Tufts Veterinary School, and there I met her and Duncan for the first time. Duncan paced anxiously in the consulting room as Nancy related her tale of woe and described her now hermitlike existence. Here was a case of separation anxiety pure and simple—or was it? I probed beneath the surface to see what additional information might emerge.

Although Nancy's supposition was that Duncan's separation anxiety had been precipitated by her taking him to work, that didn't explain some of the other anxiety attacks that had occurred previously. Apparently, for years Duncan had periodically engaged in seemingly random acts of destruction when left alone. Nancy attributed one of these destructive incidents to the unexpected arrival of a propane delivery person, but the cause of the other incidents was something of a mystery. Something must have triggered them—but what? A dog doesn't show separation anxiety and panic because it is alone on one occasion and then spontaneously compose itself for weeks thereafter. Separation anxiety is usually an ongoing problem, though it can fluctuate somewhat in intensity from day to day. I explained this to Nancy, and that's when she informed me of another variety of "panic attack" that Duncan had evidenced, even in her presence. The catalyst for these panic attacks was the sound of wind, and sometimes other sounds, not separation.

Here, in Nancy's own words, is a report of such panic attacks:

> On windy days he often jumps at windows, pulling down shades, scratching at a desk in front of the window, and pulling papers off the desk. He has scratched and damaged a door, too, perhaps trying to get out. I don't think he likes to hear high wind when he is in the house. One day Duncan woke me at 3 A.M., breathing fast, whining, seemingly unwilling to stand. I took him to the vet, but by the time we got there he had calmed right down. The vet could find nothing wrong with him. It was very windy that night. On May 5 Duncan woke at 6 A.M., breathing fast, shaken, and he climbed onto my bed and sat on my pillow. It took him an hour to settle down. His reaction was the same as it is on windy nights, though this time it was not windy.

Careful questioning revealed that Duncan suffered from other noise sensitivities, including the sound of icicles falling in the winter, the warning beeps of a smoke detector running down, and even the sound made by some squeaky toys. Curiously, he wasn't that bothered by thunder at the time of our meeting. It was clear that Duncan's fear of being alone was not his only dread. He was also sound-phobic. He was the kind of dog who would cringe if admonished by means of a "shake-can" (a penny-containing soda can) or cower when a smoke detector went off. For a dog to have more than one fear is quite common. Dogs who are frightened of people are often unnerved by "things that go bump in the night." Also, many dogs with a thunderstorm phobia display separation anxiety, and vice versa. When multiple fears are present in a dog, I term the condition "global fear," and that diagnosis was certainly appropriate in Duncan's case.

Duncan had been able to contain himself when he was alone prior to a certain date but became completely unhinged after one or two particularly disturbing incidents. From the ancillary history presented, it seemed likely that Duncan's separation anxiety was precipitated by scary sounds, such as wind noise or thunder, occurring while he was alone. Although Duncan might have been able to deal with some of his fears when Nancy was around, the sound of the wind howling or the clatter of a burglar entering the house might have been more than he could handle while he was alone. Duncan would learn from such events that bad things might happen while he was on his own and separated from the only one who could console him. This experience—that being home alone is occasionally associated with pure terror—would certainly exacerbate a mildly disconcerting situation. For dogs like Duncan with compounded phobias, it is no longer a matter of treating separation anxiety alone but one of treating noise phobia, too. Even if the separation anxiety problem is successfully reversed by means of a retraining program designed to instill self-confidence, it only takes the minor huffing and puffing of a windstorm to bring the straw house down again. A tricky problem to be sure.

I ran this by Nancy and she sat there looking at me for a few seconds before responding.

"Oh, I see," she said, "so we have a double problem, one feeding into the other. How do you go about fixing that?"

"It's not going to be easy," I had to admit. "Sound phobia alone is difficult to get completely under control, and separation anxiety can be quirky, too." Nancy winced.

Without further discussion, I outlined the treatment program and stressed the importance of following the recommendations precisely. There wasn't much I had to add that Nancy hadn't already been told about the treatment of separation anxiety, but I recapped the essential features of independence training and pointed out the background benefits of providing Duncan with plenty of exercise, a healthy diet, and positive training experiences. As far as the noise phobia was concerned, I focused on the primary problem, wind noise, and advised Nancy on how to desensitize Duncan to wind noise using a high-quality tape recording of such noise. The idea was to expose Duncan to ever-increasing volumes of wind noise while simultaneously rewarding him for remaining calm and composed.

In addition, I put Duncan on an antidepressant, clomipramine, to stabilize his mood and reduce his fearfulness. I did this in part for humane reasons (why should Duncan suffer when he doesn't have to?) but also to expedite his rehabilitation for Nancy's sake. After all, she was having a pretty tough time of it, too, with her social life in tatters.

I next spoke to Nancy some two to three weeks later as a matter of routine follow-up. Duncan was far from cured at this point, but at least there were some early signs of improvement. She had not left him alone for any extended period since her visit with me, choosing to place him in the relative security of doggy day care. This made it difficult to assess his progress, but Nancy had the distinct impression that he was a lot calmer when she dropped him off at day care. Previously he had pulled on his lead and struggled to go with her as she left. Now he stood quietly, his lead slack and tail wagging slowly, as she pulled out of the parking lot. He also seemed a lot more composed when she picked him up in the evening. She said that now when she went to collect him he would lead her all around the center at the end of the day, as if to show her where he had been and what he had been doing. The staff also reported a noticeable improvement in Duncan's demeanor. They were particularly impressed that he had stopped soiling his run when he had to be left unattended while other dogs were walked. At home, Nancy had occasionally left Duncan alone for short periods of time—for example, to get something from her car—and she had noticed that he no longer tried to throw himself between her and the door as if trying to escape with her. All in all, the general impression we both had was that Duncan was on the road to recovery.

In the weeks that followed, Nancy's confidence was still not sufficiently high for her to try anything more ambitious than brief stints away from Duncan. The memory of his escape and the sight of her trashed apartment still loomed large in her mind. Also, she became concerned because, for the first time in his life, Duncan had shown signs of anxiety during a thunderstorm, seeking out her company and appearing distraught. This, she correctly assessed, indicated a continuing problem. I reminded her that the effects of the medication could take several more weeks to peak, and that primary or secondary thunderstorm phobia can often be contained. Sensing Nancy's frustration, I urged her not to give up on behavior modification therapy and tried to encourage her compliance with all aspects of the program. She admitted that she had not been able to locate a tape recording of wind sound that was sufficiently realistic to fool Duncan, and thus had not been able to start desensitizing him to sounds. More diligence was due from Nancy if we were to succeed.

I was reasonably happy with the early feedback from Nancy but knew it would be quite some time before she would be able to leave Duncan alone for any longer than a few minutes. Even if the first home trial was successful, there was still the acid test to come: leaving Duncan alone during a windstorm. She would need to work hard on that aspect of his reconditioning.

In the meantime, I started to reflect on the extraordinarily similar predicaments and emotional challenges facing Duncan *and* his owner. Reading between the lines, I had the impression that Nancy's life was not an easy one. She had alluded to this more than once in our conversation and it showed in her demeanor. She struck me as needing a clear focus for her obvious passion and intensity. Here she was, an intelligent and sensitive person, with a seemingly empty life, and with Duncan as her one true friend. It was as if she had thrown herself into the management of Duncan's problem as a diversion from some other less malleable issues. Not that Nancy would have wished Duncan's problem on him. But since the problem already existed, rehabilitating Duncan had become an all-consuming project for her. In short, it appeared that looking after Duncan was filling some void in her life and providing her with a focus.

Nancy's own temperament seemed to mirror Duncan's personality. Had dog and owner cleaved to each other because they were the same? This pair was not so much complementary as dependent. Each member of this pack of two needed and leaned heavily on the other for companionship, entertainment, and interest. There may be some biological foundation for the development of such a relationship. Both dogs and people are social creatures, slated by nature to be part of a group. Lower pack members seem particularly to crave the strength that numbers bring. The intensity of Nancy's interest in Duncan's problems might have been a reflection of a social need of her own; after all, two's company. This is not to say that Duncan's problems weren't real, simply that Duncan's need for attention fit precisely with what Nancy was primed to provide. Duncan gave her a clear purpose in life: to be there for him and to help him through his problems. It's always better to worry about someone else than to be forced to focus on your own problems, particularly when the problems are seemingly insurmountable.

The question was, did Nancy's fretting and attention help or hinder Duncan's progress? That's difficult to assess, but to shed some light on the matter, it helps to consider the fate of other needy dogs adopted from shelters. It appears that they can have one of two emotional trajectories: they either improve over time with their new adoptive owners, or their behavior deteriorates. Those who improve can do so to the point of cure. Owners of dogs who are the subject of such success stories tend to be stable, well-balanced, no-nonsense people. It is as if their confidence rubs off on the dog. On the other side of the coin are dogs whose separation anxiety deteriorates postadoption. These dogs' owners seem to be concerned individuals, like Nancy. In such cases, it seems that the owner's empathy with the dog's plight has the reverse of the desired effect. For example, whereas a more confident owner will stride out of the house wearing a smile on his face and delivering an upbeat good-bye, his more sympathetic counterpart may go through elaborate leaving and greeting rituals with their dogs in an attempt to appease them.

"Mommy will be back soon, please don't worry," or "I'm so sorry, darling, but I just have to go out for a while," are typical of such gushing pleas. Of course, the dog doesn't understand the phraseology, but will quickly pick up on the tone in which the words are uttered—one of pity. Well, there's nothing better than pity to guarantee to make a person or dog feel worse about his plight. The emotional roller coaster of separation anxiety is set in action at the time of departure and fueled by exuberant greetings on the owner's return.

The very essence of most behavior modification programs devised to deal with separation anxiety is that they encourage a more pragmatic relationship between the owner and the dog. The dog will not change by itself. Some behaviorists recommend a "planned departure technique" in which the owners are told to leave the dog for ever-increasing periods of time. The dog learns that the owner will return before too long, hopefully not noticing the gradual increase in the time the owner is away. This is a no-nonsense program where often the dog is instructed to sit or lie quietly while the owner walks toward and finally out the door. In severe cases, cues that the owner is about to leave—singing, car keys, putting on a coat or shoes—are rehearsed at various times of the day when the owner is not going to leave. It is the owner who must change his or her behavior, going through the motions of leaving without fuss or commotion. Other behaviorists recommend a "nothing in life is free/working for a living" program (see Appendix 2, the "12-Step Leadership Program for Dominant Dogs") as a means of teaching the owner to treat the dog like a dog, to build leadership, mutual respect, and trust. It is impossible to "baby" a dog who is subjected to this "tough love" program, which relies on obedience to a command before any of the luxuries or necessities of life are provided.

Finally the independence-training program that we employ at Tufts University School of Veterinary Medicine is virtually identical to the one that was recommended for Duncan by Georgie Wade. It is based on breaking down attachments based on sympathy and dependence and replacing them with functional relationships based on independence and trust. It helps owners understand what we are trying to achieve if we tell them we are helping the dog to "stand on its own four feet" without continuous support from them.

Every behaviorist knows the look on an owner's face when he or she is told, as a part of an independence-training program:

"No, he shouldn't sleep *on* your bed anymore,"

or "Do not allow him to lean against you or sit next to you while you are watching television,"

or "Do not pet him unless he does something to deserve it."

And then there's the hardest one of all:

"Totally ignore him for twenty minutes before you leave and for twenty minutes after you return home."

"What?" they gasp. "I couldn't do that."

"But you must," is the reply, "if you want to help your dog get over the problem."

Sometimes it takes a lot of convincing to get owners to enforce this program, and in some cases you just know it isn't going to happen. Overly kind people, if there can be such a thing, just can't help themselves, even after I've explained to them that it is their own behavior that leads to the very thing they have come to me to fix. As you may have gathered, however, some people *do* steel themselves and stick with the program, and such individuals usually manage to effect significant improvements in their dog's behavior. In a formal study of treatment outcome, 50 percent of owners saw "improvement" in their dog's behavior after two months and 60 percent saw improvement after three months when an independent training program was employed. However, it is important to note that the improvement will regress if owners subsequently revert to their former indulgent ways, so determination and self-discipline are important tools in achieving sustainable results.

I wasn't quite sure where Nancy and Duncan would fall on the continuum of treatment success but I feared that they would not do too well. As determined as Nancy was, I didn't feel that she would see the program through. Her own deep feelings for Duncan would paradoxically ensnarl her progress. This may have been why she saw only marginal improvement after following Georgie Wade's advice and why she was only able to achieve temporary gains with Dr. Brenda DeVore's doorside desensitization program. So why should I fare any better than these others? Well, I wasn't sure that I would, but I did try hard to enlist the essential ingredient of Nancy's sustained compliance, contacting her frequently at every step along the way. And, in addition, I did have a different medication facilitating the program.

In my next follow-up with Nancy I asked her to tape-record Duncan during a brief absence so that we could find out exactly what, if any, improvement had been made. Although Nancy was a little nervous about the scheme, she tentatively agreed to go through with it provided that her absence was brief. She didn't want to stress Duncan too much and really didn't want to find her apartment trashed again. We settled on ten minutes and the plan was launched. The results came back in short order. As far as Nancy was concerned, the trial had not been a success. She heard Duncan pacing to and fro for a few minutes, panting and whining, his tags jingling and toenails tapping on the parquet tiles. Finally there was silence, which she attributed to his being out of microphone range of the recorder. The whole episode lasted nine long minutes. Although I agreed that the problem was not resolved, I wasn't convinced that there had been no improvement. After all, we didn't have any pretreatment tapes to compare this recording with and the silence may have indicated exactly what it appeared to indicate—Duncan settling down.

Nancy wanted to know what to do next. Duncan clearly could not be left alone for any longer than the briefest time, she insisted. I agreed with her up to a point—she may well have been completely right—but I also realized that if I disagreed, it would not fly with her. Instead I asked her to build on the improvements she had made when she left

Duncan alone for short periods. A compromise was reached and Nancy set off to start with what were, in effect, the humble beginnings of a desensitization program. Her charge was to leave Duncan for thirty seconds while she walked to her car and back. Then, provided Duncan remained calm at this level of challenge, she would try opening the car door and perhaps sitting inside the car. If this phase passed without incident, she would try starting the car engine before returning, then try rolling the car backward and forward in the drive, and so on until she was able to leave the property and return without Duncan losing his cool. It was a plan, and I had her full understanding.

Two weeks after I briefed Nancy on this incremental approach, a television producer called to ask me if I could help them illustrate the problem of separation anxiety with reference to one of my cases. Nancy and Duncan were at the forefront of my mind, so I suggested that we try to catch the slowly improving Duncan on tape. Of course, there was no way I would suddenly sic the media on Nancy without warning, so I called her first to make sure she was game.

As it turned out, not only was Nancy willing to participate in the television shoot, she was actually thrilled at the idea of Duncan and her making such a splash and was happy to allow me to pass her telephone number on to the producer. Good, I thought. That's that. But it wasn't. The producer called me back to say that Nancy was not prepared to leave Duncan alone, even for ten minutes, because that might stress him out and anyway was against *my* orders. Nancy was right in a way. I *had* suggested an incremental approach toward leaving Duncan, but two weeks had passed since that time and we were never going to find out whether Duncan was improving if we didn't try a small challenge from time to time. I called Nancy to inquire how Duncan had been doing and to hear her objections firsthand. The word on Duncan was good. He continued to show little or no distress when she tried mock departures and was maintaining his cool at day care. I suggested that we might learn a lot about Duncan's attitude from the videotape and indicated that I thought the filming would be a great opportunity to find out exactly what we were dealing with. I also pointed out that the challenge would only be for ten minutes and would probably not stress Duncan much. Somewhat reluctantly, Nancy agreed to the filming.

The cameras duly arrived on the appointed day, and after a lengthy setup period, the trial began. Duncan was left completely unattended for a good ten minutes and the whole episode was caught on tape through a wide-angle lens. I didn't hear about the results of the filming until the next day, when the crew arrived to interview me.

"So how did it go?" I asked, almost before they crossed the vet school threshold.

"He didn't do anything," replied the cameraman indifferently as he unpacked his equipment.

"Nothing at all?" I exclaimed.

"Well, Ms. Crighton thought he was a bit stressed, but actually he just sat and looked at the door."

"Really," I mused.

I knew that Duncan's staring at the door did not indicate a totally relaxed state of mind. He was probably thinking about his mistress's sudden departure, but then again, he wasn't so stressed that he was pacing, panting, whining, or trying to bust out (as was the case previously). I was delighted with the improvement but still had to convince Nancy that we were on the right track. This I managed to do, but imparting the good news was like trying to roll a rock up a steep slope. It was almost as if she was programmed to receive only bad news. I couldn't help thinking she was a bit like Eeyore in *The House at Pooh Corner*. Poor Eeyore always expected, and thus usually got, the worst of everything. From receiving an empty honey pot and a burst balloon for his birthday to falling in the river and floating downriver on his back, nothing went right for Eeyore. He was primed for failure. That's how Nancy seemed to me—a real pessimist in almost every situation. It bothered me that she felt so negative about everything so I tried to cheer her on with talk of success. I made some limited progress with this approach and ultimately managed to keep her on the straight and narrow regarding Duncan's rehabilitation.

The program aired showing Duncan relaxed, but not jubilant, about being left alone, and a couple of weeks passed. Nancy was interviewed about Duncan and, on camera, she spoke frankly about the life she had been forced to lead because of Duncan's shenanigans.

"Don't you pretty much have to plan your whole life around the fact that Duncan cannot be left alone?" the interviewer asked.

"I do," Nancy replied. "I leave him at day care when I go to work, and for short spells as part of a retraining program, but that's it. I'm with him the rest of the time."

"So you haven't been to the movies recently?" the interviewer pressed.

"No, I haven't," said Nancy.

"Or out to eat?"

Nancy thought for a moment.

"No, I guess I haven't. Not for a while anyway. Not since Duncan."

"But don't you miss these things that other people enjoy and take for granted?"

"Not really . . . well, a bit," Nancy finally admitted. "I couldn't leave Duncan when he needs me so much. He's more important than movies or meals out. I stay at home for Duncan's sake . . . because I love him and I don't want to see him suffer."

The interviewer was dumbstruck.

I called Nancy a couple of weeks later to find out what, if anything, had been going on in the meantime and was delighted to hear some good news. Apparently Duncan had behaved well during several short absences ranging from ten minutes to about twenty minutes. This was excellent news, but to cap it off, Nancy added that Duncan remained calm during one absence when there had been a high wind, the remnants of a severe hurricane. He had not suffered his usual meltdown, she reported ecstatically. In fact, he had not displayed any signs whatsoever of becoming upset and was not even panting when she returned. It was indeed a day for celebration. Both dog and owner seemed to have turned a metaphorical corner and were heading in a healthier direction. I was delighted for them. Of course, the medication would have to be continued for several more months before I would dare wean Duncan off it, but I felt positive about the future and at this stage things couldn't have been going any better.

I began to wonder how Nancy would fare without Duncan's problem to preoccupy her. Her whole existence, her whole routine, had been structured around tending to Duncan's special needs. Without that necessity she would have to find some other focus for her attention. Perhaps she would now be able to go out with some people from the office or catch a movie with a friend. Perhaps she would make new acquaintances or develop a hobby. One thing I suggested Nancy should pursue was the acquisition of another dog. This would provide another focus for her and company for Duncan—an insurance policy, if you will. Although, in general, the strategy of getting a dog for your dog doesn't work to bolster a dog's confidence, there are some instances when it can make a major difference. A new dog slightly lower on the totem pole than Duncan, but one without a dysfunctional background, would be ideal. If Duncan and the new dog bonded closely, Duncan would have some company when Nancy had to leave for a while. Not only do some dogs benefit from the additional company, they also can learn from watching each other. The hope would be that Duncan would become the top dog and lead his new follower by example. Nancy has not taken me up on my last suggestion, at least not yet.

Behavior modification is a dynamic process. Anxious dispositions don't go away, but the problems they create can be managed in an ongoing way, retaining those aspects of the program that work and jettisoning those that do not. I expect to hear from Nancy again sometime, and when I do, I'll push the pack-of-three concept again. Somehow, whatever it takes, I'll try to help her to remain relatively free and to avoid being held prisoner in her own home, if that is indeed what she wants.

14

SAM'S STORY

His name is First Friend, because he will be our friend for always and always and always.—*Rudyard Kipling*

Sam, a rambunctious yellow Labrador pup, was bought from a registered breeder by a young couple who lived in a small apartment. This proved to be a serious mistake. Unexpectedly, the wife became pregnant shortly after Sam's arrival, and as her girth began to expand, so Sam also grew large and became a real handful, more than they could, in fact, manage. He was so boisterous, charging around clumsily from room to room, knocking things over, stealing food, and jumping up on people, that the couple soon decided they couldn't keep him. At the young age of six months, Sam was to be turfed out. The couple advertised and interviewed to find him a home, but that didn't yield much. Eventually, through talking with people in the neighborhood, they found a family with two school-age children in a nice single-family home with a fenced-in yard who said they would take him. The mom and dad in that family worked full-time and the kids were in school. Now, why would such a family agree to take a six-month-old Lab? Everyone knows that pups are a lot of work and require fairly constant attention if they are to be schooled correctly.

There's also the humane consideration of getting a dog when you're going to have to leave it alone all day. The situation Sam was about to be deposited into was, in fact, worse than the one he was vacating.

The new family took over Sam one June day. Things weren't too bad over the summer, as the kids were home with the baby-sitter and Sam could romp outside. In his spare time, Dad, a typical family man right down to the leather-patched elbows of his aging sweater, began constructing a wire "kennel," a cage about six by twelve feet, and, when it was complete, put a plastic doghouse in it to protect Sam from the weather. Sam might have been allowed in the house a little at first, but such invitations became progressively less frequent. Once the kids were back at school, busying themselves with fourth- and sixth-grade homework respectively, nine-month-old Sam spent most of his time in his prison. The wife didn't want him soiling in the house and, like his previous owners, found him too rambunctious. Naturally, Sam barked steadily all day and night, and soon the neighbors started to complain. When Sam wasn't kenneled, he was tied up with a yellow rope, and he chewed up his plastic doghouse until nothing was left. For reasons that were a complete mystery to me, Sam was not neutered at this time and was fed a "high-performance" ration. He just kept getting bigger and bigger. His head became absolutely massive, like a polar bear's, his paws and chest were big, and his body as a whole was huge. Sam's sire had been a big handsome guy, too, so he obviously took after his "dad."

By this stage Sam spent his days alone; he was not allowed in the house at all, and fall was approaching. The leaves were turning on the maples surrounding the family's wire-fenced half-acre lot and the autumn skies were a deep ozone blue. The neighbors continued to gripe about the racket, and eventually began to complain in writing. The family decided that Sam just had to go, repeating the same old sequence by which owners default in their duties and then the dog suffers for their sins. Rather optimistically, Dad posted signs around town, but no one responded. Finally, the next February, he took Sam to the pound, where Sam was locked in a tiny concrete cell, about two by three feet, with nothing but a water dish. Beside and across from him were other massive dogs, the kinds favored by ego-defective males, huge Rottweilers and German shepherds, all of whom seemed very vicious. The pound only had five cells. After three weeks, it was nearly time to kill Sam, since no one had taken him. While he was incarcerated, Sam became psychologically traumatized and seriously depressed.

Over this period, a charming couple in the bloom of middle age, Ernie and Mary Fowler, were battling cash flow problems in their small souvenir business and were both feeling a little low. Their shop had done well over the summer, but the couple were now facing a dramatic late-season slowing of trade, as often occurred in early fall, except that this year it was more marked. The Fowlers had no children at home and for some time had been considering that a dog might fill a gap and lift their spirits. They had watched every television show they could find on dogs. After watching one show about rescuing dogs, they decided that they would save a life by adopting an adult dog from the pound. Also, they figured that this ploy would spare them the intensive puppyhood phase, but they had no idea what lay ahead.

Without telling Mary, Ernie started visiting the pound from time to time, looking over the dogs there. It pained him deeply to leave some of them but Ernie was looking for a particular dog, one he thought Mary could get on with, and one with no obvious behavior problems. He had to look past the now familiar sign "L.D.," denoting a dog's last day, and into the future for Mary and himself. Responsible person that he was, he didn't want to bring home a dog he might have to return the next day. Nothing clicked for a while. Despite evening discussions on the subject, he and Mary couldn't even decide what breed would be right for them. Then, one Saturday morning, Mary saw a television show about the ten best family dogs in the United States and learned that the Labrador retriever was considered the number one breed. The Lab's popularity, it was stated, was due to its stable personality, good humor, sociability, and devotion to its owner. Mary decided that this was the type of dog she wanted—a Lab, preferably female. When Ernie came home that evening she told him what she had decided. "That's great," he said, "because I just saw one at the pound. He's an unneutered male, fourteen months old, and his name is Sam."

"I wanted a female," Mary replied, "but let's take a look at him anyway. How about Monday?"

Monday morning came around and they set off to see Sam. Mary had never told Ernie this, but she had been afraid of dogs all her life, especially big dogs, even though she had a desire to own one. She wouldn't go for a walk alone for fear that a dog might come after her, but off she went to the pound anyway.

When the couple arrived, they couldn't help noticing that the place smelled foul and that the "prison cells" were small and ugly. In one cell there was a hunched-down, sad, depressed-looking yellow dog, called Sam. Mary gave Ernie some dog kibble and he offered it to Sam, who accepted it meekly. Mary tried to feed him, too. Timorously, she held out her hand and said, "Sit, Sam."

He sat immediately and, head down, waited for her to hand him the treat. This was the humble beginning of the lifelong love affair between Mary and Sam.

The pound booked Sam for neutering the next day, and the Fowlers had to wait until this had been done to pick him up. Mary drove her beat-up Ford Escort over to the pound and Ernie went in and got Sam. On his return, he opened the back door of the car and said, "Hop in, Sammy," and Sam obliged without fuss. On the way home, it occurred to Mary that Sam's large head was perched directly over her shoulder and that there was dog spit everywhere (she has since learned to live with that). This dog whom she didn't know, who was drooling and who reeked of the pound, was breathing right down her neck. And she was scared of dogs.

The pound later said that Sam was a Lab cross. They thought he looked half pit bull because of his massive head, a speculation that did little to alleviate Mary's fear of him. Sam was so used to rejection that he put on a big show for the Fowlers when they got him home, leaping and dancing around like a dog on a tear. The Fowlers immediately took steps to enroll him in an obedience class. Sam had a lot to deal with that first week and acted uptight. He would glare at Mary, body stiff and pupils dilated, the sight of which made the hairs on her neck stand up. If the Fowlers tied Sam outside, for even a few minutes, he would bark ferociously, tail high and stiff, body rigid, giving them what seemed like an evil eye, his pupils widely dilated and head cocked to one side. This scared Mary so profoundly that she always asked Ernie to bring him in. Sam commuted with the Fowlers an hour each way to and from work. He rapidly became "shop dog" to the employees. Everyone adored him. The pound told Mary that Sam's previous owner had fed him a "high-performance" dog food, so she did the same. The Fowlers embarked on the first hundred days of becoming Sam's parents.

The Fowlers e-mailed Dr. Stanley Coren, the host of the *Good Dog* television show, and asked him what they could do to bring Sam into line. Sam was wild and hyper, and tore around the house like a whirling dervish. He seemed aggressive and a law unto himself. His only redeeming quality was that he was quiet in the car, and the Fowlers were grateful for that. In addition to his other problems, Sam had no idea how to ask to go out to relieve himself, had no communication skills, was poorly socialized, and didn't seem to know how to behave himself indoors. Mary reported that he had growled at them a few times when he was disturbed while resting and that she was terrified of sleeping with him in their room. All her friends told her, "He's a pack animal, you have to let him sleep in the bedroom," but she felt sure he was going to attack her. Sam went berserk whenever he saw another dog, barking wildly and lunging. Then, when he got near, he became extremely friendly and would start wagging his tail.

For the Fowlers, he was an enigma. Sam knew no commands other than "sit" and "shake a paw." In the kitchen he would be all over the place. He once leapt a foot in the air when Mary turned on the dishwasher. It wasn't so much that he was sound-sensitive as that he was not familiar with indoor life. Once he put his nose on the stove while she was cooking—but only once. He was so big he seemed to fill the room. The way he moved and stood, he conveyed the message that he owned the room. The Fowlers bought him a kennel to sleep in at night but he couldn't stand it. They thought it made him angry but later found out that he was just anxious about going in there. They tried letting him sleep in the laundry room until Mary could get used to him, but he tore that apart. They could not eat in front of him as he would put his face into everything. He would also run off all the time, so they had to keep him leashed, and he would pull so hard on walks they felt they were fresh-air skiing. Mary hurt her ankle, knee, shoulder, and arm at various times while trying to walk him.

Dr. Coren recommended that Mary read the chapters on aggression in my book *The Dog Who Loved Too Much*. The description of dominance aggression she found in the first chapter described Sam's personality precisely. Mary was intrigued but scared by what she read. What she did not understand was that dominant dogs won't hurt you unless you interfere with them in some way. In fact, it is quite easy to work around dominance aggression by avoiding the circumstances that cause it, though this is usually not a satisfactory permanent solution. Mary also failed to appreciate that dominance and aggression are not synonymous and can sometimes move in opposite directions. Some of the most dominant dogs I have known are not aggressive at all, just willful, while dominants lacking in confidence and with something to prove (subdominants, if you will) can be quite dangerous to live with if you don't know what you're doing. Fortunately, the Fowlers' trainer gave Mary some advice to bolster her flagging confidence and she soldiered on.

Shortly after this regrouping experience, Mary stumbled across the Tufts Web site and downloaded our dominance aggression questionnaire (see Appendix 1). From this chart, she determined that Sam showed only a few signs of classical dominance aggression as measured by actual aggressive signaling, though he certainly threw his weight around. All in all, Mary felt the evaluation was equivocal, as is sometimes the case. She then took Sam to her local vet and asked him if *he* thought Sam was aggressive. He pulled and pushed Sam and grabbed him and handled him quite roughly, but Sam just stood there. He said, "I don't think this dog is aggressive at all." Mary began to relax upon hearing her vet's proclamation. It's lucky that she didn't understand more about dominance or she might have remained on edge. People who appear dominant (to the dog), especially unfamiliar people whom the dog hasn't had much chance to assess, can often get away with things that more familiar folk can't. Familiarity, it seems, breeds contempt. Dominance aggression tends to be directed almost exclusively toward family members and young children (but not infants, who are considered too insignificant to pose a real threat). Anyway, her fears dispelled, Mary started working with Sam with renewed vigor and confidence.

About a month after the Fowlers adopted Sam, they met a man in a parking lot who showed great interest in him. The man looked inside Sam's earflaps and declared that Sam was a registered full-blooded Lab (the man knew because he had two Labs of his own). Mary felt much better knowing that he wasn't a mixed-breed dog, especially not one with the feared pit bull genes. Ernie enrolled Sam in an obedience class and considered himself the pupil. Mary went along to observe. The Fowlers reported that Sam was still obsessive about other dogs, and would always initially engage in his barking, lunging, tail-wagging routine, but otherwise things went pretty smoothly.

For reasons they can't remember, they decided to feed him a different dog food, called "Technical." After a few weeks on this new diet they noticed that Sam seemed much calmer. They reasoned, "It must be the neutering, the obedience classes, or perhaps he's just getting used to us." Whatever was responsible, Sam's behavior changed dramatically over the next four to six weeks, but he was experiencing very loose stools and had several accidents in the house. The vet recommended that they switch back to the "high-performance," high-protein ration to fix the problem. So they did, and almost immediately Sam was back to his old self, running around wildly, barking at everything, seemingly unable to relax. In this mode, Sam would stick his face in Mary's and bark demandingly at her; he would then dash about crazily, sometimes push the Fowlers around, and then run off. The change in his behavior was so dramatic that the Fowlers were amazed. They decided to switch him back to the Technical in stages. By the time they achieved a half-and-half mix, Sam was already calming down. When on one hundred percent Technical he was still rambunctious, but in a nice way, playful and at times giddy, but no longer crazed and hyperkinetic. Diet did seem to make a big difference.

During this period, the Fowlers were teaching Sam some social skills and manners, taking him to the leash-free park so that he could get used to other dogs, and teaching him how to play. When he saw a ball for the first time, he just looked at it and had no idea what to do with it. This indifference to a ball in a Labrador *retriever*? It just didn't seem right. The Fowlers believe he had never been given any toys. As time went by he learned to enjoy all kinds of toys: stuffed animals, plastic bottles, tennis balls, soccer balls, squishy balls, sticks, and the like.

In time Sam would play baseball by lying on the landing and "snicking" the tennis ball down the stairs (bump, bump, bounce, bump), staring at it in fascination till Mary pitched it back to him. He would then catch it and snick it down again, sometimes with his nose, sometimes with his cheek or paw. He also learned to play soccer with Mary's grandsons and he asked the Fowlers to do things for him when he couldn't help himself. When his ball or toy became stuck under something, he would come and ask one of his humans to help him, all the way from another room, using his body language to beg. Sometimes he would bring them his Garfield toy, toss it on Mary's computer keyboard, and cock his head to one side as if to say, "Come play with me." Mary loved this cheeky, fun-loving, slightly pushy side of Sam. When she was working and couldn't be disturbed, Mary would often have to surround herself with chairs and desks in her office to prevent Sam from throwing his stuffed animals onto the keyboard. Taking no for an answer was difficult for him, so he would sometimes go and get a tennis ball, put it on the floor, and "snick" it under her chair with his nose. There was no stopping him.

According to Mary, the most wonderful thing that happened to Sam over time was that his stiff, rigid body posture started to soften. Previously he had never wagged his tail, never wriggled in anticipation of anything, and never did that wiggle-walk a dog will do when it's happy to see you. In his third month with the Fowlers, Sam began to really appreciate them, even love them. He started to run to the Fowlers when he saw them, ears down, tail wagging low and fast, a smile on his big polar bear face, wriggling and dancing toward them. It was a warm and submissive greeting. He learned to sleep peacefully, on his own blankets on the floor of the Fowlers' bedroom, and would greet them warmly in the morning. Mary could, by this time, touch him anywhere, wrestle with him, and hug him. He loved it. The bonding between them strengthened by the day. Originally Sam had no idea what "stick around and come when you are called" meant, but in time he stayed near the shop in the backyard (no fence, lots of distractions, a ravine and creek behind him) and would bound toward the Fowlers whenever they beckoned.

One hundred days after they rescued Sam, the Fowlers took stock of the situation and realized that Sam wasn't the only one who was learning a lot, they were too. They found him incredibly intelligent and perceptive, and felt that the love he offered them was immense, despite the fact that Mary had been so afraid of him earlier on that she'd been almost ready to give up on him. At first she didn't understand him at all, but now Sam was fast becoming a close and cherished friend. He even helped Ernie deal with his fiscal worries by constantly reminding him, through his presence and the warmth of his affection, that there were more important things in life than money. Ernie loved him for that, too.

Two lesser problems remained after the initial difficult phase had passed and Sam had become a much loved and much happier dog. The first was that Sam would not give anything up (i.e., drop it) without guarding it and then grabbing it again and taking it away. But Mary pointed out that she could take his food away and put her hand in his mouth or face while he was eating, so she didn't think Sam was trying to signal his dominance. This "object guarding" meant that the Fowlers couldn't play games with him that required him to drop the object, e.g., fetch. Sam would roll or "snick" a ball toward them when they played baseball, but that was about as generous as he got. He would get a toy and roll it or snick it along a surface in play, but if the toy was in his mouth there was no way they could get it from him. Problem number two was his obsession with, and wild barking at, other dogs. The Fowlers are still trying to resolve these residual problems, especially the latter, because Sam would even display this behavior in the car when he saw other dogs. One night he threw himself out of a car window that was rolled down twelve to fifteen inches while they were driving along at thirty miles an hour, slamming himself into a parked car, in an effort to get at two dogs.

One thing that resonated in the Fowlers' minds was the profound effect the high-performance food had on Sam. They felt sure that if they put him back on this food the aggressive, frenetic signs would return. "He's not really aggressive," Mary argued on Sam's behalf, "but the crazy behavior made him seem to be." She called the manufacturer and tried to explain her concerns, but apparently they couldn't have cared less. This gentle, affectionate, problem-solving, soccer-playing Lab had almost been put to sleep on account of his food-induced overboisterousness. It was fortuitous for Sam that the long series of errors and poor judgments that nearly ended his life prematurely were offset by chance events and erroneous advice that had allowed him to survive.

Mrs. Fowler shared Sam's story with me because the chapter on dominance aggression in my first book had almost led her to take Sam back to the pound. She had worried that, like the woman in my book, she might wind up victimized by her dominant aggressive dog. Sam was definitely stubborn and strong-willed, but in his case there wasn't any serious overt aggression, and no battle for dominance. He would stiffen and posture aggressively if challenged but never followed through. Somewhere down the line, Sam had learned bite inhibition, meaning that he had learned not to clamp his jaws down and puncture the skin of humans or indeed other animals. He didn't drive his point home with a sledgehammer but rather by posturing and demonstrating his feelings. This is the way a well-educated dog pack member should behave. Even with other dogs, Sam's aggression, though loud and menacing, never amounted to more than symbolism and attempts at intimidation.

These days Sam is a model dog. His remaining stubbornness, Mary believes, is just a factor of his adolescence. He gets more cooperative and obedient by the day. Mary and Ernie were, and obviously are, sending the right signals to Sam and his remarkable turnaround attests to this. Mary believes that if you have not owned a dog from puppyhood, factors other than dominance may cause the dog to "act out" like her Sam. Her take on Sam was that he felt so alone that he showed dominance aggression out of anxiety ("Watch out, I'm a big tough dog"), even though he really just had something to prove to himself. This is one of the latest theories of dominance aggression—that it is fueled by underlying anxiety—and Mary came up with it on her own.

Mary explained to me that Sam still hates yellow rope, and that he can undo even the most intricate knot. Also, he hates being tied outside, or being tied at all. This, she reasons, is because he was constantly tied in his last "home," which for him was a prison. At first Sam would threaten Mary fiercely if she approached him while he was tied. She and Ernie had thought it would be good for him to spend thirty minutes at a time outdoors on his own, but instead he felt lonely. Now he tolerates being tied much better, and when Mary approaches him when he's tied he wiggles, wags his tail, sits "pretty," and waits for her to untie him. He still displays some anxiety if Mary moves out of sight, probably fearing abandonment again. The Fowlers can tie him to a post or bike outside a restaurant while they have lunch, and as long as he can see them, he sits calmly and watches what goes on. If left alone in the car, Sam is content. Only being tied with a rope and left alone makes him slightly anxious.

Nowadays, people from every walk of life are attracted to Sam. His joyous barking out the car window, ears flying in the wind, makes people smile at him. At stoplights, children spot him in the car and their faces light up. Police officers approach the car when the Fowlers stop at the coffee shop just to say hello to Sam. In fact, Sam makes everyone happy because he's such a happy-go-lucky dog. One day he went bounding into a house across the street from the Fowlers', a home where the father is deaf and the mother (of three) is deaf and blind. He introduced himself, and this kicked off a long-term relationship between Sam and the family. The father now smiles and waves at Ernie every time he goes sailing by on his bike with Sam at his side. There's no leash anymore. When Ernie says, "Go right," Sam goes right, and when he says, "Go left," Sam goes left.

Mary acknowledges that Sam has become integral to the Fowlers' lives, helping them through tough times, and that he's always there for them. "There isn't a mean bone in this lovable dog's body," she says. "He has lost completely all of the signs of so-called dominance aggression. The problem was that he just hadn't learned how to play, to wiggle, and to smile. He had been tied, caged, and isolated. Please tell people not to own a dog for which they cannot care. Our lives have changed. They now revolve around the 'Wag Park,' bike rides, playing ball, and finding new ways to challenge his problem-solving talent and exercise his ever active mind."

Sam also brought wonder to the Fowlers' lives. One evening Mary's sister, who is in the hospital eight hundred miles away, told Mary over the phone that a CT scan had shown she had a brain tumor. As Mary lay there in bed worrying and unable to sleep for many long hours, Sammy pushed closer and closer to her (he was on the floor on her side of the bed). He had never done that before. It was as if he knew, she told me. Mary kept her hand on him, and there was, she thought, a miraculous communication between the two of them. She felt he really knew she was upset. I'm sure she was right.

The pound in the Fowlers' town of ninety thousand people has limited "cells," and the Fowlers have never forgotten that Sam was going into his fourth week there. Sam had little time remaining. Ernie always recalls that he had been to the pound several times but when he first saw Sammy, his feeling was, Here is my dog.

"God works in mysterious ways," he wrote to me subsequently. "I am all choked up, tears in my eyes, just telling you how he has helped us."

Sam loves to learn a new skill, and it's a good thing, too, because Mary later found out that she had a progressive arthritic condition. She is now teaching Sam assistive skills as she may well need his help even more in the future. Sam, like most other dogs, is far happier when he has a job. Perhaps assisting Mary will enrich his life even further and at the same time give Mary the strength and ability to be able to carry on. I hope for Mary's sake that she doesn't have to rely on Sam's skills too heavily, but I know that if she ever does, she could have no better assistant than Sam.

EPILOGUE

The animal, that inevitable enigma, is the opposite of us in its very likeness.—*Paul Valéry*

The force that brings people and their pets together and later seals the bond derives its energy from the similarities between the species. The similarities stem from the fact that we share certain biological characteristics and have remarkable genetic similarities, but it is the psychological resemblance that is so astonishing and so fundamental to the interspecies connection. Somewhere along the continuum of vertebrate evolution, societies formed, self-awareness dawned, and understanding the intentions and mood of others became imperative for survival. It is this awareness of self and others in particular that has paved the way for mutual understanding between certain species.

The potential for bonding between humans and other mammalian species is not just confined to our interactions with dogs and cats, but also applies to our interactions with horses, cattle, sheep, birds, rats, and, of course, other primates. One woman whose herd of dairy cattle had to be destroyed because of the foot-and-mouth disease epidemic in England, wept as she related the tale of their destruction. She knew all of the cows by name; apparently each had a unique personality and responded to her with great affection and knowing. She even had a favorite whom she regarded more as a pet than as a farm animal, and felt she had a particularly close relationship with this leader cow. The woman couldn't bear to watch the executions of the cows but thought she owed it to "her girls" to be there for them up to the last moment. At each shot of the captive bolt pistol, she shuddered and felt as if her soul was being torn from her body. Her cattle weren't just her business, they were her family. Though financially ruined, she could only think of them, of what they had suffered, and dwelled on the fact that she could never replace the individuals she had lost. She would start a new business someday but would never consider dairying a second time. The memories of the slaughter would haunt her forever and she couldn't stand being reminded every day by the sight of another herd.

Sometimes bonds develop between nonhuman species. Koko the chimp and the cat to whom he bonded provide a classical example. In my last book I related the tale of a dog who fell in love with a rat. Relationships between horses and goats or donkeys can become so close that they experience separation anxiety when they have to be separated. People bonding with dogs and cats, and vice versa, is just one more example of interspecies bonding where the animals in question share some common social needs and can, in some way, communicate with each other.

Dogs and cats are more similar to us than they are different. Both species are capable of social behavior and need to be able to communicate their preferences and needs to other group members, just as we do. Eyes have a lot to do with this communication. In dogs, cats, and people, they can be most expressive. Sam's owner (see "Sam's Story") said of him, "People comment on his eyes, that they're not like a dog's eyes but like a person's eyes. They are so human, brown and gold, expressive. He can communicate so much with those eyes." This ability to communicate by means of expression is not confined to dogs, cats, and humans. An immunology researcher at Tufts University modified his research because the primates with whom he was working were too good at communicating in this way. His experiment mandated that he strap the monkeys down, so that they were unable to move a muscle, and then give them various injections designed to affect them in unpleasant ways. But at the last moment, he would see the monkey's eyes looking up at him, the creature unmistakably pleading with him to stop doing what he was doing. He gave up the research because of this experience.

Body language is another method by which animals communicate with us, or at least attempt to. In all social species, it seems, forward body movement represents resolve or can be a threat; head held high reflects confidence; head held low or to one side means shame or deference; and taut musculature indicates stress. It's much more complicated than that when one includes the communicative significance of blinking, yawning, ear position (humans are not talented in this respect), open versus closed mouth, and species-specific body language like dogs' "play bow" and dogs' and cats' tail positions and movement. The differences in body language between different species can be countered by learning. We can learn how a dog or cat looks when it wants to play, and they can learn that we're not always angry because our ears are pressed close to our heads. We can learn that when a dog tucks its tail it is scared, and dogs can relate our body posture to our mood and intentions.

Then there's vocal communication. Dogs and cats can quickly learn the significance of individual human sounds (words); we can learn that a dog wants attention when it barks in a specific way; we can also appreciate a cat's distress cries as distinct from its happy purring sounds and chirps. I know a dog, a deaf dalmatian called Hogan, who has learned forty-four words of American Sign Language, but he actually understands a lot more than his impressive vocabulary suggests. I won't go into details of the extraordinary story of Irene Pepperberg's parrot, Alex, who has a vocabulary and a sense of concepts greater than some five-year-old children. Suffice it to say that Alex is not unique among parrots in his ability to understand language and concepts.

I am not suggesting that nonhuman animals are more intelligent, in our sense of the word, than humans, just that some species, at least, are clearly sentient and are quite capable of sometimes subtle communication with us. This is what makes so many of them good pets. Pet owners discover the wonder of this communication without any particular training. Intuition tells them that their perceptions are real. Scientists, however, not surprisingly, have a very difficult time coming up with anything more than rudimentary evidence of animals' communicative abilities in the laboratory. Bonds with pet animals, which are based on communication and learning, are, to a large extent, unique and individually forged through empathy and mutual understanding. Such unions, as attested to by most of the pet owners mentioned in this book, can be inspirational, life enhancing, and always unforgettable.

Empathy and understanding are not all that is necessary for the successful development of a strong bond between a human and a nonhuman animal. Successful relationships are also based on trust and experience. Trust arises from knowledge and belief: belief that the other partner in the relationship is going to respond in positive ways because of consistancy in the past. Trust also stems from dependability and kindness, and flows naturally from more sensitive, caring individuals as their contribution to the equation. In relationships with animals, it appears to be true that what you sow, so shall you reap.

My mother had the trust of the wild birds in her garden. She came to know them as unique individuals, fed them, spoke to them daily, was patient with them, and was consistently kind to them. As a result, she became affectionately known to them and was an important figure in their daily lives. She understood their difficulties, their fears, and their pleasures, and worried about their well-being to the point of having bird-sitters tend to their needs when she visited me in the United States. When my mom walked into her garden, she was always surrounded by a constellation of birds, like a modern-day St. Francis of Assisi. Admittedly, she would feed them, but it was still remarkable that they were so devoid of fear that the braver ones would fly into our kitchen and hop around on the kitchen counter as she chopped up their food. Growing up, I always found it astonishing to enter the kitchen to find thrushes and blackbirds hopping around on the surfaces. The trust that existed between these birds and my mother allowed her to gain insight into their "personal" lives that would otherwise have been impossible. She learned more about wild birds because of her interactions with them, and among them, than she could ever have learned by spying on them from a hide. In her own way, over several decades of bird-tending in an English country garden, she developed a familiarity and understanding with her birds akin to the relationships Dr. Jane Goodall must have developed with her chimps in the Gombe.

An elegantly dressed client of mine came out of a store one day with her stunningly handsome, now well-behaved golden retriever at her side when a man in his forties and his seven-year-old son approached her. The boy asked if he could pet her dog—a fairly regular request, as it happened. While the boy petted the dog, his father told the woman that his family had owned a yellow Labrador for twelve years and that the dog had died two and a half years previously. He then took out his wallet and showed her a head-and-shoulders picture of his dog. She was overcome by emotion when she realized that this big burly guy had for over two years kept his dog's photo in his wallet and felt comfortable enough to show her the picture. With a nod, he then bent down and petted and touched the dog with a faraway look in his eyes as if he were communicating with an old friend.

It's curious what you see when you take a step back and consider the special relationship people have with their pets. The bond is rooted in an affinity between different species, not just pride of ownership or some other utilitarian association. Not everybody with a pet develops a strong bond of mutual appreciation and understanding, but many do. Close relationships, however, do seem to be the rule rather than the exception, perhaps because of the unconditional, non-judgmental affection that pets offer. So are these people deluding themselves when they think their pets understand them and respond to their various moods? I don't think so, and neither do they. That's why the people I have written about in these chapters were prepared to go to such extraordinary lengths to help their pets. They saw in their pets something that parents see in their children and to which unattached people apparently are blind.

Nature has equipped us to bond closely with family members and to support them no matter what. People with pets often view their animals in this light and see the good in them no matter how they behave. Even dominant aggressive dogs, like Sam and Tucker, have their good side. Owners often tell me, speaking of this type of dog, "He's a perfect dog ninety-eight percent of the time but then he suddenly becomes mean." I am consulted about the two percent who are mean. It's a 24/7 commitment for owners to a new way of interacting with their pet if problems are to be resolved. Having owners change their own behavior toward a dominant dog or pushy cat, making resources conditional and setting consistent limits, is one of the hardest things I can ask them to do, but that's exactly what has to be done.

A dog with separation anxiety, like Nancy Crighton's dog, Duncan, though it may be incredibly destructive to the home in the owner's absence, usually makes one of the most doting and dependent pets. Trying to train such a dog to be independent is more painful for the owner than it ever is for the dog. If such a dog barks constantly during its owner's absence, the owner may find himself or herself threatened with eviction if the problem can't be resolved expeditiously. And the owner may have to put up with thousands of dollars' worth of material damage if they don't pay the emotional price of therapy—not much of a choice. Also, there's the dog's suffering to consider, because separation anxiety undoubtedly causes feelings of panic, despair, even depression, in affected pets. Dogs or cats exhibiting obsessive-compulsive behavior, another anxiety-based behavioral disorder, can be an enigma to their owners but their problem behaviors do not usually detract from the strong bond they share with their owners. Many owners of such disturbed animals, like Mona's owner, will go to any lengths to resolve the emotional problems underpinning their pet's compulsive disorder, even to the point of giving them psychotropic medications, and that's often what it takes. Friends do not necessarily understand why the owner is going to such lengths to help their pet, but the owner is quite clear in his or her mind and I understand perfectly.

Some pets are not only adored as family members but also serve an invaluable function. Remember the dog Belle in the chapter "The Dog Who Hated Men"? Belle warned her diabetic owner of impending blood sugar crises and basically kept her alive. There are guide dogs for the blind and "hearing ear" dogs for the deaf. These dogs provide a service but are also often their owners' best friends. What lengths would the owners of such dogs not go to in order to resolve medical or behavioral issues? Police working dogs (K9s) often have extremely close bonds with their handlers. Police officers have come to me regarding various behavior problems their dogs have exhibited, and it is obvious they have been touched by their dogs' troubles. These men are just as dedicated to their dogs' welfare as they would be to that of a human police partner, if not more so. One time in Massachusetts, the state ruled that live-at-home police working dogs would have to be kenneled to save the state money. It was the police handlers themselves who complained most bitterly, since these dogs weren't just working dogs but were also integrated family members. I was asked by the handlers to make a case against the dogs being taken away from their homes and institutionalized. This I did, publicly stating the problems arising from confinement, but it made no difference to the authorities in charge. The dogs were incarcerated, causing the handlers much heartache and no doubt leading to a considerable deterioration in the dogs' quality of life. I don't mean to omit service cats from this discussion. There are cats whose owners tour them through old people's homes and hospitals for the enrichment of elderly and incapacitated people. For these cats, a close relationship with the owner is a given. It is the joy and healing they bring to others that is most remarkable. Old faces light up and arthritic fingers get some physiotherapy in the form of petting. Old folk who would have sat motionless and emotionless in armchairs suddenly find themselves mentally active and enjoying a pleasurable interaction with a pet.

It is not a weakness to develop a close and loving relationship with a pet. Quite the reverse: it indicates loyalty, caring, and strength of character. Understanding pet owners are better people than their animal-unfriendly counterparts. They are more likely to treat fellow human beings with dignity and respect and are less likely to solve their problems using aggression. Pet owners will continue to be denigrated by some as anthropomorphic until science comes up with a way of measuring and validating the bond. In the meantime, as some compensation, believers in the bond, the recipients of pets' affections, will be able to enjoy their lot while their more pragmatic counterparts will be alone in their skepticism. In ending, I would like to add that if pet lovers controlled the world, it would probably be a better place.

APPENDIX 1

Is Your Dog Dominant? A Dominance Assessment Test for Dogs

Check the appropriate box if your dog exhibits any of the listed behaviors at any time when you or any member of the family do the following:

	Growl	Lift lip	Snap	Bite	No aggressive response	Not tried
Touch dog's food or add food while eating						
Walk past dog while eating						
Take away real bone, rawhide, or delicious food						
Walk by dog when it has a real bone/rawhide						
Touch delicious food while the dog is eating it						
Take away a stolen object						
Physically wake dog up or disturb resting dog						

(continued on next page)

	Growl	Lift lip	Snap	Bite	No aggressive response	Not tried
Restrain dog when it wants to go someplace						
Lift dog						
Pet dog						
Medicate dog						
Handle dog's face/mouth						
Handle dog's feet						
Trim dog's toenails						
Groom dog						
Bathe or towel off						
Take off or put on collar						
Pull dog back by the collar or scruff						
Reach for or grab dog by the collar						
Hold dog by the muzzle						
Stare at dog						
Reprimand dog in loud voice						
Visually threaten dog: newspaper or hand						
Hit dog						
Walk by dog in crate						
Walk by/talk to dog on furniture						

	Growl	Lift lip	Snap	Bite	No aggressive response	Not tried
Remove dog from furniture: physically or verbally						
Make dog respond to command						

Guide to Scoring and Interpreting Results

Growl scores 1 point
Lift lip scores 2 points
Snap scores 4 points
Bite scores 8 points
Put one score in each line (maximal response)

Total score less than 5 = not dominant aggressive
Total score 5–15 = mildly dominant
Total score 15–30 = moderate
Greater than 30 = severe

APPENDIX 2

12-Step Leadership Program for Dominant Dogs

1. Avoid Confrontation

Make a list of circumstances that elicit aggression from your dog, including those that cause growling, lip lifts, snaps, and bites. Once you have compiled your list, you need to think about how to avoid such situations. Avoiding aggression is an *essential* component of the rehabilitation program, and if not employed, will undermine the other measures applied.

2. Feed Your Dog Only When He Responds to a Command

Since food is such a valued commodity within the pack, it is imperative to make the dominant dog realize you control this asset. Food must no longer appear like manna from heaven, but be offered only (and obviously) by you. Your dog must earn all food (including treats) from you by responding positively to a command given by you.

3. Do Not Pet Your Dog Indiscriminately

The tactile stimulus of petting, and the acknowledgment that goes with it, is a powerful reward for most dogs and should be rationed in the same way as food.

4. Praise

Depending on the dog in question, praise can be another highly valued asset for which dominant dogs should be required to work.

5. Remove All Valued Assets

You do not want your dog to have anything it may want to protect from you. You can easily prevent possessive aggression by removing *all* of your dog's valued possessions, such as toys, bones, and rawhides. The provision of toys is a privilege for which dominant dogs must work.

6. Games

Games are fun and a positive experience for your dog. As such, they should be rationed.

7. Demanding Behavior

Demanding what they want, and getting it, is one of the ways that dominant dogs exercise control over compliant owners. Constantly responding to your dog's demands will undermine your authority and create an atmosphere conducive to the expression of dominance aggression.

8. Company

Your company and close physical presence should be rationed in the same way as everything else your dog values and should only be provided as a reward for deferential behavior.

9. High Places

The simple rule for dominant dogs is *no high places*, including furniture and bed.

10. Freedom

Freedom, for dogs, is one of life's privileges which a dominant dog should have to earn.

11. Exercise

15 to 20 minutes of aerobic exercise daily is a minimal requirement (health permitting). Exercise generates serotonin which stabilizes the dog's mood and reduces aggression.

12. Diet

It is probably worthwhile to try feeding a low protein (16% to 22%), artificial-preservative-free diet for a trial period of 2 to 4 weeks to see if there is any improvement in your dog's behavior. Caveats apply with regard to young dogs (less than 6 months of age), pregnant and nursing bitches, and in some medical conditions. Consult your veterinarian before making the switch. Diet changes should be made gradually (over 3–4 days) to avoid gastrointestinal upset.

APPENDIX 3

How to Retrain a Fearful or Fear-Aggressive Dog

The steps in the program are as follows:

1. Prevent any uncontrolled exposure to strangers.
2. Teach the dog a "sit and watch me" command or, alternatively, to remain in a relaxed down-stay position.
3. Reward the dog's compliance with food treats and/or petting and warm praise.
4. With the dog on lead and under control, introduce a mildly fear-inducing person at a distance. Reward the dog for remaining calm.
5. As long as the dog remains relaxed, ask the person to move a little closer and repeat the exercise.
6. If the dog is resistant to remaining still, an alternative strategy is to have the person stand still and walk the dog around the person in progressively smaller circles.
7. Once the dog is able to remain quiet when the person is walking past, the person can then walk by and drop a treat for the dog. If the dog consumes the treat, this is an indication that the dog is fairly relaxed. Later the person can walk past and hold out a treat and see if the dog takes it. *Never* force the issue.
8. During the early stages of training, assistants should be advised

not to make direct eye contact with the dog and not to approach the dog directly. Instead they should be advised to approach at an angle or with a curved trajectory, to move slowly but purposefully, and to avert their gaze, looking perhaps at the dog's ears or nose rather than directly into its eyes. Such an approach is less threatening to most dogs. It is unwise to reach toward the dog at this stage.

9. If the dog cannot maintain a controlled "sit" or "down" position, focusing on its owner because it is tense, barking, or lunging at the stranger, then the owner should return to an earlier phase of training. Ideally, during the training process, no one should come close enough to the dog to trigger a fearful or aggressive response
10. Repeat procedures 3 times a week initially (20-minute sessions). Eventually exposures may be reduced to 2 to 4 times a month.

In-home procedures and precautions

1. For dogs who are fearful when people come to the house, the dog can be isolated at first, then, once everyone is seated, the dog can be brought into the room and restrained on leash. If this approach is employed, the dog should be removed from the room before the guests prepare to leave, in the early stages of retraining.
2. Once the dog is able to relax with people quietly sitting in the home, it should be taught to remain calm when people move around in the home. Dogs who display fear-driven aggressive behavior have a tendency to snap at people when they are moving away, for example, as they are preparing to leave. Start by having the guest slowly stand up and then sit down again. Reward the dog for not reacting. Next have the person stand up and sit down more quickly, and so on.
3. If all goes well, the person can progress to taking a few steps around his or her seat. Gradually increase the amount of movement the dog can tolerate while remaining relaxed. Reward each progression with a jackpot of food treats.

4. It is not a good idea to have the person attempt to pet or reach out toward the dog at this stage; however, if the dog is relaxed, the person can toss a food treat in the dog's general direction. The goal is to teach the dog to associate visitors with pleasant experiences.
5. Once the dog is able to relax in the visitors' presence and is accepting food treats from them, it may be allowed to interact with them while secured by means of a ten-foot-long nylon training leash. The dog should be the one to initiate all interactions with the visitors, not the other way around. If it chooses to approach a guest, have the person quietly offer his or her hand for the dog to sniff and/or passively hold out a food treat. Never advance your hand rapidly toward the dog's muzzle.
6. If the dog indicates that it would like to be petted, the visitor may do so, briefly, but should avoid reaching up and over the dog's head and should avoid prolonged eye contact.
7. These exercises should be repeated with a variety of mildly fear-promoting volunteers who should engage in progressively more ambitious interactions with the dog.

Note

The use of a head halter, such as a Gentle Leader (or "snout loop"), is highly recommended for this type of training. Head halters permit exquisite control and send biologically appropriate signals of the owner's leadership.

APPENDIX 4

Predilections for Various Behaviors Based on Breed

DOGS

Biting: Top 4: German shepherd, chow,[1] cocker spaniel, golden retriever.[2] Also ran: Akita, American Eskimo, springer spaniel, Rottweiler, pit bull, Lhasa apso, bichon frise, corgi. (Note: Cocker spaniel and golden retriever may be overrepresented because of breed popularity.)

Lethal attacks: Top 4: pit bull, Rottweiler, German shepherd, Husky-Malamute type.[3] Also ran: mastiff-type, canary dogs, chow, Doberman, St. Bernard, Great Dane.

Interdog aggression: terriers in general; e.g., bull breeds, Airedale, Irish terrier, Kerry Blue.[4]

Fearful behavior: herding breeds;[5] certain lines of golden retriever.

Compulsive behaviors:

Acral lick dermatitis: German shepherd, Great Dane, Labrador retriever, St. Bernard,[6] Doberman.[7]

Light chasing/shadow chasing: Old English sheepdog, West Highland white, wirehaired fox terrier, Rottweiler.[4]

Fly snapping: German shepherd, cavalier King Charles spaniel, Norwich terrier.[4]

Compulsive drinking: boxers.[4]

Tail chasing: bull terriers, German shepherds.[8]

Nursing (sucking): dachshunds, Dobermans.[4,7]

Barking/howling: hounds in general, beagles in particular;[9,10] huskies, Malamutes, Dobermans.[11]

Digging: Northern breeds;[9] terriers.

Coprophagia: retrievers.[4]

House-soiling: terriers in general.[4]

Chasing things: Border collie, Sheltie, German shepherd, Rottweiler.[11]

CATS

Aggression: Can be line specific but does not appear to be breed specific, except perhaps in Turkish Angoras.[12]

Fearful behavior: Genetic factors tend to be line specific, and are heavily influenced by early nurtural experiences.[12]

Compulsive behaviors: Oriental breeds: Siamese, Burmese, Tonkinese, Singapura, etc.; exotic breeds: Ocicat, Ajos Azules, Munchkins.[7,12]

References

1. K. A. Gershmann et al., "Which Dogs Bite? A Case-Control Study of Risk Factors," *Pediatrics* 93:913–17 (1994).
2. Communication from Humane Society of the United States.
3. Special Report, *Journal of the American Veterinary Medical Association* 217:6 (2000).
4. Tufts Behavior Clinic experience.
5. E. Cornwall McCobb et al., "Thunderstorm Phobia in Dogs: An Internet Survey of 69 Cases," *Journal of the American Animal Hospital Association* 37:319–24 (2001).
6. J. L. Rapoport, "Drug Treatment of Canine Acral Lick," *Archives of General Psychiatry* 49 (July 1992).
7. N. H. Dodman et al., "Veterinary Models of OCD," in *Obsessive-Compulsive Disorders* (New York: Marcel Dekker, Inc., 1997).
8. J. K. Blackshaw, "Abnormal Behaviour in Dogs," *Australian Veterinary Journal* 65(12):393–94 (December 1988).
9. B. Kilcommons and S. Wilson, *Paws to Consider* (New York: Warner Books, 1999).
10. B. Fogle, *The Dog's Mind* (Middlesex, England: Pelham Books, 1992).
11. Legend and genetics.
12. S. Pflueger, chairman of the World Cat Genetics Committee, personal communi cation (August 2001).

ABOUT THE AUTHOR

Dr. Nicholas H. Dodman graduated from Glasgow University Veterinary School in 1970 and was appointed as a "house surgeon" at the school following graduation. After this stint, he visited a veterinary practice in San Francisco for six months and then returned to Scotland as a lecturer in surgery and anesthesia at Glasgow University Veterinary School for the next ten years, prepping himself for his eventual return to the United States in 1981.

Although he was interested in animal behavior prior to returning to the United States, it was only after joining the faculty of Tufts University School of Veterinary Medicine in Grafton, Massachusetts, that this interest flourished and turned into a passion. Dr. Dodman founded the Animal Behavior Clinic at Tufts Veterinary School in the late 1980s and began seeing clinical patients there. He was board certified in animal behavior by the American College of Veterinary Behaviorists in 1996 and continues his specialty practice of animal behavior at Tufts Veterinary School to this day.

During the ten to fifteen years that Dr. Dodman has been intimately involved in the study and practice of animal behavioral medicine, he has published over one hundred scientific papers and has written five books on the subject. He also holds six United States patents relating to behavioral modification techniques and medications. His popular-press books have reached best-seller lists and brought him national recognition. He has appeared on numerous national television and radio shows, including *Good Morning America*, the *Today* show, *Dateline*, *48 Hours*, *20/20*, CNN's *Headline News*, NPR's *Fresh Air*, and *The Oprah Winfrey Show*.